Fodor's InFocus

O'AHU

1st Edition

Portions of this book appear in *Fodor's Hawai'i*

Fodor's Travel Publications New York, Toronto, London, Sydney, Auckland

www.fodors.com

Be a Fodor's Correspondent

Your opinion matters. It matters to us. It matters to your fellow Fodor's travelers, too. And we'd like to hear it. In fact, we *need* to hear it. When you share your experiences and opinions, you become an active member of the Fodor's community. Here's how you can help improve Fodor's for all of us.

Tell us when we're right. We rely on local writers to give you an insider's perspective. But our writers and staff editors also depend on you. Your positive feedback is a vote to renew our recommendations for the next edition.

Tell us when we're wrong. We update most of our guides every year. But things change. If any of our descriptions are inaccurate or inadequate, we'll incorporate your changes in the next edition and will correct factual errors at fodors.com *immediately.*

Tell us what to include. You probably have had fantastic travel experiences that aren't yet in Fodor's. Why not share them with a community of like-minded travelers? Share your discoveries and experiences with everyone directly at fodors.com. Your input may lead us to add a new listing or a higher recommendation.

Give us your opinion instantly at our feedback center at www.fodors.com/feedback. You may also e-mail editors@fodors.com with the subject line "In Focus O'ahu Editor." Or send your nominations, comments, and complaints by mail to In Focus O'ahu Editor, Fodor's, 1745 Broadway, New York, NY 10019.

Happy Traveling!

Tim Jarrell, Publisher

FODOR'S IN FOCUS O'AHU

Editor: Jess Moss
Series Editor: Douglas Stallings

Production Editor: Astrid deRidder

Maps & Illustrations: David Lindroth, Ed Jacobus, Mark Stroud; *cartographers*; Bob Blake and Rebecca Baer, *map editors;* William Wu, *information graphics*

Design: Fabrizio La Rocca, *creative director*; Guido Caroti, *art director*; Ann McBride, *designer*; Melanie Marin, *senior picture editor*

Cover Photo: Polynesian Cultural Center

Production Manager: Amanda Bullock

1st Edition

ISBN 978-1-4000-0890-2
ISSN 1943-0183

SPECIAL SALES

This book is available for special discounts for bulk purchases for sales promotions or premiums. Special editions, including personalized covers, excerpts of existing books, and corporate imprints, can be created in large quantities for special needs. For more information, write to Special Markets/Premium Sales, 1745 Broadway, MD 6-2, New York, New York, NY 10019, or e-mail specialmarkets@randomhouse.com.

AN IMPORTANT TIP & AN INVITATION

Although all prices, opening times, and other details in this book are based on information supplied to us at press time, changes occur all the time in the travel world, and Fodor's cannot accept responsibility for facts that become outdated or for inadvertent errors or omissions. **So always confirm information when it matters,** especially if you're making a detour to visit a specific place. Your experiences—positive and negative—matter to us. If we have missed or misstated something, **please write to us.** We follow up on all suggestions. Contact the In Focus O'ahu editor at editors@fodors.com or c/o Fodor's at 1745 Broadway, New York, NY 10019.

PRINTED IN CHINA
10 9 8 7 6 5 4 3 2 1

CONTENTS

MAPS

DID YOU KNOW?

Some people say O'ahu has the best of both worlds—dynamic, exciting cities such as Waikīkī and Honolulu as well as mountains and waterfalls.

ABOUT THIS BOOK

Our Ratings

We wouldn't recommend a place that wasn't worth your time, but sometimes a place is so experiential that superlatives don't do it justice. These sights and properties get our highest rating, **Fodor's Choice**, indicated by orange stars throughout this book. Black stars highlight places we deem **Highly Recommended** places that our writers, editors, and readers praise again and again for consistency and excellence. Care to nominate a place or suggest that we rate one more highly? Visit our feedback center at www.fodors.com/feedback.

Credit Cards

Want to pay with plastic? **AE, D, DC, MC, V** following restaurant and hotel listings indicate if American Express, Discover, Diner's Club, MasterCard, and Visa are accepted.

Restaurants

Unless we state otherwise, restaurants are open for lunch and dinner daily. We mention dress only when there's a specific requirement and reservations only when they're essential or not accepted—it's always best to book ahead.

Hotels

Hotels have private bath, phone, TV, and air-conditioning and operate on the European Plan (aka EP, meaning without meals), unless we specify otherwise.

Many Listings

★ Fodor's Choice
★ Highly recommended
⊠ Physical address
✛ Directions
🗐 Mailing address
☎ Telephone
🖷 Fax
⊕ On the Web
✑ E-mail
🗐 Admission fee
☉ Open/closed times
Ⓜ Metro stations
🖃 Credit cards

Hotels & Restaurants

🏨 Hotel
🛏 Number of rooms
⚴ Facilities
🍽 Meal plans
✕ Restaurant
⚶ Reservations
⤱ Smoking
🍷 BYOB
✕🏨 Hotel with restaurant that warrants a visit

Outdoors

🏌 Golf
⛺ Camping

Other

☺ Family-friendly
⇨ See also
⊠ Branch address
☞ Take note

Experience O'ahu

WHAT'S WHERE

1 **West O'ahu:** (which includes Central O'ahu highlands, the Leeward coast, and the Hawaiian communities of Nānākuli and Wai'anae): is finding a new identity as a "second city" of suburban homes and tech firms, coexisting with agriculture and traditional lifestyles.

2 **The North Shore:** is a melange of farmers and surfers, vacation homes and plantation villages, culminating in a tumble of black rocks at Ka'ena Point, where, according to tradition, souls meet eternity.

3 **Windward O'ahu:** with its offshore islands and remnants of ancient fishponds, is where the beachlovers live, and Hawaiians on their ancestral lands.

4 **Southeast O'ahu:** encompasses Honolulu's bedroom communities crawling up the steep-sided valleys, snorkelers' favorite Hanauma Bay, and a string of wild and often hidden beaches (including that steamy one in *From Here to Eternity*).

5 **The capital city of Honolulu:** holds the nation's only royal palace, free concerts under the tamarind trees in the financial district, and the galleries and open markets of Nu'uanu and Chinatown.

6 **Waikīkī:** is the dream that sells Hawai'i as the place to surf, swim, and sail by day and dine, dance, and party by night.

NORTH SHORE

2

Pu'uomahuka Heiau

Waimea Bay

Waimea Valley Audobon Center

83

Hale'iwa

Waialua Bay

Dillingham Airfield

930

KA'ENA POINT

Yokohama Bay

WAI'ANAE

WEST O'AHU

1

Kaala

Mākaha

93

Wai'anae

Mā'ili

803

Dole Plantation

80

MOUNTAINS

Palikea

Puu Manawahua

750

Nānākuli

H1

Kō 'Ōlina Resort & Marina

93

'Ewa

Kapolei

0   5 mi
0   5 km

Waiale'e

Kahuku

La'ie

Polynesian Cultural Center

Hau'ula

Punalu'u

Ka'a'awa

KO'OLAU

CENTRAL O'AHU

Wahiawā

Wheeler Air Force Base

Mililani Town

Puu Kaaumakua

MOUNTAINS

Kahalu'u

WINDWARD O'AHU

3

830

Kāne'ohe

Kāne'ohe Bay Marine Corps Base

MŌKAPU PT.

Kāne'ohe Bay

MŌKAPU PENINSULA

Kailua Bay

Kailua

Bellows Air Force Base

Pearl Harbor

'Aiea

78

63

61

Mt. Olomana

Waimānalo

72

Kaau Crater

Puu Lanipo

4

Pearl Harbor Naval Base

Punchbowl Crater

5

HONOLULU

SOUTHEAST O'AHU

Koko Crater

Honolulu International Airport

Mamala Bay

H1

72

Maunalua Bay

Hawai'i Kai

Hanauma Bay

Waikīkī

DIAMOND HEAD

6

KOKO HEAD

Diamond Head Crater

PLANNER

When You Arrive

Honolulu International Airport is 20 minutes from Waikīkī (40 during rush hour). Car rental is across the street from baggage claim. A cumbersome airport taxi system requires you to line up to a taxi wrangler who radios for cars (about $25 to Waikīkī). Other options: TheBus ($2, one lap-size bag allowed) or public airport shuttle ($8). Ask the driver to take H1, not Nimitz Highway, at least as far as downtown, or your introduction to paradise will be Honolulu's industrial backside.

Timing Is Everything

Winter brings whales (November through March) and waves (surf competitions December through February). In June, the Islands honor the king who made them a nation, and in September, the Aloha Festivals celebrate island culture.

Renting a Car

If you plan on getting outside of Waikīkī and Honolulu, renting a car is a must. But renting a Mustang convertible is a sure sign that you're a tourist and practically begs "come burglarize me." A good rule of thumb: When the car is out of your sight even for a moment, it should be empty of anything you care about.

■TIP→**Reserve your vehicle in advance, especially during the Christmas holidays.** This will not only ensure that you get a car, but also that you get the best rates. *See O'ahu Essentials for more information on renting a car and driving.*

Dining & Lodging on O'ahu

Hawai'i is a melting pot of cultures, and nowhere is this more apparent than in its cuisine. From luaus and "plate lunch" to sushi and steak, there's no shortage of interesting flavors and presentations.

Whether you're looking for a quick snack or a multicourse meal, turn to Chapter 6 to find the best eating experiences the island has to offer. Jump in, and enjoy!

Choosing vacation lodging is a tough decision, but fret not—our expert writers and editors have done most of the legwork.

Looking for a tropical forest retreat, a big resort, or a private vacation rental? Chapter 7 gives you the details you need to book a place that suits your style. Quick tips: Reserve your room far in advance and ask about discounts and special packages (hotel Web sites often have Internet-only deals).

Seeing Pearl Harbor

Pearl Harbor is a must-see for many. Consider whether you want to see only the Arizona Memorial, or the USS *Bowfin* and USS *Missouri* as well. Plan to arrive early—tickets for the Arizona Memorial (free) are given out on a first-come, first-served basis and can disappear within an hour.

Note that children under four are not allowed on the *Bowfin* and may not enjoy the crowds and waiting in line at other sights.

Island Driving Times

Driving from your hotel in Waikīkī to the North Shore, say, will take longer than you'd think from glancing at a map.

Areas around Honolulu can have traffic jams that rival Southern California. Heavy traffic toward downtown Honolulu begins as early as 6:30 AM and lasts until 9 AM. In the afternoon, expect traffic departing downtown to back up around 3 PM until approximately 7 PM.

Here are average driving times—without traffic—that will help you plan your excursions accordingly.

Waikīkī to Kō'Ōlina	1 hour
Waikīkī to Hale'iwa	45 minutes
Waikīkī to Hawai'i Ka	25 minutes
Waikīkī to Kailua	30 minutes
Waikīkī to Downtown Honolulu	10 minutes
Waikīkī to Airport	25 minutes
Kne'ohe to Turtle Bay	1 hour
Hawai'i Kai to Kailua	25 minutes
Hale'iwa to Turtle Bay	20 minutes

Island Hopping

Should you try to fit another island into your trip or stay put in O'ahu? Tough call. Although none of the Islands are more than 30 minutes away from another by air, security hassles and transport swallow up precious vacation hours. If you've got less than a week, do O'ahu well and leave the rest for the next trip. With a week, you can give three days to O'ahu (Pearl Harbor, Honolulu, and one rural venture), then head to a Neighbor Island for some beach time and maybe an adventure or two.

If you do decide to island-hop, book in advance; you'll get a better fare by packaging your travel. Don't compare the Neighbor Islands to Honolulu and never call them "the outer islands"—that's insultingly O'ahu-centric.

TOP ATTRACTIONS

That Beach

Kailua is the beach you came to Hawai'i for: wide and gently sloped, glowing golden in the sun, outfitted with a couple of well-placed islets to gaze at, and fronted by waters in ever-changing shades of turquoise. The waves are gentle enough for children. Kayakers are drawn to the Mokulua Islands offshore. Small convenience stores and restaurants are within walking distance. And there's just enough wind to keep you from baking. Paradise, but civilized.

Finding Shangri La

Wealth allowed heiress Doris Duke to acquire the lavish seaside estate she called Shangri La. For most, that would have been enough. But Duke had a passion—Islamic art and architecture—and determination as well as money. She had a vision of courtyards and pleasure gardens and rooms that are themselves works of art. And she presided over every detail of the never-quite-finished project. The property, now a center for Islamic studies, is utterly unique and quite simply not to be missed.

O'ahu After Hours

Yes, you can have an umbrella drink at sunset. But in the multicultural metropolis of Honolulu, there's so much more to it than that. Sip a glass of wine and listen to jazz at Formaggio, join the beach-and-beer gang at Duke's Canoe Club, or head to Zanzabar, where DJs spin hip-hop and techno. Sample the sake at an *izakaya* (Japanese tavern) or listen to a performance by a Hawaiian musician. Snack on pūpū, and begin your journey toward that unforgettable tropical sunrise.

Hiking to Ka'ena Point

If we had but one day to spend in rural O'ahu, we'd spend it walking the back road along the rocky shore at the island's northern tip. Ka'ena, a state park as well as a protected natural area, comprises 850 acres of undeveloped coastline that centers on the point where it is said the souls of the ancient dead leapt into the eternal darkness. The views are incomparable; shells can be scavenged in keyhole coves in calm weather; whales spout offshore during winter; and threatened native plants flourish. It's a trek that will change your mind about O'ahu being "too crowded."

Catching a Wave

Taking a surfing lesson from a well-muscled beach boy has been a Honolulu must-do since the first gay divorcée stepped off the first cruise ship. Waikīkī, with its well-shaped but diminutive waves, remains the perfect spot for grommets (surfing newbies), though surf schools operate at beaches (and

many hotels) around the island. Most companies guarantee at least one standing ride in the course of a lesson. And catching that first wave? We guarantee you'll never forget it.

Exploring Chinatown

Chinatown is like one of those centerpiece lazy susans: turn it this way, and you find one thing; turn it another, and there's something else. The various guided tours of this busy neighborhood each offer up a different dish: one focuses on food and restaurants, another shines a light on cultural attractions, and the occasional architect-led AIA tour delves into the area's design character. Take your pick or wander on your own. Just don't miss this unique mixed plate.

Hula with Heart

Professional hula dancers—the ones in poolside hotel shows and dinner extravaganzas—are perfection: hands like undulating waves, smiles that never waiver. But if you want to experience hula with heart, scan the newspapers for a hula school fund-raiser, or ask the activities desk about local festivals. You may see some missteps and bumbles, but you'll also experience different hula styles and hear songs and chants deeply rooted in the culture, all the while surrounded by the scents of a hundred homemade lei.

Listening to a Living Legend

Auntie Genoa Keawe can hold a note longer than anyone. Drop by the Moana Terrace of the Waikīkī Marriott hotel any Thursday between 6 and 9 to hear for yourself. Keawe is an octogenarian dynamo and the living embodiment of the falsetto singing style that Hawaiians so relish. You'll feel like you dropped in on a backyard party.

A Sail on the Wild Side

Who wouldn't want these memory snapshots to take home: the seemingly amused eye of a spinner dolphin as it arcs through the wake of the catamaran in which you're riding; the undulating form of an endangered green sea turtle swimming below you; the slap and splash and whoosh of a humpback whale breaching in full view on indigo seas. Wild Side Specialty Tours can't promise these specific encounters, but their ecologically conscious daily excursions in a quiet, uncrowded catamaran do guarantee good memories.

A Day on the North Shore

"Hano Hano, Hale'iwa," the song says—Beautiful Hale'iwa. Also fun, funky, fast-moving, family-friendly Hale'iwa—an easy place in which to while away half a day. Visit the quirky surf museum, wander through the surf shops, choose from half a dozen good but cheap

TOP ATTRACTIONS

restaurants, suck up some refreshing shave ice, find one-of-a-kind clothes and gifts, and charter a catamaran or fishing boat. Then head back the long way to town (along the east side of the island) along a route that takes you past world-renowned surf spots.

A Trip to Japan

Little known outside O'ahu's growing community of Japanese nationals is a class of small restaurant/bars called *izakaya* or Japanese taverns. Even newer on the scene are *okonomi,* hip spots that specialize in Osaka-style grilled omelets and potent Japanese spirits. Both are like a visit to Japan, minus the long plane ride, and, though pricey, the à la carte menus are unfailingly excellent—if distinctly odd. A must-notch in any foodie's belt.

A Plate-Lunch Picnic

Take a break the way the locals do: get a plate lunch (typically meat with two scoops of macaroni salad and two scoops of rice), then find a park or beach. Don't pack a ton of stuff, don't stick to a schedule. Eat, talk-story (local slang for chatting), or take a nap—then explore, walk, swim, or snorkel. Some options: Mitsu-Ken Catering, then a picnic on the grounds of the nearby Bishop Museum; Fukuya Delicatessen, then Kahala Beach Park; Diamond Head Market and Grill, then Waikīkī Beach or Kapi'olani Park; L&L Drive-Inn, then Kailua Beach.

Walking in the Rain Forest or to a Waterfall

Wend your way through the hillside neighborhood of 'Aiea, northwest of Honolulu, and suddenly you're in a cool, green park, scented with astringent eucalyptus. This is the 3½-mi 'Aiea Loop Trail and if you're committed to squeezing a hike into a short O'ahu stay, you couldn't do better for glimpses of hidden valleys and the experience of an island forest.

If waterfalls are more your speed, then head straight to the back of Manoa Valley, 3 mi mauka (or toward the mountains from Waikīkī) and you'll find a 1½-mi trail along a well-worn path following Manoa stream through native trees and flowers to the Manoa Falls.

Like Jurassic Park with plant identification labels, Hoomaluhia Botanical Garden is a series of half-wild botanical zones broken up by lawns for picnicking. There are craft courses, a visitor center with an art gallery, and a campground. If there's a painter, photographer, or plant nut in the party, plan a long, long stay.

WHEN TO GO

Long days of sunshine and fairly mild year-round temperatures make Hawai'i an all-season destination. Most resort areas are at sea level, with average afternoon temperatures of 75°F–80°F during the coldest months of December and January; during the hottest months of August and September the temperature often reaches 90°F. Higher "Upcountry" elevations typically have cooler and often misty conditions. Only at mountain summits does it reach freezing.

Moist trade winds drop their precipitation on the north and east sides of the Islands, creating tropical climates, whereas the south and west sides remain hot and dry with desertlike conditions. Rainfall can be high in winter, particularly on the north and east shores.

Most travelers head to the Islands in winter, specifically from mid-December through mid-April. This high season means that fewer travel bargains are available; room rates average 10% to 15% higher during this season than the rest of the year.

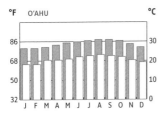

°F   O'AHU   °C

GREAT ONE-DAY ITINERARIES

To experience even a fraction of O'ahu's charms, you need a minimum of four days and a bus pass. Five days and a car is better: Waikīkī is at least a day, Honolulu and Chinatown another, Pearl Harbor the better part of another. Each of the rural sections can swallow a day each, just for driving, sightseeing, and stopping to eat. And that's before you've taken a surf lesson, hung from a parasail, hiked a loop trail, or visited a botanical garden. The following itineraries will take you to our favorite spots on the island.

First Day in Waikīkī

You'll be up at dawn due to the time change and dead on your feet by afternoon due to jet lag. Have a dawn swim, change into walking gear, and head east along Kalākaua Avenue to Monsarrat Avenue, and climb Diamond Head. After lunch, nap in the shade, do some shopping, or visit the nearby East Honolulu neighborhoods of Mō'ili'ili and Kaimukī, rife with small shops and good, little restaurants. End the day with an early, interesting, and inexpensive dinner at one of these neighborhood spots.

Southeast & Windward Exploring

For sand, sun, and surf, follow H1 east to keyhole-shape Hanauma Bay for picture-perfect snorkeling, then round the southeast tip of the island with its windswept cliffs and the famous Hālona Blowhole. Fly a kite or watch body surfers at Sandy Beach. Take in Sea Life Park. In Waimānalo, stop for local-style plate lunch, or punch on through to Kailua, where there's intriguing shopping and good eating.

The North Shore

Hit H1 westbound and then H2 to get to the North Shore. You'll pass through pineapple country, then drop down a scenic winding road to Waialua and Hale'iwa. Stop in Hale'iwa town to shop, to experience shave ice, and to pick up a guided dive or snorkel trip. On winding Kamehameha Highway, stop at famous big-wave beaches, take a dip in a cove with a turtle, and buy fresh Island fruit at roadside stands.

Pearl Harbor

Pearl Harbor is an almost all-day investment. Be on the grounds by 7:30 AM to line up for Arizona Memorial tickets. Clamber all over the USS *Bowfin* submarine. Finally, take the free trolley to see the "Mighty Mo" battleship. If it's Wednesday or Saturday, make the five-minute drive mauka (toward the mountains) for bargain-basement shopping at the sprawling Aloha Stadium Swap Meet.

WEDDINGS & HONEYMOONS

There's no question that Hawai'i is one of the country's foremost honeymoon destinations. Romance is in the air here: the white, sandy beaches, swaying palm trees, and balmy tropical breezes put people in the mood for love. It's easy to understand why Hawai'i is fast becoming a popular wedding destination as well, and new resorts and hotels entice visitors. You can plan a traditional ceremony followed by a reception at an elegant resort, or you can go barefoot on the beach and celebrate at a lū'au. The Islands are brimming with many wedding planners, which makes it easy to wed in paradise, and then stay here to honeymoon.

The Big Day

Choosing the Perfect Place. When choosing a location, remember that you really have two choices to make: the ceremony location and where to have the reception, if you're having one. For the former, there are beaches, bluffs overlooking beaches, gardens, private residences, resort lawns, and, of course, places of worship. As for the reception, there are these same choices, as well as restaurants and even lū'au. If you decide to go outdoors, remember the seasons—yes, Hawai'i has seasons. If you're planning a winter wedding outdoors, be sure you have a backup plan (such as a tent), in case it rains. Also, if you're planning an outdoor wedding at sunset—which is very popular—be sure you match the time of your ceremony to the time the sun sets at that time of year.

Finding a Wedding Planner. An on-island wedding planner can help select a location, help design the floral scheme and recommend a florist, and suggest any Hawaiian traditions to incorporate into your ceremony. Many planners have relationships with vendors, providing packages—which mean savings.

Most resorts have on-site wedding coordinators; however, there are many independents around the island and even those who specialize in certain types of ceremonies—by locale, size, religious affiliation, and so on. A simple "Hawai'i weddings" Google search will reveal dozens. What's important is that you feel comfortable with your coordinator. Ask for references—and call them. Share your budget. Get a proposal—in writing. Request a detailed list of the exact services they'll provide. If your idea of your wedding doesn't match their services, try someone else.

Getting Your License. The good news about marrying in Hawai'i is that there's no waiting period, and no residency or citizenship requirements. However, both the bride and groom must appear together in person before a marriage license agent to apply for a

WEDDINGS & HONEYMOONS

marriage license. You'll need proof of age—the legal age to marry is 18. (If you're 19 or older, a valid driver's license will suffice; if you're 18, a certified birth certificate is required.) Upon approval, a marriage license is immediately issued and costs $60, cash only. After the ceremony, your officiant will mail the marriage license to the state. For more detailed information, visit www.hawaii.gov or call 808/241–3498.

Also—this is important—the person performing your wedding must be licensed by the Hawai'i Department of Health, even if he or she is a licensed minister. Be sure to ask.

Wedding Attire. In Hawai'i, basically anything goes, from long, formal dresses with trains to white bikinis. For the men, tuxedos are not the norm; a pair of solid-colored slacks with a nice aloha shirt is. In fact, tradition in Hawai'i for the groom is a plain white aloha shirt (they do exist) with slacks or long shorts and a colored sash around the waist. If you're planning a wedding on the beach, barefoot is the way to go.

If you decide to marry in a formal dress and tuxedo, you're better off making your selections and alterations on the mainland and hand-carrying them aboard the plane.

Local Customs. When it comes to traditional Hawaiian wedding customs, the most obvious is the lei exchange in which the bride and groom take turns placing a lei around the neck of the other—with a kiss. Bridal lei are usually floral, whereas the groom's is typically made of maile, a green leafy garland that drapes around the neck and is open at the ends. Brides often also wear a haku lei—a circular floral headpiece. Other Hawaiian customs include the blowing of the conch shell, hula, chanting, and Hawaiian music.

The Honeymoon

Do you want champagne and strawberries delivered to your room each morning? A five-star restaurant in which to dine? Then a resort is the way to go. A B&B is a good option if you're on a tight budget or don't plan to spend much time in your room. On the other hand, maybe you want a little more privacy. In that case, a private vacation-rental home or a condominium resort is the answer. That's another beautiful thing about Hawai'i: the lodging accommodations are almost as plentiful as the beaches, and there's one to match your tastes and your budget.

KIDS & FAMILIES

With dozens of adventures, discoveries, and fun-filled beach days, Hawai'i is a blast with kids. Even better, the things to do here do not appeal only to small fry. The entire family, parents included, will enjoy surfing, discovering a waterfall in the rain forest, and snorkeling with sea turtles. And there are plenty of organized activities for kids that will free parents' time for a few romantic beach strolls.

Choosing a Place to Stay

Resorts: All of the big resorts make kids' programs a priority, and it shows. When you are booking your room, ask about "kids eat free" deals and the number of kids' pools at the resort. Also check out the size of the groups in the children's programs, and find out whether the cost of the programs includes lunch, equipment, and activities.

In Waikīkī your best bet for kids is the Hilton Hawaiian Village, where there's a large beach and loads of kids' programs. Another good choice is the Waikīkī Beach Marriott Resort, which has a variety of programs for kids as well. Other options include the Waikīkī Beach Hotel and the Sheraton Princess Kaiulani.

Condos: Condo and vacation rentals are a fantastic value for families vacationing in Hawai'i. You can cook your own food, which is cheaper than eating out and some-

times easier, and you'll get twice the space of a hotel room for about a quarter of the price. Be sure to ask about the size of the complex's pool (some try to pawn a tiny soaking tub off as a pool) and whether barbecues are available.

For the ultimate condo experience on O'ahu Marriott's Ko Olina Beach Club's sheltered beaches, four pools, barbecue and children's play areas, large kitchens and on-site grocery store can't be beat. In Waikīkī, the Castle Waikīkī Shore is the only beachfront condo property. Outrigger Luana offers barbecues, a pool, and recreational areas near Fort DeRussy on Waikīkī beach.

Ocean Activities

Hawai'i is all about getting your kids outside—away from TV and video games. And who could resist the turquoise water, the promise of spotting dolphins or whales, and the fun of boogie boarding or surfing?

On the Beach: Most people like being in the water, but toddlers and school-age kids tend to be especially enamored of it. There are several beaches in Hawai'i that are nearly as safe as a pool—completely protected bays with pleasant white-sand beaches.

In Waikīkī, your best bets for young children are Kūhiō Beach

KIDS & FAMILIES

Park and Fort DeRussy Beach Park. Both have water protected from a strong shore break and a wide stretch of sand. On the Windward side, your best bets are Kailua Beach park with its shade trees and good bathroom and shower facilities or ultracalm Lanikai beach. North Shore beaches are only recommended for children in the summer months. On the Leeward side of the island, Kō'Ōlina's protected beaches are great for families with small children.

On the Waves: Surf lessons are a great idea for older kids, especially if mom and dad want a little quiet time. Beginner lessons are always on safe and easy waves and last anywhere from two to four hours.

Waikīkī is *the* place for everyone to learn to surf, including kids. Some hotels, including the Waikīkī Beach Marriott Resort and Spa, offer in-house surf schools. Or, for a unique experience, try Hawaiian Fire, Inc. These off-duty Honolulu fire fighters teach water safety in addition to surfing in their two-hour lessons near Barber's Point (starting at $97).

The Underwater World: If your kids are ready to try snorkeling, Hawai'i is a great place to introduce them to the underwater world.

On O'ahu the quintessential snorkeling experience can be had at Hanauma Bay. After viewing an educational film about Hawai'i's underwater world, and descending into a half-submerged volcano, kids have an opportunity not only to see hundreds of species of fish in protected waters but to enjoy a wide stretch of beach as well.

Land Activities

O'ahu is fortunate to have the largest variety of land-based experiences in the Islands. Kids can visit the Honolulu Zoo for a sleepover, touch fishy friends at the Waikīkī Aquarium, help in a dolphin training session at Sea Life Park, or even learn to husk a coconut at the Polynesian Culture Center.

After Dark

At night, younger kids get a kick out of lū'aus, and many of the shows incorporate young audience members, adding to the fun. If you're planning on hitting a lū'au with a teen in tow, we highly recommend going the modern route. Cirque du Soleil's Waikīkī production (opening summer 2008) will keep even teens in your family entertained, while the Paradise Cove Lū'au offers fire dancers and kid-friendly games.

Exploring O'ahu

WORD OF MOUTH

"On O'ahu, you'll want to see Pearl Harbor, and drive up to the North Shore beaches, maybe Diamond Head and the Pali lookout. Then there's the beach, and relaxing, and shopping, and eating!!!"
—dmlove

By Trina
Kudlacek

O'ahu is one-stop Hawai'i—all the allure of the Islands in a chop-suey mix that has you kayaking around offshore islets by day and sitting in a jazz club 'round midnight, all without ever having to take another flight or repack your suitcase. It offers both the buzz of modern living in jam-packed Honolulu (the state's capital), and the allure of slow-paced island life on its northern and eastern shores. It is, in many ways, the center of the Hawaiian universe.

There are more museums, staffed historic sites, and walking tours here than you'll find on any other island. And only here do a wealth of renovated buildings and well-preserved neighborhoods so clearly spin the story of Hawai'i's history. It's the only place to experience island-style urbanity, since there are no other true cities in the state. And yet you can get as lost in the rural landscape and be as laid-back as you wish.

O'ahu is home to Waikīkī, the most famous Hawaiian beach with some of the world's most famous surf on the North Shore; and the Islands' best known historical site—Pearl Harbor. If it's isolation, peace, and quiet you want, O'ahu is probably not for you, but if you'd like a bit of spice with your piece of paradise, this island provides it.

GEOLOGY

Encompassing 597 square mi, O'ahu is the third-largest island in the Hawaiian chain. Scientists believe the island was formed about 4 million years ago by two volcanoes: Wai'anae and Ko'olau. Wai'anae, the older of the two, makes up the western side of the island, whereas Ko'olau shapes the eastern side. Central O'ahu is an elevated plateau bordered by the two mountain ranges, with Pearl Harbor to the south. Several of O'ahu's most famous natural landmarks, including Diamond Head and Hanauma Bay, are tuff rings and cinder cones formed during a renewed volcanic stage (roughly 1 million years ago).

FLORA & FAUNA

Due to its elevation, the eastern (Ko'olau) side of O'ahu is much cooler and wetter than the western side of the island, which tends to be dry and arid. The island's official flower, the little orange *ilima*, grows predominantly in the east, but leis throughout the island incorporate *ilima*. Numerous tropical fish call the reef at Hanauma Bay home, migrating humpback whales can be spotted off the coast past Waikīkī and Diamond Head from December through April, spinner dolphins pop in and out of the island's bays, and

Kick back in a hammock in Waikīkī and gaze off at Diamond Head in the distance.

dozens of islets off Oʻahu's eastern coast provide refuge for endangered seabirds.

HISTORY

Oʻahu is the most populated island because early tourism to Hawaiʻi started here. Although Kīlauea volcano on Hawaiʻi was a tourist attraction in the late 1800s, it was the building of the Moana Hotel on Waikīkī Beach in 1901 and subsequent advertising of Hawaiʻi to wealthy San Franciscans that really fueled tourism in the islands. Oʻahu was drawing tens of thousands of guests yearly when, on December 7, 1941, Japanese Zeros appeared at dawn to bomb Pearl Harbor. Though tourism understandably dipped during the war (Waikīkī Beach was fenced with barbed wire), the subsequent memorial only seemed to attract more visitors, and Oʻahu remains hugely popular with tourists to this day.

DIAMOND HEAD & KAPIʻOLANI PARK

Diamond Head Crater is perhaps Hawaiʻi's most recognizable natural landmark. It got its name from sailors who thought they had found precious gems on its slopes; these later proved to be calcite crystals, or fool's gold. Hawaiians saw a resemblance in the sharp angle of the crater's seaward slope to the oddly shaped head of the ʻahi fish and so called

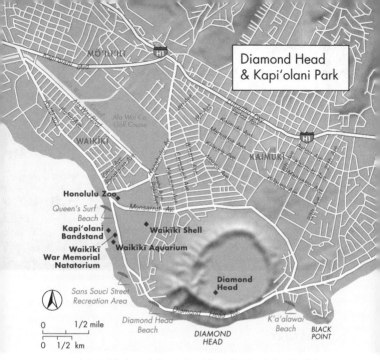

it Lēʻahi, though later they Hawaiianized the English name to Kaimana Hila. It is commemorated in a widely known hula—"*A ʻike i ka nani o Kaimana Hila, Kaimana Hila, kau mai i luna*" ("We saw the beauty of Diamond Head, Diamond Head set high above").

Kapiʻolani Park lies in the shadow of the crater. King David Kalākaua established the park in 1887, named it after his queen, and dedicated it "to the use and enjoyment of the people." Kapiʻolani Park is a 500-acre expanse where you can play all sorts of field sports, enjoy a picnic, see wild animals at the Honolulu Zoo, or hear live music at the Waikīkī Shell or the Kapiʻolani Bandstand.

TOP ATTRACTIONS

Diamond Head State Monument and Park. Panoramas from this 760-foot extinct volcanic peak, once used as a military fortification, extend from Waikīkī and Honolulu in one direction and out to Koko Head in the other, with surfers and windsurfers scattered like confetti on the cresting waves below. This 360-degree perspective is a great orientation for first-time visitors. On a clear day, look to your left past Koko Head to glimpse the outlines of the islands of

Maui and Moloka'i. To enter the park from Waikīkī, take Kalākaua Avenue east, turn left at Monsarrat Avenue, head a mile up the hill, and look for a sign on the right. Drive through the tunnel to the inside of the crater. The ¾-mi trail to the top begins at the parking lot. New lighting inside the summit tunnel and a spiral staircase eases the way, but be aware that the hike to the crater is a strenuous upward climb; if you aren't in the habit of getting much exercise, this might not be for you. Take bottled water to ensure that you stay hydrated under the tropical sun. ■TIP→To beat the heat and the crowds, rise early and do the hike before 8 AM. As you walk, note the color of the vegetation; if the mountain is brown, Honolulu has been without significant rain for a while; but if the trees and undergrowth glow green, you'll know it's the wet season (winter) without looking at a calendar. This is when rare Hawaiian marsh plants revive on the floor of the crater. Keep an eye on your watch if you're there at day's end, because the gates close promptly at 6. ⊠*Diamond Head Rd. at 18th Ave., Waikīkī* ☎*808/587–0285* ⊕*www.hawaiistateparks.org* ☎*$1 per person, $5 per vehicle* ⊙*Daily 6–6.*

♺ **Honolulu Zoo.** To get a glimpse of the endangered *nēnē*, the Hawai'i state bird, check out the Kipuka Nēnē Sanctuary. Though many animals prefer to remain invisible, the monkeys appear to enjoy being seen and are a hoot to watch. It's best to get to the zoo right when it opens, since the animals are livelier in the cool of the morning. There are bigger and better zoos, but this one, though showing signs of neglect due to budget constraints, is a lush garden and has some great programs. The Wildest Show in Town, a series of concerts ($2 donation), takes place on Wednesday evening in summer. You can have a family sleepover inside the zoo during Snooze in the Zoo on a Friday or Saturday night every month. Or just head for the petting zoo, where kids can make friends with a llama or stand in the middle of a koi pond. There's an exceptionally good gift shop. On weekends, the Zoo Fence Art Mart, on Monsarrat Avenue on the Diamond Head side outside the zoo, has affordable artwork by contemporary artists. Metered parking is available all along the *makai* (ocean) side of the park and in the lot next to the zoo. TheBus, O'ahu's only form of public transportation, makes stops here along the way to and from Ala Moana Center and Sea Life Park (routes 22 and 58). ⊠*151 Kapahulu Ave., Waikīkī* ☎*808/971–7171* ⊕*www.honoluluzoo.org* ☎*$8* ⊙*Daily 9–4:30.*

Kapi'olani Bandstand. Victorian-style Kapi'olani Bandstand, which was originally built in the late 1890s, is Kapi'olani Park's stage for community entertainment and concerts. The nation's only city-sponsored band, the Royal Hawaiian Band, performs free concerts on Sunday afternoons. Local newspapers list event information. ⊠*Near intersection of Kalākaua and Monsarrat Aves., Waikīkī.*

☼ **Waikīkī Aquarium.** This amazing little attraction harbors more than 2,500 organisms and 420 species of Hawaiian and South Pacific marine life, including endangered Hawaiian monk seals, sharks, and the chambered nautilus. The Edge of the Reef exhibit showcases five different types of reef environments found along Hawai'i's shorelines. Check out the Northwestern Hawaiian Islands exhibit (opening in late 2008), Ocean Drifters jellyfish exhibit, outdoor touch pool, and the self-guided audio tour, which is included with admission. The aquarium offers programs of interest to adults and children alike, including the Aquarium after Dark when visitors grab a flashlight and view fish going about their rarely observable nocturnal activities. Plan to spend at least an hour at the aquarium, including 10 minutes for a film in the Sea Visions Theater. ⊠*2777 Kalākaua Ave., Waikīkī* ☎*808/923-9741* ⊕*www.waquarium.org* ⊡*$9* ☉*Daily 9–4:30.*

Waikīkī Shell. Locals bring picnics and grab one of the 6,000 "grass seats" (lawn seating) for music under the stars (there are actual seats, as well). Concerts are held May 1 to Labor Day, with a few winter dates, weather permitting. Check newspaper Friday entertainment sections to see who is performing. ⊠*2805 Monsarrat Ave., Waikīkī* ☎*808/924–8934* ⊕*www.blaisdellcenter.com.*

HONOLULU

Here is Hawai'i's only true metropolis, its seat of government, center of commerce and shipping, entertainment and recreation mecca, a historic site and an evolving urban area—conflicting roles that engender endless debate and controversy. For the visitor, Honolulu is an everyman's delight: Hipsters and scholars, sightseers and foodies, nature lovers and culture vultures all can find their bliss.

Once there was the broad bay of Mamala and the narrow inlet of Kou, fronting a dusty plain occupied by a few thatched houses and the great Pakaka *heiau* (shrine).

DID YOU KNOW?

Waikīkī Beach stretches from Hilton Hawaiian Village to Kapi'olani Park and Diamond Head, and if you surf here you'll be hanging ten with the best of 'em.

Nosing into the narrow passage in the early 1790s, British sea captain William Brown named the port Fair Haven. Later, Hawaiians would call it Honolulu, or "sheltered bay." As shipping traffic increased, the settlement grew into a Western-style town of streets and buildings, tightly clustered around the single freshwater source, Nu'uanu Stream. Not until piped water became available in the early 1900s did Honolulu spread across the greening plain. Long before that, however, Honolulu gained importance when King Kamehameha I reluctantly abandoned his home on the Big Island to build a chiefly compound near the harbor in 1804 to better protect Hawaiian interests from the Western incursion.

Two hundred years later, the entire island is, in a sense, Honolulu—the City and County of Honolulu. The city has no official boundaries, extending across the flatlands from Pearl Harbor to Waikīkī and high into the hills behind.

CHINATOWN

Chinatown occupies 15 blocks immediately north of downtown Honolulu—it's flat, compact, and easily explored in half a day. ■TIP➔The best time to visit is morning, when the popos (grandmas) shop—it's cool out, and you can enjoy a cheap dim-sum breakfast. Chinatown is a seven-days-a-week operation. Sunday is especially busy with families sharing dim sum in raucous dining hall–size restaurants.

The name Chinatown has always been a misnomer. Though three-quarters of O'ahu's Chinese lived closely packed in these 25 acres in the late 1800s, even then the neighborhood was half Japanese. Today, you hear Vietnamese and Tagalog as often as Mandarin and Cantonese, and there are touches of Japan, Singapore, Malaysia, Korea, Thailand, Samoa, and the Marshall Islands, as well.

Perhaps a more accurate name is the one used by early Chinese: Wah Fau ("Chinese port") signifying a landing and jumping-off place. Chinese laborers, as soon as they completed their plantation contracts, hurried into the city to start businesses here. It's a launching point for today's immigrants, too: Southeast Asian shops almost outnumber Chinese; stalls carry Filipino specialties like winged beans and goat meat; and in one tiny space, knife-wielding Samoans skin coconuts to order.

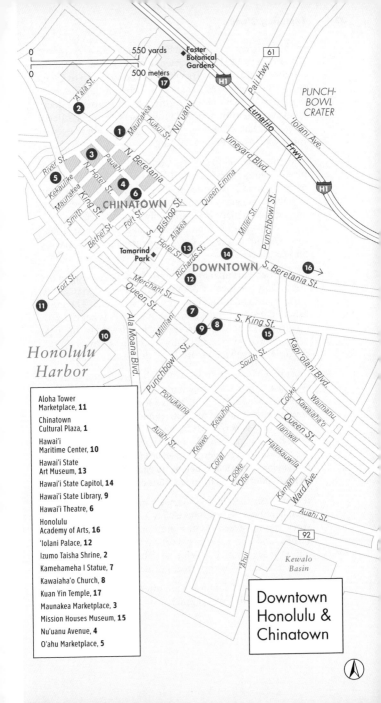

0
550 yards
0
500 meters

Foster
Botanical
Gardens

61

H1

PUNCH-
BOWL
CRATER

Pali Hwy.

Iolani Ave.

Lunalilo Frwy.

Maunakea St.

Kukui St.

Nuʻuanu Ave.

Vineyard Blvd.

Aʻala St.

N. Beretania St.

Pauahi St.

River St.

Kekaulike

N. Hotel St.

Maunakea

King St.

Smith St.

Bethel St.

Fort St.

Queen Emma St.

Miller St.

Punchbowl St.

CHINATOWN

Bishop St.

Alakea St.

Hotel St.

Tamarind
Park

Richards St.

DOWNTOWN

S. Beretania St.

Merchant St.

Queen St.

Mililani St.

Fort St.

Honolulu
Harbor

S. King St.

Punchbowl St.

South St.

Kapiʻolani Blvd.

Ala Moana Blvd.

Pohukaina

Auahi St.

Keawe

Coral

Cooke

Ohe

Keauhou

Kamani

Iliniwai

Waimanu

Kawaiahaʻo

Queen St.

Halekauwila

Ward Ave.

Auahi St.

Ahui

92

Kewalo
Basin

Aloha Tower
Marketplace, **11**

Chinatown
Cultural Plaza, **1**

Hawaiʻi
Maritime Center, **10**

Hawaiʻi State
Art Museum, **13**

Hawaiʻi State Capitol, **14**

Hawaiʻi State Library, **9**

Hawaiʻi Theatre, **6**

Honolulu
Academy of Arts, **16**

ʻIolani Palace, **12**

Izumo Taisha Shrine, **2**

Kamehameha I Statue, **7**

Kawaiahaʻo Church, **8**

Kuan Yin Temple, **17**

Maunakea Marketplace, **3**

Mission Houses Museum, **15**

Nuʻuanu Avenue, **4**

Oʻahu Marketplace, **5**

Downtown
Honolulu &
Chinatown

In the half-century after the first Chinese laborers arrived in Hawai'i in 1851, Chinatown was a link to home for the all-male cadre of workers who planned to return to China rich and respected. Merchants not only sold supplies, they held mail, loaned money, wrote letters, translated documents, sent remittances to families, served meals, offered rough bunkhouse accommodations, and were the center for news, gossip, and socializing.

Though much happened to Chinatown in the 20th century—beginning in January 1900, when almost the entire neighborhood was burned to the ground to halt the spread of bubonic plague—it remains a bustling, crowded, noisy, and odiferous place bent primarily on buying and selling, and sublimely oblivious to its status as a National Historic District or the encroaching gentrification on nearby Nu'uanu Avenue.

Chinatown's original business district was made up of dry goods and produce merchants, tailors and dressmakers, barbers, herbalists, and dozens of restaurants. The meat, fish, and produce stalls remain but the mix is heavier now on gift and curio stores, lei stands, jewelry shops and bakeries, with a smattering of noodle makers, travel agents, Asian-language video stores, and dozens of restaurants.

A caution: Hotel Street was Honolulu's red-light district and A'ala Park, just across the Nu'uanu stream, shelters many homeless people and more than a few drug users. A police station in the heart of the district has tamped down crime, and the area is perfectly safe by day—even panhandling is rare. But at night, park in a well-lighted place, travel with the crowds, and be alert. ■TIP→**Look for well-marked municipal parking lots on Smith, Bethel, Nu'uanu, and Beretania; these charge a third of what the private lots demand.**

If you're here between January 20 and February 20, check local newspapers for Chinese New Year activities. Bakeries stock special sweets, stores and homes sprout bright-red scrolls, and lion dancers cavort through the streets feeding on *li-see* (money envelopes). The Narcissus Queen is chosen, and an evening street fair draws crowds.

Weekly tours of Chinatown are offered on Tuesday by the Chinese Chamber of Commerce.

DID YOU KNOW?

Just north of downtown Honolulu is Chinatown, where you can explore temples, eat authentic cuisine, and watch Chinese New Year festivities.

Shopping in Chinatown

Chinatown is rife with ridiculously inexpensive gifts: folding fans for $1 and coconut purses for $5 at **Maunakea Marketplace**, for example. Curio shops sell everything from porcelain statues to woks, ginseng to Mao shoes. If you like to sew, or have a yen for a brocade cheongsam, visit the Hong Kong Supermarket in the Wo Fat Chop Sui building (at the corner of N. Hotel and Maunakea) for fresh fruit, crack seed (Chinese dried fruit popular for snacking), and row upon row of boxed, tinned delicacies with indecipherable names. Narrow, dim, and dusty **Bo Wah Trading Co.** (1037 Maunakea) is full of inexpensive cooking utensils. **Chinatown Cultural Plaza** offers fine-quality jade. Chinatown is Honolulu's lei center, with shops strung along Beretania and Maunakea; every local has a favorite shop where they're greeted by name. In spring, look for gardenia nosegays wrapped in ti leaves.

TOP ATTRACTIONS

❶ Chinatown Cultural Plaza. This sprawling multistory shopping square surrounds a courtyard with an incense-wreathed shrine and Moongate stage for holiday performances. The Chee Kung Tong Society has a beautifully decorated meeting hall here; a number of such *tongs* (meeting places) are hidden on upper floors in Chinatown. Outside, near the canal, local members of the community play cards and mahjong. ⊠ *100 N. Beretania, Chinatown.*

❷ Izumo Taisha Shrine. From Chinatown Cultural Plaza, cross a stone bridge to visit Okuninushi No Mikoto, a *kami* (god) who is believed in Shinto tradition to bring good fortune if properly courted (and thanked afterward). ⊠ *N. Kukui and Canal, Chinatown.*

⓱ Kuan Yin Temple. A couple of blocks *mauka* (toward the mountains) from Chinatown is the oldest Buddhist temple in the Islands. Mistakenly called a goddess by some, Kuan Yin, also known as Kannon, is a bodhisattva—one who chose to remain on earth doing good even after achieving enlightenment. Transformed from a male into a female figure centuries ago, she is credited with a particular sympathy for women. You see representations of her all over the Islands: holding a lotus flower (symbolizing beauty in the form of the flower that grows from the mud of human frailty), as at the temple; pouring out a pitcher of oil (like mercy flowing); or as a sort of Madonna with a child. Visitors are permitted, but be aware this is a practicing place of worship. ✉ *170 N. Vineyard, Downtown Honolulu* ☎ *No phone.*

❸ **Maunakea Marketplace.** On the corner of Maunakea and Hotel streets is this plaza surrounded by shops, an indoor market, and a food court. Within the Marketplace, the **Hawaiian Chinese Cultural Museum and Archives** (✆ *$2* ⊙ *Mon.– Sat. 10–2*) displays historic photographs and artifacts.■ **TIP →** **If you appreciate fine tea, visit the Tea Hut, an unpretentious counter inside a curio shop.** ✉ *1120 Maunakea St., Chinatown* ☎ *808/524–3409.*

❺ **O'ahu Marketplace.** Here is a taste of old-style Chinatown, ★ where you're likely to be hustled aside as a whole pig, ready for roasting, is carried through the crowd and where glassy-eyed fish of every size and hue lie stacked on ice. Try the bubble tea (juices and flavored teas mixed with bead-like tapioca pieces) or pick up a magenta dragonfruit for breakfast. ✉ *N. King St. at Kekaulike, Chinatown.*

ALSO WORTH SEEING

❻ **Hawai'i Theatre.** Opened in 1922, this theater earned rave reviews for its neoclassical design, with Corinthian columns, marble statues, and plush carpeting and drapery. Nicknamed the "Pride of the Pacific," the facility was rescued from demolition in the early 1980s and underwent a $30-million renovation. Listed on both the State and National Register of Historic Places, it has become the centerpiece of revitalization efforts of Honolulu's downtown area. The 1,200-seat venue hosts concerts, theatrical productions, dance performances, and film screenings. ✉ *1130 Bethel St., Chinatown* ☎ *808/528–0506* ✆ *$5* ⊙ *1-hr guided tours Tues. at 11.*

❹ **Nu'uanu Avenue.** Here on Chinatown's southern border and on Bethel Street, which runs parallel, are clustered art galleries, restaurants, a wine shop, an antiques auctioneer, a dress shop or two, one tiny theater space (the Arts at Mark's Garage), and one historic stage (the Hawai'i Theatre). **First Friday** art nights, when galleries stay open until 9 PM, draw crowds. If you like art and people-watching and are fortunate enough to be on O'ahu the first Friday of the month, this event shouldn't be missed. ✉ *Nu'uanu Ave., Chinatown.*

DOWNTOWN HONOLULU

Honolulu's past and present play a delightful counterpoint throughout the downtown sector. Postmodern glass-and-steel office buildings look down on the Aloha Tower, built in 1926 and, until the early 1960s, the tallest structure in Honolulu. Hawai'i's history is told in the architecture of these few blocks: the cut-stone turn-of-the-20th-century storefronts of Merchant Street, the gracious white-columned American-Georgian manor that was the home of the Islands' last queen, the jewel-box palace occupied by the monarchy before it was overthrown, the Spanish-inspired stucco and tile-roofed Territorial Era government buildings, and the 21st-century glass pyramid of the First Hawaiian Bank Building.

Plan a couple of hours for exploring downtown's historic buildings, more if you're taking a guided tour or walk. The best time to visit is in the cool and relative quiet of morning or on the weekends when downtown is all but deserted except for the historic sites. To reach Downtown Honolulu from Waikīkī by car, take Ala Moana Boulevard to Alakea Street and turn right; three blocks up on the right, between South King and Hotel, there's a municipal parking lot in Ali'i Place on the right. You can also take route 19 or 20 of TheBus to the Aloha Tower Marketplace or take a trolley from Waikīkī.

TOP ATTRACTIONS

★ **Fodor'sChoice 'Iolani Palace.** America's only royal residence was
 built in 1882 on the site of an earlier palace, and it contains the thrones of King Kalākaua and his successor (and sister) Queen Lili'uokalani. Bucking the stereotype of the primitive islander, the palace had electricity and telephone lines installed even before the White House. Downstairs galleries showcase the royal jewelry, and kitchen and offices of the monarchy. The palace is open for guided or self-guided audio tours, and reservations are essential. ■TIP→If you're set on taking a guided tour, call for reservations a few days in advance. The gift shop was formerly the 'Iolani Barracks, built to house the Royal Guard. ⊠*King and Richards Sts., Downtown Honolulu* ☎*808/522–0832* ⊕*www.iolani palace.org* ⊠*$20 guided tour, $12 audio tour, $6 downstairs galleries only* ⊘*Tues.–Sat. 9–2, guided tours every 15 mins 9–11:15, self-guided audio tours 11:45–3:30.*

⑦ Kamehameha I Statue. Paying tribute to the Big Island chieftain who united all the warring Hawaiian Islands into one kingdom at the turn of the 18th century, this statue, which stands with one arm outstretched in welcome, is one of three originally cast in Paris, France, by American sculptor T.R. Gould. The original statue, lost at sea and replaced by this one, was eventually salvaged and is now in Kapaʻau, on the Big Island, near the king's birthplace. Each year on the king's birthday, June 11, the more famous copy is draped in fresh lei that reach lengths of 18 feet and longer. A parade proceeds past the statue, and Hawaiian civic clubs, the women in hats and impressive long holokū dresses and the men in sashes and cummerbunds, pay honor to the leader whose name means "The Lonely One." ⊠*417 S. King St., outside Aliʻiōlani Hale, Downtown Honolulu.*

❽ Kawaiahaʻo Church. Fancifully called Hawaiʻi's Westminster Abbey, this 14,000-coral-block house of worship witnessed the coronations, weddings, and funerals of generations of Hawaiian royalty. Each of the building's coral blocks was quarried from reefs offshore at depths of more than 20 feet and transported to this site. Interior woodwork was created from the forests of the Koʻolau Mountains. The upper gallery has an exhibit of paintings of the royal families. The graves of missionaries and of King Lunalilo are adjacent. Services in English and Hawaiian are held each Sunday, and the church members are exceptionally welcoming, greeting newcomers with lei; their affiliation is United Church of Christ. Although there are no guided tours, you can look around the church at no cost. ⊠*957 Punchbowl St., at King St., Downtown Honolulu* ☎*808/522–1333* ⌐*Free* ☉*English service Sun. at 8 AM and Wed. at 6 PM, Hawaiian service Sun. at 10:30 AM.*

ALSO WORTH SEEING

⓫ Aloha Tower Marketplace. Two stories of shops and kiosks sell island-inspired clothing, jewelry, art, and home furnishings. The Marketplace also has indoor and outdoor restaurants and live entertainment. For a bird's-eye view of this working harbor, take a free ride up to the observation deck of Aloha Tower. Cruise ships dock at Piers 9 and 10 alongside the Marketplace and are often greeted and sent out to sea with music and hula dancing at the piers' end. ⊠*1 Aloha Tower Dr., at Piers 10 and 11, Downtown Honolulu* ☎*808/528–5700, 808/566–2337 entertainment info* ⊕*www.alohatower.com* ☉*Mon.–Sat. 9–9, Sun. 9–6; restaurants open later.*

⑩ Hawai'i Maritime Center. The story of the Islands begins
☾ on the seas. The King **Kalākaua's Boathouse Museum,**
★ a branch of the Bishop Museum, has interactive exhibits
where you can learn about Hawai'i's whaling days and
the history of Honolulu Harbor, the Clipper Seaplane, and
the voyaging canoe *Hōkūle'a* (often absent at the museum
and out touring the Pacific) that helped spark the Hawaiian cultural renaissance and proved that Hawaiians were
masters of craftsmanship and navigation. Also featured is
the Northwestern Hawaiian Islands exhibit, with information about the unique flora and fauna of the national
monument which was established in 2006. Moored next to
the Boathouse is a 1778 four-masted, square-rigged ship,
the *Falls of Clyde,* which once brought tea from China
to the U.S. West Coast. Self-guided audio tours are available. ✉*Ala Moana Blvd. at Pier 7, Downtown Honolulu*
☎*808/521–2829* ⊕*www.bishopmuseum.org/exhibits/hmc/
hmc.html* ▣*$7.50* ☉*Daily 8:30–5.*

⑬ Hawai'i State Art Museum. Hawai'i was one of the first states
in the nation to legislate that a portion of the taxes paid on
commercial building projects be set aside for the purchase
of artwork. A few years ago, the state purchased an ornate
period-style building (built to house the headquarters of
a prominent developer) and dedicated 12,000 feet on the
second floor to the art of Hawai'i in all its ethnic diversity. The **Diamond Head Gallery** features new acquisitions
and thematic shows from the State Art Collection and the
State Foundation on Culture and the Arts. The **'Ewa Gallery** houses more than 150 works documenting Hawai'i's
visual-arts history since becoming a state in 1959. Also
included are a sculpture gallery as well as a café, a gift
shop, and educational meeting rooms. ✉*250 S. Hotel St.,
2nd fl., Downtown Honolulu* ☎*808/586–0900 museum,
808/536–5900 restaurant* ⊕*www.hawaii.gov/sfca* ▣*Free*
☉*Tues.–Sat. 10–4.*

⑭ Hawai'i State Capitol. The capitol's architecture is richly
symbolic: the columns resemble palm trees, the legislative
chambers are shaped like volcanic cinder cones, and the
central court is open to the sky, representing Hawai'i's open
society. Replicas of the Hawai'i state seal, each weighing
7,500 pounds, hang above both its entrances. The building, which in 1969 replaced 'Iolani Palace as the seat of
government, is surrounded by reflecting pools, just as the
Islands are embraced by water. A pair of statues, often
draped in lei, flank the building: one of the beloved queen

Lili'uokalani and the other of the sainted Father Damien de Veuster. ✉*215 S. Beretania St., Downtown Honolulu* ☎*808/586–0146* ✆*Free* ☉*Guided tours on request weekday afternoons; call for availability.*

❾ Hawai'i State Library. This beautifully renovated main library was built in 1913. Its Samuel M. Kamakau Reading Room, on the 1st floor in the Mauka (Hawaiian for "mountain") Courtyard, houses an extensive Hawai'i and Pacific book collection and pays tribute to Kamakau, a missionary student whose 19th-century writings in English offer rare and vital insight into traditional Hawaiian culture. ✉*478 King St., Downtown Honolulu* ☎*808/586–3500* ✆*Free* ☉*Mon. and Wed. 10–5, Tues., Fri., and Sat. 9–5, Thurs. 9–8.*

⑯ Honolulu Academy of Arts. Originally built around the collection of a Honolulu matron who donated much of her estate to the museum, the academy is housed in a maze of courtyards, cloistered walkways, and quiet low-ceilinged spaces. An impressive permanent collection includes Hiroshige's *ukiyo-e* Japanese prints, donated by James Michener; Italian Renaissance paintings; and American and European art. The newer Luce Pavilion complex, nicely incorporated into the more traditional architecture of the place, has a traveling-exhibit gallery, a Hawaiian gallery, an excellent café, and a gift shop. The Academy Theatre screens art films. This is also the jumping-off place for tours of Doris Duke's estate, Shangri La. Call or check the Web site for special exhibits, concerts, and films. ✉*900 S. Beretania St., Downtown Honolulu* ☎*808/532–8700* ⊕*www.honolulu academy.org* ✆*$10, free 1st Wed. and 3rd Sun. of month* ☉*Tues.–Sat. 10–4:30, Sun. 1–5.*

⑮ Mission Houses Museum. The determined Hawai'i missionaries arrived in 1820, gaining royal favor and influencing every aspect of island life. Their descendants became leaders in government and business. You can walk through their original dwellings, including Hawai'i's oldest wooden structure, a white frame house that was prefabricated in New England and shipped around the Horn. Certain areas of the museum may be seen only on a one-hour guided tour. Docents give an excellent picture of what mission life was like. Rotating displays showcase such arts as Hawaiian quilting, portraits, even toys. ✉*553 S. King St., Downtown Honolulu* ☎*808/531–0481* ⊕*www.missionhouses.org* ✆*$10* ☉*Tues.–Sat. 10–4; guided tours at 11 and 2:45.*

PEARL HARBOR

December 7, 1941. Every American then alive recalls exactly what he or she was doing when the news broke that the Japanese had bombed Pearl Harbor, the catalyst that brought the United States into World War II.

Although it was clear by late 1941 that war with Japan was inevitable, no one in authority seems to have expected the attack to come in just this way, at just this time. So when the Japanese bombers swept through a gap in O'ahu's Ko'olau Mountains in the hazy light of morning, they found the bulk of America's Pacific fleet right where they hoped it would be: docked like giant stepping stones across the calm waters of the bay named for the pearl oysters that once propered there. More than 2,000 people died that day, including 49 civilians. A dozen ships were sunk. And on the nearby air bases, virtually every American military aircraft was destroyed or damaged. The attack was a stunning success, but it lit a fire under America, which went to war with "Remember Pearl Harbor" as its battle cry. Here, in what is still a key Pacific naval base, the attack is remembered every day by thousands of visitors, including many curious Japanese, who for years heard little World War II history in their own country. In recent years, the memorial has been the site of reconciliation ceremonies involving Pearl Harbor veterans from both sides.

★ **Fodor's Choice USS *Arizona* Memorial.** Snugged up tight in a row of seven battleships off Ford Island, the USS *Arizona* took a direct hit that December morning, exploded, and rests still on the shallow bottom where she settled. A visit to the Memorial begins prosaically—a line, a ticket that assigns you to a group and tour time, a wait filled with shopping, visiting the museum, and strolling the grounds. When your number is called, you watch a 23-minute documentary film then board the ferry to the memorial. The swooping, stark-white memorial, which straddles the wreck of the USS *Arizona,* was designed by Honolulu architect Alfred Preis to represent both the depths of the low-spirited, early days of the war, and the uplift of victory. After the carnival-like courtyard, a somber, contemplative mood descends upon visitors during the ferry ride; this is a place where 1,777 people died. Gaze at the names of the dead carved into the wall of white marble. Scatter flowers (but no leis—the string is bad for the fish). Salute the flag. Remember Pearl Harbor. ⊠*National Park Service, Pearl Harbor* ☎*808/422–0561*

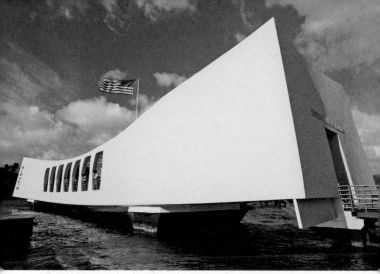

The USS Arizona took a direct hit in the attack on Pearl Harbor. A swooping memorial now straddles the ship's wreck, which lies beneath the blue waters.

⊕*www.nps.gov/usar* ✉*Free. Add $5 for museum audio tours.* ☞*Tour tickets distributed on a first-come, first-served basis, with 1- to 3-hr waits common; arrive early, tickets are sometimes gone by noon* ◷*Daily 8–3.*

Battleship *Missouri* Memorial. Together with the *Arizona* Memorial, the *Missouri's* presence in Pearl Harbor perfectly bookends America's WWII experience that began December 7, 1941, and ended on the "Mighty Mo's" starboard deck with the signing of the Terms of Surrender. To begin your visit, go to the parking area behind the USS *Bowfin* Museum and board a jitney for the breezy, eight-minute ride to Ford Island and the teak decks and towering superstructure of the *Missouri*. You'll find her docked for good in the very harbor from which she first went to war on January 2, 1945. The last battleship ever built, the *Missouri* famously hosted the final act of WWII, the signing of the Terms of Surrender. The commission that governs this floating museum has surrounded her with buildings tricked out in WWII style—a Canteen that serves as an orientation space for tours, a WACs and WAVEs Lounge with a flight simulator the kids will love ($5 for one person, $18 for four), Truman's Line restaurant serving Navy-style meals, and a Victory Store housing a souvenir shop and covered with period mottos ("Don't be a blabateur.").

The *Missouri* is all about numbers: 209 feet tall, six 239,000-pound guns, capable of firing up to 23 mi away.

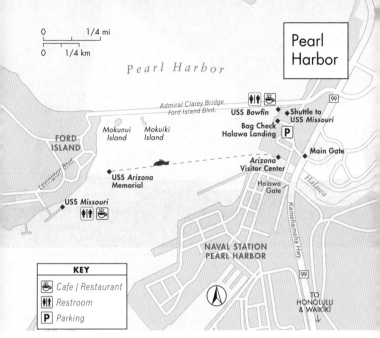

Pearl Harbor

Absorb these during the tour, then stop to take advantage of the view from the decks. The Mo is a work in progress, with only a handful of her hundreds of spaces open to view. ⊠*Pearl Harbor* ☎*808/423–2263 or 888/877–6477* ⊕*www.ussmissouri.com* ≈*$16 adults, $8 children. Add $6 for chief's guided tour or audio tour; add $33 for in-depth, behind-the-scenes tours* ⊙*Daily 9–5.*

USS *Bowfin* Memorial. Launched one year to the day after the Pearl Harbor attack, the USS *Bowfin* sank 44 enemy ships during WWII and now serves as the centerpiece of a museum honoring all submariners. Although the *Bowfin* no less than the *Arizona* Memorial commemorates the lost, the mood here is lighter. Perhaps it's the childlike scale of the boat, a metal tube just 16 feet in diameter, packed with ladders, hatches, and other obstacles, like the naval version of a jungle gym. Perhaps it's the World War II–era music that plays in the covered patio. Or it might be the Museum's touching displays—the penciled sailor's journal, the Vargas girlie posters. Aboard the boat nick-named Pearl Harbor Avenger, compartments are fitted out as though "Sparky" was away from the radio room just for a moment, and "Cooky" might be right back to his pots and pans. The

Plan Your Pearl Harbor Day

MAKING THE MOST OF YOUR TIME

Expect to spend at least half a day; a whole day is better.

At the *Arizona* Memorial, you'll get a ticket, be given a tour time, and then have to wait anywhere from 15 minutes to 3 hours. You must pick up your own ticket so you can't hold places. If the wait is long, skip over to the *Bowfin* to fill the time.

WHAT TO BRING

Picture ID is required during periods of high alert; bring it just in case.

You'll be standing, walking, and climbing all day. Wear something with lots of pockets and a good pair of walking shoes. No purses, packs or bags are allowed. Take only what fits in your pockets. Cameras are okay but without the bags. A private bag storage booth is located in the parking lot near the visitors' center. Leave nothing in your car; theft is a problem despite bicycle security patrols.

KIDS

This might be the day to enroll younger kids in the hotel children's program. Older kids enjoy the *Bowfin* and *Missouri*, especially.

SUGGESTED READING

Pearl Harbor and the USS Arizona Memorial, by Richard Wisniewski. $5.95. 64-page magazine-size quick history.

Bowfin, by Edwin P. Hoyt. $14.95. Dramatic story of undersea adventure.

The Last Battleship, by Scott C. S. Stone. $11.95. Story of the Mighty Mo.

---

museum includes many artifacts to spark family conversations, among them a vintage dive suit that looks too big for Shaquille O'Neal. A caution: the *Bowfin* could be hazardous for very young children; no one under 4 allowed. ⊠*11 Arizona Memorial Dr., at Pearl Harbor* ☎*808/423–1341* ⊕*www.bowfin.org* ⊠*$10 adults, $4 children. Add $2 for audio tours. Children under 4 may go into the museum but not aboard the Bowfin* ☉*Daily 8–4:30.*

The Pacific Aviation Museum. This new museum opened on December 7, 2006, as phase one of a four-phase tribute to the air wars of the Pacific. Located on Ford Island in Hangar 37, an actual seaplane hangar that survived the Pearl Harbor attack, the museum is made up of a theater where a short film on Pearl Harbor kicks off the tour, an education center, a shop, and a restaurant. Exhibits—many of which are interactive and involve sound effects—include an authentic Japanese Zero in a diorama setting and a chance to don a flight suit and play the role of a World War II pilot using one of six flight simulators. Various aircrafts are employed to narrate the graet battles: the Doolittle Raid on Japan, the Battle of Midway, Guadalcanal, and so on. The actual Stearman N2S-3 in which President George H. W. Bush soloed is another exhibit. ☎808/441-1000 ⊕www. pacificaviationmuseum.org ⊒$14.

AROUND HONOLULU

Downtown Honolulu and Chinatown can easily swallow up a day's walking, sightseeing, and shopping. Another day's worth of attractions surrounds the city's core. To the north, just off H1 in the tightly packed neighborhood of Kalihi, explore a museum gifted to the Islands in memory of a princess. Immediately mauka (toward the mountain), off Pali Highway, are a renowned resting place and a carefully preserved home where royal families retreated during the doldrums of summer. To the south, along King Street and Wai'alae Avenue, are a pair of neighborhoods chock-a-block with interesting restaurants and shops. Down the shore a bit from Diamond Head, visit O'ahu's ritziest address and an equally upscale shopping center.

One reason to venture farther afield is the chance to glimpse Honolulu's residential neighborhoods. Species of classic Hawai'i homes include the tiny green-and-white plantation-era house with its corrugated tin roof, two windows flanking a central door and small porch; the breezy bungalow with its swooping Thai-style roofline and two wings flanking screened French doors through which breezes blow into the living room. Note the tangled "Grandma-style" gardens and many 'ohana houses—small homes in the backyard of a larger home or built as apartments perched over the garage, allowing extended families to live together. Carports, which rarely house cars, are the Island version of rec rooms, where parties are held and neighbors sit to "talk story." Sometimes you see gallon jars on the flat roofs of garages or carports: these are pickled lemons fermenting in the sun. Also in the neighborhoods, you find the folksy restaurants and takeout spots favored by Islanders.

■TIP→For those with a Costco card, the cheapest gas on the island is at the Costco station on Arakawa Street between Dillingham Boulevard and Nimitz Highway. Gas gets more expensive the farther you are from Honolulu.

2

★ **Bishop Museum.** Founded in 1889 by Charles R. Bishop as a memorial to his wife, Princess Bernice Pauahi Bishop, the museum began as a repository for the royal possessions of this last direct descendant of King Kamehameha the Great. Today it's the Hawai'i State Museum of Natural and Cultural History and houses almost 25 million items that tell the history of the Hawaiian Islands and their Pacific neighbors. The latest addition to the complex is a natural-science wing with state-of-the-art interactive exhibits. Venerable but sadly aging Hawaiian Hall, is undergoing a multimillion-dollar renovation; it houses Polynesian artifacts: lustrous feather capes, the skeleton of a giant sperm whale, photography and crafts displays, and an authentic, well-preserved grass house inside a two-story 19th-century Victorian-style gallery. Closed for renovations at this writing, the Hall is scheduled to reopen in early 2008. Also check out the planetarium, daily hula and science demonstrations, special exhibits, and the Shop Pacifica. The building alone, with its huge Victorian turrets and immense stone walls, is worth seeing. ⊠*1525 Bernice St., Kalihi* ☎*808/847–3511* ⊕*www.bishopmuseum.org* ⊠*$15.95* ⊙*Daily 9–5.*

Mō'ili'ili. Packed into the neighborhood of Mō'ili'ili are flower and lei shops (especially Le Fleur), restaurants (Spices, Fukuya Delicatessen), and little stores such as Kuni Island Fabrics, a great source for Hawaiian quilting and other crafting materials; Siam Imports, for goodies from Thailand; and Revolution Books, Honolulu's only leftist book shop. ⊠*S. King St., between Hausten and Wai'alae Ave., Honolulu.*

National Memorial Cemetery of the Pacific. Nestled in the bowl of Puowaina, or Punchbowl Crater, this 112-acre cemetery is the final resting place for more than 48,000 U.S. war veterans and family members. Among those buried here is Ernie Pyle, the famed World War II correspondent who was killed by a Japanese sniper on Ie Shima, an island off the northwest coast of Okinawa. Puowaina, formed 75,000–100,000 years ago during a period of secondary volcanic activity, translates as "Hill of Sacrifice." Historians believe this site once served as an altar where ancient Hawaiians offered sacrifices to their gods. ■TIP➜**The cemetery has unfettered views of Waikīkī and Honolulu—perhaps the finest on O'ahu.** ⊠*2177 Puowaina Dr., Nu'uanu* ☎*808/532–3720* ⊕*www. cem.va.gov/cem/cems/nchp/nmcp.asp* ⊠*Free* ⊙*Mar.–Sept., daily 8–6:30; Oct.–Feb., daily 8:30–5:30.*

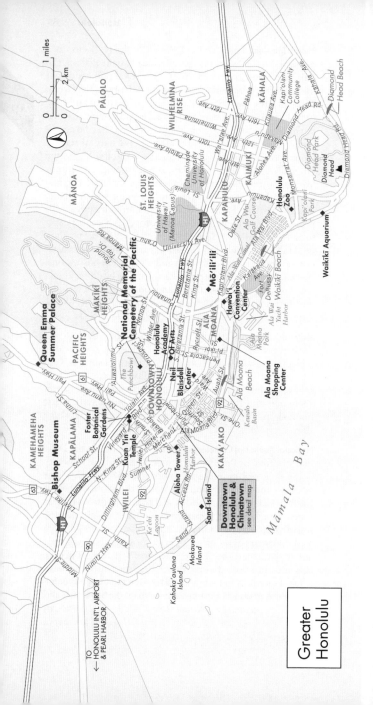

Greater Honolulu

2

Queen Emma Summer Palace. Queen Emma and her family used this stately white home, built in 1848, as a retreat from the rigors of court life in hot and dusty Honolulu during the mid-1800s. It has an eclectic mix of memorabilia, European, Victorian, and Hawaiian furnishings, and excellent examples of Hawaiian quilts and koa furniture. ⊠*2913 Pali Hwy., Nu'uanu* ☎*808/595–3167* ⊕*www. daughtersofhawaii.org* ⊑*$6* ⊙*Self-guided or guided tours daily 9–4; last entry at 3.*

EN ROUTE. A few minutes and a world away from Waikīkī and Honolulu, the scenic Tantalus and Round Top Scenic Drive shaded by vine-draped trees has frequent pullouts with views of Diamond Head and the Ewa Beach side of Honolulu. It's a nice change of pace from urban life below. At Puu Ualakaa Park, stop to see the sweeping view from Manoa Valley to Honolulu. The road beyond the park is blocked off, so turn around here to head back to Honolulu. To start the drive, go to Punchbowl Memorial Cemetery and follow Tantalus Drive as it climbs uphill.

SOUTHEAST O'AHU

Driving southeast from Waikīkī on busy four-lane Kalaniana'ole Highway, you'll pass a dozen bedroom communities tucked into the valleys at the foot of the Ko'olau Range, with just fleeting glimpses of the ocean from a couple of pocket parks. Suddenly, civilization falls away, the road narrows to two lanes, and you enter the rugged coastline of Koko Head and Ka Iwi.

This is a cruel coastline: dry, windswept, and rocky shores, with untamed waves that are notoriously treacherous. While walking its beaches, do not turn your back on the ocean, don't venture close to wet areas where high waves occasionally reach, and do heed warning signs.

At this point, you're passing through Koko Head Regional Park. On your right is the bulging remnant of a pair of volcanic craters that the Hawaiians called Kawaihoa, known today as Koko Head. To the left is Koko Crater and an area of the park that includes a hiking trail, a dryland botanical garden, a firing range, and a riding stable. Ahead is a sinuous shoreline with scenic pullouts and beaches to explore. Named the Ka Iwi Coast (*iwi,* "ee-vee," are bones—sacred to Hawaiians and full of symbolism) for the channel just offshore, this area was once home to a ranch and small fishing enclave that were destroyed by a tidal wave in the 1940s.

Driving straight from Waikīkī to Makapu'u Point takes from a half to a full hour, depending on traffic. There aren't a huge number of sights per se in this corner of O'ahu, so a couple of hours should be plenty of exploring time, unless you make a lengthy stop at a particular point.

Hālona Blowhole. Below a scenic turnout along the Koko Head shoreline, this oft-photographed lava tube sucks the ocean in and spits it out. Don't get too close, as conditions can get dangerous. ■TIP→**Look to your right to see the tiny beach below that was used to film the wave-washed love scene in *From Here to Eternity*.** In winter this is a good spot to watch whales at play. Offshore, the islands of Moloka'i and Lāna'i call like distant sirens, and every once in a while Maui is visible in blue silhouette. Take your valuables with you and lock your car, because this scenic location is a hot spot for petty thieves. ⊠*Kalaniana'ole Hwy., 1 mi east of Hanauma Bay.*

★ **Fodor's**Choice **Hanauma Bay Nature Preserve.** The exterior wall ⊙ of a volcanic crater collapsed thousands of years ago, opening it to the sea and thereby giving birth to O'ahu's most famous snorkeling destination. Even from the overlook, the horseshoe-shape bay is a beauty, and you can easily see the reefs through the clear aqua waters. The wide beach is a great place for sunbathing and picnics. This is a marine conservation district, and regulations prohibit feeding the fish. Visitors are required to go through the Education Center before trekking down to the bay. The center provides a cultural history of the area and exhibits about the importance of protecting its marine life. Check out the "Today at the Bay" exhibit for up-to-date information on daily tides, ocean safety warnings, and activities. Food concessions and equipment rentals are also on-site. ■TIP→**Come early to get parking, as the number of visitors allowed per day is limited.** Also note that the bay is best in the early hours before the waters are churned up. Call for current conditions. Thursday evening lectures, Saturday morning field trips, and Saturday night Hanauma Bay by Starlight events (extending opening hours to 10 PM) are held weekly. ⊠*7455 Kalaniana'ole Hwy.* ☎*808/396–4229* ⊕*www.honolulu. gov/parks/facility/hanaumabay/index.htm* ⊴*$5; parking*

DID YOU KNOW?

The Bishop Museum in Honolulu is the state's natural and cultural heritage museum, and has more than 24.7 million items inside.

CLOSE UP

Shangri La

The marriage of heiress Doris Duke, at age 23, to a man much older than herself didn't last. But their around-the-world honeymoon tour did leave her with two lasting loves: Islamic art and architecture, which she first encountered on that journey; and Hawai'i, where the honeymooners made an extended stay.

Today visitors to her beloved Islands—where she spent most winters—can share both loves by touring her home. The sought-after tours, which are coordinated by and begin at the downtown Honolulu Academy of Arts, start with a visit to the Arts of the Islamic World Gallery. A short van ride then takes small groups on to the house itself, on the far side of Diamond Head.

In 1936 Duke bought 5 acres at Black Point, down the coast from Waikīkī, and began to build and furnish the first home that would be all her own. She called it **Shangri La.** For more than 50 years, the home was a perpetual work in progress as Duke traveled the world, buying furnishings and artifacts. When she died in 1993, Duke left instructions that her home was to become a center for the study of Islamic art, open to the public for tours.

To walk through the house and its gardens—which have remained much as Duke left them with only some minor conservation-oriented changes—is to experience the personal style of someone who saw everything as raw material for her art.

With her trusted houseman, Jin de Silva, she built, by her own hand, the elaborate Turkish (or Damascus) Room, trimming tiles and painted panels to fit the walls and building a fountain of her own design.

One aspect of the home that clearly takes its inspiration from the Muslim tradition is the entry: an anonymous gate, a blank white wall, and a wooden door that bids you "Enter herein in peace and security" in Arabic characters. Inside, tiles glow, fountains tinkle, and shafts of light illuminate artworks through arches and high windows.

The house is open by guided tour only; tours take 2½ hours. Children under 12 are not admitted. All tours begin at the Academy of Arts.

✉️*Academy of Arts, 900 S. Beretania, Kahala* ☎️*808/532–3853 Academy of Arts* ⊕ *www. honoluluacademy.org* 💲*Tours $25* 🕐*Tours Wed.–Sat. by reservation*; first tour 8:30 AM, last tour 1:30 PM.

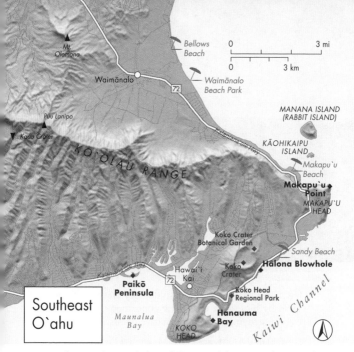

$1; mask, snorkel, and fin rental $6; tram from parking lot $1.50 round-trip ⊙ Wed.–Mon. 6–6.

Scenic lookout. Just past Hanauma Bay as you head toward Makapu'u Point, you'll see a turnout with some fine views of the coastline and, in winter, you'll have an opportunity to see storm-generated waves crashing against lava cliffs. This is also a popular place for winter whale-watching so bring your binoculars, some sunscreen, and a picnic lunch and join the small crowd scanning for telltale white spouts of water only a few hundred yards away. ⊠ *Kalaniana'ole Hwy., just past Hanauma Bay, Koko Head.*

Makapu'u Point. This spot has breathtaking views of the ocean, mountains, and the Windward islands. The point of land jutting out in the distance is **Mōkapu Peninsula**, site of a U.S. Marine base. The spired mountain peak is **Mt. Olomana**. In front of you on the long pier is part of the **Makai Undersea Test Range**, a research facility that's closed to the public. Offshore is **Manana Island (Rabbit Island)**, a picturesque cay said to resemble a swimming bunny with its ears pulled back. Coincidentally, Manana Island was once overrun with rabbits, thanks to a rancher who let a

If you're a snorkeler, head straight for Hanauma Bay, the best and most popular place to snorkel on O'ahu.

few hares run wild on the land. They were eradicated in 1994 by biologists who grew concerned that the rabbits were destroying the island's native plants.

Nestled in the cliff face is the **Makapu'u Lighthouse,** which became operational in 1909 and has the largest lighthouse lens in America. The lighthouse is closed to the public, but near the Makapu'u Point turnout you can find the start of 1-mi-long paved road (closed to traffic). Hike up to the top of the 647-foot bluff for a closer view of the lighthouse and, in winter, a great whale-watching vantage point. ⊠*Kalaniana'ole Hwy., 2 mi past Sandy Beach, Koko Head.*

Paikō Peninsula. Secluded within the confines of the bay, private and quiet, this slim spit of land is a lovely place to spend a morning or afternoon swimming, snorkeling, reading, and dozing. The peninsula is reached by a narrow residential road that dead-ends at the Paikō Lagoon State Reserve. The reserve is off-limits to the public, but all beaches in Hawai'i are public to the high-water line, and there is a beach-access pathway a few houses before the road's end. Turn left when you get to the beach and find your spot near where the houses end. ⊠*Paikō Dr., off Kalaniana'ole Hwy., just past Niu Valley on right.*

WINDWARD O'AHU

Looking at Honolulu's topsy-turvy urban sprawl, you would never suspect the Windward side existed. It's a secret Oahuans like to keep, so they can watch the awe on the faces of their guests when the car emerges from the tunnels through the mountains and they gaze for the first time on the panorama of turquoise bays and emerald valleys watched over by the knife-edged Ko'olau ridges. Jaws literally drop. Every time. And this just a 15-minute drive from downtown.

It is on this side of the island that many Native Hawaiians live. Evidence of traditional lifestyles is abundant in crumbling fishponds, rock platforms that once were altars, taro patches still being worked, and throw-net fishermen posed stock-still above the water (though today, they're invariably wearing polarized sunglasses, the better to spot the fish).

Here, the pace is slower, more oriented toward nature. Beach-going, hiking, diving, surfing, and boating are the draws, along with a visit to the Polynesian Cultural Center, and poking through little shops and wayside stores.

You can easily spend an entire day exploring Windward O'ahu, or you can just breeze on through, nodding at the sights on your way to the North Shore. Waikīkī to Windward is a drive of less than half an hour; to the North Shore via Kamehameha Highway along the Windward Coast is one hour, minimum.

TOP ATTRACTIONS

Byodo-In Temple. Tucked away in the back of the Valley of the Temples cemetery is a replica of the 11th-century Temple at Uji in Japan. A 2-ton carved wooden statue of the Buddha presides inside the main temple building. Next to the temple building are a meditation pavilion and gardens set dramatically against the sheer, green cliffs of the Ko'olau Mountains. You can ring the 5-foot, 3-ton brass bell for good luck and feed some of the hundreds of carp that inhabit the garden's 2-acre pond. ✉ *47-200 Kahekili Hwy., Kāne'ohe* ☎*808/239–9844* ✉*$2* ☉*Daily 8–5.*

NEED A BREAK? Generations of children have purchased their beach snacks and sodas at Kalapawai Market (✉ *306 S. Kalāheo Ave.*), near Kailua Beach. A Windward landmark since 1932, the green-and-white market has distinctive charm. You'll see slipper-clad locals sitting in front sharing a cup of coffee and talking story at picnic tables or in front of the market. It's a good source for your carryout lunch, since there's no concession stand at the beach. Or, grab a cup of coffee and have a seat at the wooden tables outside. With one of the better selections of wine on the island, the market is also a great place to pick up a bottle.

Nu'uanu Pali Lookout. This panoramic perch looks out to Windward O'ahu. It was in this region that King Kamehameha I drove defending forces over the edges of the 1,000-foot-high cliffs, thus winning the decisive battle for control of O'ahu. ■TIP→From here you can see views that stretch from Kāne'ohe Bay to Mokoli'i ("little lizard"), a small island off the coast, and beyond. Temperatures at the summit are several degrees cooler than in warm Waikīkī, so bring a jacket along. Hang on tight to any loose possessions; it gets extremely windy at the lookout. Lock your car and take valuables with you; break-ins are common. ⊠Top of Pali Hwy. ⊗Daily 9–4.

EN ROUTE. As you drive the Windward and North Shores along Kamehameha Highway, you'll note a number of interesting geological features. At Kualoa look to the ocean and gaze at the uniquely shaped little island of **Mokoli'i** ("little lizard"), a 206-foot-high sea stack also known as Chinaman's Hat. According to Hawaiian legend, the goddess Hi'iaka, sister of Pele, slew the dragon Mokoli'i and flung its tail into the sea, forming the distinct islet. Other dragon body parts—in the form of rocks—are scattered along the base of nearby Kualoa Ridge. ■TIP→In Lā'ie, if you turn right on Anemoku Street, and right again on Naupaka, you come to a scenic lookout where you can see a group of islets, dramatically washed by the waves.

☾ **Polynesian Cultural Center.** Re-created individual villages showcase the island lifestyles and traditions of Hawai'i, Tahiti, Samoa, Fiji, the Marquesas Islands, New Zealand, and Tonga. Focusing on individual islands within its 42-acre center, 35 mi from Waikīkī, the Polynesian Cultural Center was founded in 1963 by the Church of Jesus Christ of Latter-day Saints. It houses restaurants, hosts lū'aus, and demonstrates cultural traditions such as tribal tattooing, fire dancing, and ancient customs and ceremonies. The expansive open-air shopping village carries Polynesian handicrafts. ■TIP→If you're staying in Honolulu, see the center as part of a bus tour so you won't have to drive home late at night after the two-hour evening show. Various packages are avail-

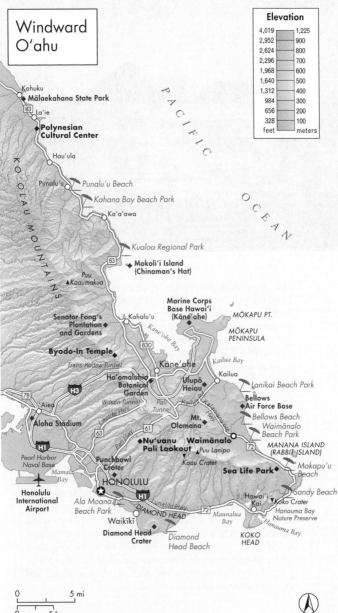

Windward O'ahu

Elevation

feet	meters
4,019	1,225
2,952	900
2,624	800
2,296	700
1,968	600
1,640	500
1,312	400
984	300
656	200
328	100
feet	meters

PACIFIC OCEAN

KO'OLAU MOUNTAINS

Kahuku
Mālaekahana State Park
83
La'ie
Polynesian Cultural Center
Hau'ula
Punalu'u
Punalu'u Beach
Kahana Bay Beach Park
Ka'a'awa
Kualoa Regional Park
83
Mokoli'i Island (Chinaman's Hat)
Puu Kaaumakua
Marine Corps Base Hawai'i (Kāne'ohe)
MŌKAPU PT.
MŌKAPU PENINSULA
Senator Fong's Plantation and Gardens
Kahalu'u
Kane'ohe Bay
Byodo-In Temple
830
Trans-Kodaw Tunnel
Ho'omaluhia Botanical Garden
Kāne'ohe
Kailua Bay
Kailua
Lanikai Beach Park
Ulupō Heiau
Wilson Tunnel
'Aiea
H3
Pali Tunnel
Bellows Air Force Base
Bellows Beach
Waimānalo Beach Park
78
Likelike Hwy
Mt. Olomana
63
Aloha Stadium
61
Nu'uanu Pali Lookout
Waimānalo
MANANA ISLAND (RABBIT ISLAND)
Pearl Harbor Naval Base
Pali Hwy
Punchbowl Crater
Puu Lanipo
72
Makapu'u Beach
Kaau Crater
Sea Life Park
Mamala Bay
HONOLULU
H1
Hawai'i Kai
Sandy Beach
Honolulu International Airport
Ala Moana Beach Park
Lunalilo Hwy
DIAMOND HEAD
72
Koko Crater
Maunalua Bay
Hanauma Bay Nature Preserve
Waikīkī
Diamond Head Crater
Diamond Head Beach
KOKO HEAD
Hanauma Bay

0 — 5 mi
0 — 5 km

You can catch a great sunset over Manana Island, otherwise known as "Rabbit Island," located on the Windward side of O'ahu.

able, from basic admission to an all-inclusive deal. Every May, the PCC hosts the World Fire Knife Dance Competition, an event that draws the top fire-knife dance performers from around the world. ✉ *55-370 Kamehameha Hwy., Lā'ie* ☎ *808/293–3333 or 800/367–7060* ⊕ *www.polynesia. com* 💲 *$50–$230* ⊗ *Mon.–Sat. 12:30–9:30. Islands exhibits close at 6:30.*

Windward Villages. Tiny villages—generally consisting of a sign, store, a beach park, possibly a post office, and not much more—are strung along Kamehameha Highway on the Windward side. Each has something to offer. In **Waiahole,** look for fruit stands and an ancient grocery store. In **Ka'a'awa,** there's a lunch spot and convenience store/gas station. In **Punalu'u,** stop at the gallery of fanciful landscape artist Lance Fairly and the woodworking shop, Kahaunani Woods & Crafts, plus venerable Ching General Store or the Shrimp Shack. Kim Taylor Reece's photo studio, featuring haunting portraits of hula dancers, is between Punalu'u and Hau'ula. **Hau'ula** has Hau'ula Gift Shop and Art Gallery, formerly yet another Ching Store, now a clothing shop where sarongs wave like banners and, at Ha'ula Kai Shopping Center, Tamura Market, with excellent seafood and the last liquor before Mormon-dominated Lā'ie.

ALSO WORTH SEEING

🐾 **Sea Life Park.** Dolphins leap and spin, penguins frolic, and a killer whale performs impressive tricks at this marine-life attraction 15 mi from Waikīkī at scenic Makapu'u Point. The park has a 300,000-gallon Hawaiian reef aquarium, the Hawaiian Monk Seal Care Center, and a breeding sanctuary for Hawai'i's endangered *Honu* sea turtle. Join the Stingray or Dolphin Encounter and get up close and personal in the water with these sea creatures (don't worry, the rays' stingers have been removed) or go on an underwater photo safari. ✉ *41-202 Kalaniana'ole Hwy., Waimānalo* ☎ *808/259–7933 or 886/365–7446* ⊕ *www.sealifepark hawaii.com* 🎟 *$29* ⏱ *Daily 10:30–5.*

Waimānalo. The biggest draws of this modest little seaside town flanked by chiseled cliffs are its beautiful beaches, with glorious views to the Windward side. **Bellows Beach** is great for swimming and bodysurfing, and **Waimānalo Beach Park** is also safe for swimming. Down the side roads, as you head mauka, are little farms that grow a variety of fruits and flowers. Toward the back of the valley are small ranches with grazing horses. ■TIP➔**If you see any trucks selling corn and you're staying at a place where you can cook it, be sure to get some in Waimānalo. It may be the sweetest you'll ever eat, and the price is the lowest on O'ahu.** ✉ *Kalaniana'ole Hwy.*

THE NORTH SHORE

An hour from town and a world away in atmosphere, O'ahu's North Shore, roughly from Kahuku Point to Ka'ena Point, is about small farms and big waves, tourist traps and otherworldly landscapes. Parks and beaches, roadside fruit stands and shrimp shacks, a bird sanctuary, and a valley preserve offer a dozen reasons to stop between the one-time plantation town of Kahuku and the surf mecca of Hale'iwa.

Hale'iwa has had many lives, from resort getaway in the 1900s to plantation town through the 20th century to its life today as a surf and tourist magnet. Beyond Hale'iwa is the tiny village of Waialua, a string of beach parks, an airfield where gliders, hang-gliders, and parachutists play, and, at the end of the road, Ka'ena Point State Recreation Area, which offers a brisk hike, striking views, and whale-watching in season.

Giant, multicolored hibiscus flowers are used by many women as hair ornaments. They're easy to find around homes and hotels.

Pack wisely for a day's North Shore excursion: swim and snorkel gear, light jacket and hat (the weather is mercurial, especially in winter), sunscreen and sunglasses, bottled water and snacks, towels and a picnic blanket, and both sandals and close-toed shoes for hiking. A small cooler is nice; you may want to pick up some fruit or fresh corn. As always, leave valuables in the hotel safe and lock the car whenever you park.

From Waikīkī, the quickest route to the North Shore is H1 east to H2 north and then the Kamehameha Highway past Wahiawā; you'll hit Hale'iwa in less than an hour. The Windward route (H1 east, H3, Like Like or Pali Highway, through the mountains, or Kamehameha Highway north) takes at least 90 minutes to Hale'iwa.

TOP ATTRACTIONS

Hale'iwa. During the 1920s this seaside hamlet boasted a posh hotel at the end of a railroad line (both long gone). During the 1960s, hippies gathered here, followed by surfers from around the world. Today Hale'iwa is a fun mix of old general stores and contemporary boutiques, galleries, and eateries. Be sure to stop in at **Lili'uokalani Protestant Church,** founded by missionaries in the 1830s. It's fronted by a large, stone archway built in 1910 and covered with night-blooming cereus. ⊠*Follow H1 west from Honolulu to H2 north, exit at Wahiawā, follow Kamehameha Hwy.*

CLOSE UP

Say What?

T-shirts and bumper stickers common in O'ahu may stump you. Here's a guide:

Eddie Would Go: Inspirational reference to big-wave surfer Eddie Aikau, who lost his life attempting to save those aboard a swamped voyaging canoe.

Wala'au: "Gossip." The name of a popular Kaua'i radio show.

Kau Inoa: "Put (or place) your name." Urges Hawaiians to sign up to help organize a Native Hawaiian governing entity.

What part of a'ole don't you understand?: A'ole means "no."

If can, can; if no can, no can: Pidgin for "whatever."

Got koko?: "Got blood?," meaning, are you Hawaiian?

---

6 mi, turn left at signaled intersection, then right into Hale'iwa ⊕www.haleiwamainstreet.com.

Ka'ena Point State Recreation Area. The name means "the heat" and, indeed, this windy barren coast lacks both shade and fresh water (or any man-made amenities). Pack water, wear sturdy closed-toe shoes, don sunscreen and a hat, and lock the car. The hike is along a rutted dirt road, mostly flat and 3 mi long, ending in a rocky, sandy headland. It is here that Hawaiians believed the souls of the dead met with their family gods, and, if judged worthy to enter the afterlife, leapt off into eternal darkness at Leinaaka'uane, just south of the point. In summer and at low tide, the small coves offer bountiful shelling; in winter, don't venture near the water. Rare native plants dot the landscape. November through March, watch for humpbacks spouting and breaching. Binoculars and a camera are highly recommended. ⊠*North end of Kamehameha Hwy.*

⟳ **Waimea Valley Audubon Center.** Waimea may get lots of press
★ for the giant winter waves in the bay, but the valley itself is a newsmaker and an ecological treasure in its own right. If you visit one botanical garden on O'ahu, this is the one to see. The Office of Hawaiian Affairs is working to conserve and restore the natural habitat. Follow the Kamananui Stream up the valley through the 1,800 acres of gardens. The botanical collections here include more than 5,000 species of tropical flora, including a superb gathering of Polynesian plants. It's the best place on the island to see native species, such as the endangered Hawaiian moorhen. You

can also see the remains of the Hale O Lono *heiau* (temple) along with other ancient archaeological sites; evidence suggests that the area was an important spiritual center. At the back of the valley, **Waihī Falls** plunges 45 feet into a swimming pond. ■ TIP→ Bring your suit—a swim is the perfect way to end your hike. There's a lifeguard and changing room. Be sure to bring mosquito repellent, too; it gets buggy. ⊠ *59-864 Kamehameha Hwy., Hale'iwa* ☎*808/638–9199* ⊕*www. audubon.org* ⊉*$8, parking $2* ☉*Daily 9:30–5.*

TREAT YOURSELF. The chocolate-*haupia* (coconut) pie at Ted's Bakery (⊠ *59-024 Kamehameha Hwy., near Sunset Beach* ☎*808/638–8207*) is legendary. Stop in for a take-out pie or for a quick plate lunch or sandwich.

ALSO WORTH SEEING

Pu'uomahuka Heiau. Worth a stop for its spectacular views from a bluff high above the ocean overlooking Waimea Bay, this sacred spot was once the site of human sacrifices. It's now on the National Register of Historic Places. ⊠ *½-mi north of Waimea Bay, from Rte. 83 turn right on Pūpūkea Rd. and drive 1 mi uphill.*

CENTRAL AND WEST (LEEWARD) O'AHU

O'ahu's central plain is a patchwork of old towns and new residential developments, military bases, farms, ranches, and shopping malls, with a few visit-worthy attractions and historic sites scattered about. Central O'ahu encompasses the Moanalua Valley, residential Pearl City, and the old plantation town of Wahiawā, on the uplands halfway to the North Shore. All sights are most easily reached by either the H1 and H2 freeways.

West (or Leeward) O'ahu has the island's fledgling "second city"—the planned community of Kapolei, where the government hopes to attract enough jobs to lighten inbound traffic to downtown Honolulu—then continues on past a far-flung resort to the Hawaiian communities of Nānākuli and Wai'anae, to the beach and the end of the road at Keawe'ula, aka Yokohama Bay. West O'ahu begins at folksy Waipahu and continues past Makakilo and Kapolei on H1 and Highway 93, Farrington Highway.

If you've got to leave one part of this island for the next trip, this is the part to skip. It's a longish drive to West

O'AHU SIGHTSEEING TOURS

Guided tours are convenient; you don't have to worry about finding a parking spot or getting admission tickets. Most of the tour guides have taken special classes in Hawaiian history and lore, and many are certified by the state of Hawai'i. On the other hand, you won't have the freedom to proceed at your own pace, nor will you have the ability to take a detour trip if something else catches your attention.

BUS & VAN TOURS

Polynesian Adventure. ☎808/833-3000 ⊕www. polyad.com.

Polynesian Hospitality. ☎808/526-3565 ⊕www. kobay.com.

Roberts Hawai'i. ☎808/539-9400 ⊕www. robertshawaii.com.

THEME TOURS

Culinary Tour of Chinatown. Tours of noodle shops, dim-sum parlors, bakeries, and other food vendors start every Monday at 9:30 AM. ☎808/533-3181.

E Noa Tours. Certified tour guides conduct Circle Island, Pearl Harbor, and shopping tours. ☎808/591-2561 ⊕www.enoa.com.

Home of the Brave Hawaii Victory Tour. Narrated tours visit O'ahu's military bases and the National Memorial Cemetery of the Pacific. ☎808/396-8112 ⊕www. pearlharborhq.com.

Matthew Gray's Hawai'i Food Tours. Three different restaurant-tour itineraries include samplings of a variety of local favorites. ☎808/926-3663 ⊕www. hawaiifoodtours.com.

Mauka Makai Excursions. Visit the ancient Hawaiian archaeological, legendary, and nature sites that islanders hold sacred. ☎808/255-2206 ⊕www.hawaiianecotours.net.

Polynesian Cultural Center. An advantage of this tour is that you don't have to drive yourself back to Waikīkī after dark if you take in the evening show. ☎808/293-3333 or 808/923-1861 ⊕www. polynesia.com.

WALKING TOURS

Chinatown Walking Tour. Meet at the Chinese Chamber of Commerce for a fascinating peek into herbal shops, an acupuncturist's office, open-air markets, and specialty stores. ✉Chinese Chamber of Commerce, 76 N. King St., Suite 202, Chinatown ☎808/533-3181.

Hawai'i Geographic Society. A number of Downtown Honolulu historic-temple and archaeology walking tours are available. ☎808/538-3952.

O'ahu by island standards—45 minutes to Kapolei from Waikīkī and 90 minutes to Wai'anae—and Central O'ahu has little to offer. The attraction most worth the trek to West O'ahu is Hawai'i's Plantation Village in Waipahu, about a half hour out of town; it's a living-history museum built from actual homes of turn-of-the-20th-century plantation workers. In Central O'ahu, check out the Dole Plantation for all things pineapple.

Ko Olina. Among the many amenities at this resort that are open to the public is the challenging (and pricey) Ted Robinson–designed golf course (*see chapter 5, Golf, Hiking & Outdoor Activities*), two nice, sit-down lunch spots—Roy's Ko Olina at the golf course and the Naupaka Terrace at the JW Marriott Ko Olina Resort & Spa—and a couple of man-made swimming lagoons surrounded by lush lawns with changing and bathroom facilities. ⊠ *Farrington Hwy., at Ali'inui Dr., Kapolei* ☎ *808/676–5300 Ko'Olina Golf Club, 808/676–7697 Roy's Ko Olina, 808/679–0079 Naupaka Terr.* ⊕ *www.koolinagolf.com.*

Mākaha Beach Park. Famous as a surfing-and-boogie-boarding park, Mākaha hosts an annual surf meet and draws many scuba divers in summer, when the waves are calm, to explore underwater caverns and ledges. It's popular with families year-round but, in winter, watch for rip tides and currents; Mākaha means "fierce," and there's a reason for that. ⊠ *84-369 Farrington Hwy., Waia'anae.*

3

Beaches & Outdoor Activities

WORD OF MOUTH

"Lanikai is arguably the best beach on O'ahu; IMHO, it's probably the nicest beach in all of Hawai'i. the semi-white, powdery sand; shallow, turquoise waters; two picturesque islands to view offshore; gorgeous sunrise"

—bluefan

By Don
Chapman,
Trina
Kudlacek
& Chad
Pata

TROPICAL SUN MIXED WITH COOLING TRADE WINDS and pristine waters make Oʻahu's shores a literal heaven on earth. But contrary to many assumptions, the island is not one big beach. There are miles and miles of coastline without a grain of sand, so you need to know where you are going to fully enjoy the Hawaiian experience.

BEACHES

Much of the island's southern and eastern coast is protected by inner reefs. The reefs provide still coastline water but not much as far as sand is concerned. However, where there are beaches on the south and east shores, they are mind-blowing. In West Oʻahu and on the North Shore you can find the wide expanses of sand you would expect for enjoying the sunset. Sandy bottoms and protective reefs make the water an adventure in the winter months. Most visitors assume the seasons don't change a thing in the Islands, and they would be right—except for the waves, which are big on the South Shore in summer and placid in winter. It's exactly the opposite on the north side where winter storms bring in huge waves, but the ocean goes to glass come May and June.

WAIKĪKĪ

The 2½-mi strand called Waikīkī Beach extends from Hilton Hawaiian Village on one end to Kapiʻolani Park and Diamond Head on the other. Although it's one contiguous piece of beach, it's as varied as the people that inhabit the Islands. Whether you're an old-timer looking to enjoy the action from the shade or a sports nut wanting to do it all, you can find every beach activity here without ever jumping in the rental car.

■TIP→ **If you're staying outside the area, our best advice is to park at either end of the beach and walk in.** Plenty of parking exists on the west end at the Ala Wai Marina, where there are myriad free spots on the beach as well as metered stalls around the harbor. For parking on the east end, Kapiʻolani Park and the Honolulu Zoo both have metered parking for $1 an hour—more affordable than the $10 per hour the resorts want.

ꗃ **Duke Kahanamoku Beach.** Named for Hawaiʻi's famous Olympic swimming champion, Duke Kahanamoku, this is a hard-packed beach with the only shade trees on the sand

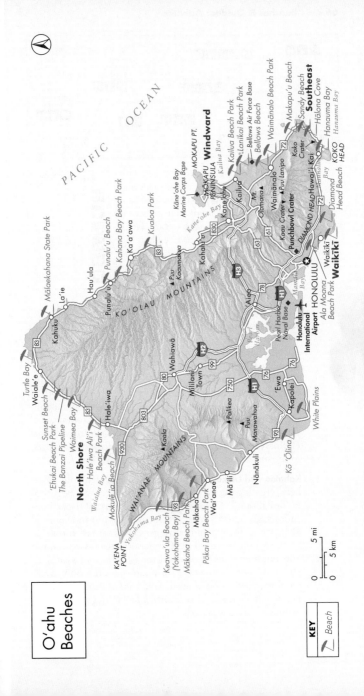

O'ahu
Beaches

PACIFIC OCEAN

North Shore

KA'ENA POINT

WAI'ANAE MOUNTAINS

KO'OLAU MOUNTAINS

MOKAPU PT.
MOKAPU PENINSULA

Windward

Southeast

KOKO HEAD

DIAMOND HEAD

Waikīkī

HONOLULU

Honolulu International Airport

KEY

⚓ Beach

0   5 mi
0   5 km

Turtle Bay
Waiale'e
Sunset Beach
'Ēhukai Beach Park
The Banzai Pipeline
Waimea Bay
Hale'iwa Ali'i Beach Park
Hale'iwa
Mokulē'ia Beach
Waialua Bay
Kaiaka

Mālaekahana State Park
Lā'ie
Hau'ula
Punalu'u Beach
Punalu'u
Ka'a'awa
Kahana Bay Beach Park
Kahana Bay
Kualoa Park

Kāne'ohe Bay Marine Corps Base
Kāne'ohe Bay
Kahalu'u
Kāne'ohe
Kailua
Kailua Beach Park
Kailua Bay
Lanikai Beach Park
Bellows Air Force Base
Bellows Beach
Waimānalo Beach Park
Makapu'u Beach
Sandy Beach
Hālona Cove
Hanauma Bay
Hanauma Bay

Kahuku
Keawa'ula Beach (Yokohama Bay)
Mākaha Beach Park
Mākaha
Mā'ili
Wai'anae
Pōkai Bay Beach Park
Yokohama Bay

Nānākuli
Kō 'Olina
'Ewa
White Plains
Kapolei

Mililani Town
Wahiawā
Pu'u Koaumakaa
Pu'u Kaala
Palikea
Pu'u Manawahua
Waipahu
Pearl Harbor Naval Base
Aiea
Ala Moana Beach Park
Mamala Bay

Waimānalo
Kāne'ohe
Koko Crater
Koko Head Beach Park
Hawai'i Kai
Maunalua Bay
Diamond Bay
Diamond Head Beach Park
Pu'u Lanipo
Mt. Olomana
Kaau Crater
Punchbowl Crater
Ka'au
Hawai'i Loa

H1 H2 H3

83 930 803 99 90 750 76 78 61 63 72 93 76

in Waikīkī. It's great for families with
young children because of the shade and
because it has Waikīkī's calmest waters,
thanks to a rock wall that creates a
semiprotected cove. The ocean clarity
here is not as brilliant as elsewhere on
Waikīkī because of the stillness of the
surf, but it's a small price to pay for
peace of mind about youngsters. ⊠*In
front of Hilton Hawaiian Village Beach
Resort and Spa* ⚲*Toilets, showers, food concession.*

BEACHES KEY

🛉	*Restroom*
🚿	*Showers*
🏄	*Surfing*
🤿	*Snorkel/Scuba*
👫	*Good for kids*
🅿	*Parking*

☾ **Fort DeRussy Beach Park.** Even before you take the two newly
refurbished beach parks into account, this is one of the finest beaches on the south side of O'ahu. Wide, soft, ultra-
white beaches with gently lapping waves make it a family
favorite for running/jumping/frolicking fun (this also happens to be where the NFL holds its rookie sand football
game every year). Add to that the heavily shaded grass grill-
ing area, sand volleyball courts, and aquatic rentals, and
this becomes a must for the active visitor. ⊠*In front of Fort
DeRussy and Hale Koa Hotel* ⚲*Lifeguard, toilets, showers,
food concession, picnic tables, grills, playground.*

Kahaloa and Ulukou Beaches. The beach widens out again
here, creating the "it" spot for the bikini crowd. Beautiful
bodies abound. This is where you find most of the sailing-
catamaran charters for a spectacular sail out to Diamond
Head or surfboard and outrigger-canoe rentals for a ride
on the rolling waves of the **Canoe** surf break. Great music
and outdoor dancing beckon the sand-bound visitor to
Duke's Canoe Club where shirt and shoes not only aren't
required, they're discouraged. ⊠*In front of Royal Hawaiian
Hotel and Sheraton Moana Surfrider* ⚲*Lifeguard, toilets,
showers, food concession.*

If you've never been on a surfboard before, O'ahu is the place to give it a try, just like these girls on Waikīkī Beach.

🐚 **Kūhiō Beach Park.** This beach has experienced a renaissance after a recent face-lift. Now bordered by a landscaped boardwalk, it's great for romantic walks any time of day. Check out the Kūhiō Beach hula mound Tuesday to Sunday at 6:30 for free hula and Hawaiian-music performances and a torch-lighting ceremony at sunset. Surf lessons for beginners are available from the beach center every half hour. ⌂*Past Sheraton Moana Surfrider Hotel to Kapahulu Ave. pier* ☞*Lifeguard, toilets, showers, food concession.*

🐚 **Queen's Surf.** So named because it was once the site of Queen Lili'uokalani's beach house, this beach draws a mix of families and gay couples—and it seems as if someone is always playing a steel drum. Many weekends, movie screens are set up on the sand, and major motion pictures are shown after the sun sets (⊕ *www.sunsetonthebeach.net*). In the daytime, banyan trees provide shade and volleyball nets attract pros and amateurs alike (this is where Misty May and Kerri Walsh play while in town). The water fronting Queen's Surf is an aquatic preserve, providing the best snorkeling in Waikīkī. ⌂*Across from entrance to Honolulu Zoo* ☞*Lifeguard, toilets, showers, picnic tables, grills.*

🐚 **Sans Souci.** Nicknamed Dig-Me Beach because of its outlandish display of skimpy bathing suits, this small rectangle of sand is a good sunning spot for all ages. Children enjoy its shallow, safe waters that are protected by the walls of the historic Natatorium, an Olympic-size saltwater swim-

Beach Safety

Yes, the beaches are beautiful, but always be cognizant of the fact that you are on a little rock in the middle of the Pacific Ocean. The current and waves will be stronger and bigger than any you may have experienced. Riptides can take you on a ride they call the "Moloka'i Express"—only problem is that it doesn't take you to the island of Moloka'i but rather into the South Pacific.

Never swim alone. It is hard for even the most attentive lifeguards to keep their eyes on everyone at once, but a partner can gain their attention if you should run into trouble. There are many safe spots, but always pay attention to the posted signs. The lifeguards change the signs daily, so the warnings are always applicable to the day's conditions. If you have any doubts, ask a lifeguard for an assessment. They're professionals and can give you competent advice.

Use sunblock early and often. The SPF you choose is up to you, but we suggest nothing lower than 30 if you plan to spend more than an hour in the sun.

---

ming arena. Serious swimmers and triathletes also swim in the channel here, beyond the reef. Sans Souci is favored by locals wanting to avoid the crowds while still enjoying the convenience of Waikīkī. ⊠*Across from Kapi'olani Park, between New Otani Kaimana Beach Hotel and Waikīkī War Memorial Natatorium* ⚲*Lifeguard, toilets, showers, picnic tables.*

HONOLULU

The city of Honolulu has only one beach, the monstrous Ala Moana. It hosts everything from Dragon Boat competitions to the Aloha State Games.

☽ **Ala Moana Beach Park.** Ala Moana has a protective reef,
★ which makes it ostensibly a ½-mi-wide saltwater swimming pool. After Waikīkī, this is the most popular beach among visitors. To the Waikīkī side is a peninsula called Magic Island, with shady trees and paved sidewalks ideal for jogging. Ala Moana also has playing fields, tennis courts, and a couple of small ponds for sailing toy boats. This beach is for everyone, but only in the daytime. It's a high-crime area after dark. ⊠*Honolulu, near Ala Moana Shopping Center and Ala Moana Blvd. From Waikīkī take Bus 8 to*

shopping center and cross Ala Moana Blvd. ☞*Lifeguard, toilets, showers, food concession, picnic tables, grills, parking lot.*

SOUTHEAST O'AHU

Much of Southeast O'ahu is surrounded by reef, making most of the coast uninviting to swimmers, but the spots where the reef opens up are true gems. The drive along this side of the island is amazing, with its sheer lava-rock walls on one side and deep-blue ocean on the other. There are plenty of restaurants in the suburb of Hawai'i Kai, so you can make a day of it, knowing that food isn't far away.

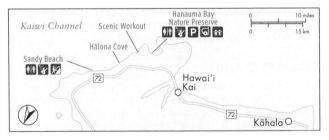

☺ **Hanauma Bay Nature Preserve.** Picture this as the world's biggest open-air aquarium. You come here to see fish, and fish you'll see. Due to their exposure to thousands of visitors every week, these fish are more like family pets than the skittish marine life you might expect. An old volcanic crater has created a haven from the waves where the coral has thrived. There's an educational center where you must watch a nine-minute video about the nature preserve before being allowed down to the bay. ■ TIP→**The bay is best early in the morning (around 7), before the crowds arrive; it can be difficult to park later in the day.** Smoking is not allowed, and the beach is closed on Tuesday.

Hanauma Bay Dive Tours (☎808/256–8956) runs snorkeling, Snuba, and scuba tours to Hanauma Bay with transportation from Waikīkī hotels on Monday, Wednesday, Thursday, and Friday only. ⊠7455 Kalaniana'ole Hwy. ☎808/396–4229 ⊕www2.hawaii.edu/~hanauma/about. htm ☞Lifeguard, toilets, showers, food concession, picnic tables, parking lot ⊠Nonresident fee $5; parking $1; mask, snorkel, and fins rental $6; tram from parking lot to beach $1.50 ☉Wed.–Mon. 6–7.

★ **Sandy Beach.** Probably the most popular beach with locals
on this side of O'ahu, the broad, sloping beach is covered
with sunbathers who come to watch the Show and soak
up rays. The Show is a shore break that's unlike any other
in the Islands. Monster ocean swells rolling into the beach
combined with the sudden rise in the ocean floor causes
waves to jack up and crash magnificently on the shore.
Expert surfers and body boarders young and old brave
this danger to get some of the biggest barrels you can
find for bodysurfing. But keep in mind that ⚠ the beach is
nicknamed "Break-Neck Beach" for a reason: many neck and
back injuries are sustained here each year. Use extreme caution when swimming here, or just kick back and watch
the drama unfold from the comfort of your beach chair.
⊠*Makai of Kalaniana'ole Hwy., 2 mi east of Hanauma
Bay* ☞*Lifeguard, toilets, showers, picnic tables.*

WINDWARD O'AHU

The Windward side lives up to its name with ideal spots
for windsurfing and kiteboarding, or for the more intrepid,
hang gliding. For the most part the waves are mellow, and
the bottoms are all sand—making for nice spots to visit
with younger kids. The only drawback is that this side
does tend to get more rain. But the vistas are so beautiful that a little sprinkling of "pineapple juice" shouldn't
dampen your experience; plus, it benefits the waterfalls
that cascade down the Ko'olaus. Beaches are listed from
south to north.

★ **Fodor's Choice Makapu'u Beach.** A magnificent beach protected
by Makapu'u Point welcomes you to the Windward side.
Hang gliders circle above the beach, and the water is filled
with body boarders. Just off the coast you can see Bird
Island, a sanctuary for aquatic fowl, jutting out of the
blue. The currents can be heavy, so check with a lifeguard
if you're unsure of safety. Before you leave, take the prettiest

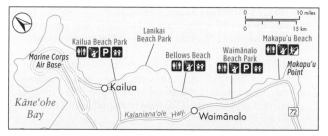

(and coldest) outdoor shower available on the island. Being surrounded by tropical flowers and foliage while you rinse off that sand is a memory you will cherish from this side of the rock. ⊠*Across from Sea Life Park on Kalaniana'ole Hwy., 2 mi south of Waimānalo* ⚲*Lifeguard, toilets, showers, picnic tables, grills.*

Waimānalo Beach Park. One of the most beautiful beaches on the island, Waimānalo is a "local" beach, busy with picnicking families and active sports fields. Expect a wide stretch of sand; turquoise, jade, and deep-blue seas; and gentle shore-breaking waves that are fun for all ages. Theft is an occasional problem, so lock your car. ⊠*South of Waimānalo town, look for signs on Kalaniana'ole Hwy.* ⚲*Lifeguard, toilets, showers, picnic tables.*

Bellows Beach. Bellows is the same beach as Waimānalo, but it's under the auspices of the military, making it more friendly for visitors. The park area is excellent for camping, and ironwood trees provide plenty of shade. ■**TIP**➔ **The beach is best before 2 PM. After 2 the trade winds bring clouds that get hung up on steep mountains nearby, causing overcast skies until mid-afternoon.** There are no food concessions, but McDonald's and other takeout fare, including *huli huli* (rotisserie) chicken on weekends, is right outside the entrance gate. ⊠*Entrance on Kalaniana'ole Hwy., near Waimānalo town center* ⚲*Lifeguard, toilets, showers, picnic tables, grills.*

★ **Lanikai Beach Park.** Think of the beaches you see in commercials: peaceful jade-green waters, powder-soft white sand, families and dogs frolicking mindlessly, offshore islands in the distance. It's an ideal spot for camping out with a book. Though the beach hides behind multimillion-dollar houses, by state law there is public access every 400 yards. ■**TIP**➔ **Look for walled or fenced pathways every 400 yards, leading to the beach. Be sure not to park in the marked bike and jogging lane.** There are no shower or bathroom facilities here—they are a two-minute drive away at Kailua Beach Park. ⊠*Past Kailua Beach Park; street parking on Mokulua Dr. for various public-access points to beach* ⚲*No facilities.*

★ **Fodor's**Choice **Kailua Beach Park.** A cobalt-blue sea, and a wide continuous arc of powdery sand make Kailua Beach Park one of the island's best beaches, illustrated by the crowds of local families that spend their weekend days here. This is like a big Lanikai Beach, but a little windier and a little wider, and a better spot for spending a full day. Kailua

Beach has calm water, a line of palms and ironwoods that provide shade on the sand, and a huge park with picnic pavilions where you can escape the heat. This is the "it" spot if you're looking to try your hand at wind- or kite-boarding. You can rent kayaks nearby at **Kailua Sailboards and Kayaks** (⊠*130 Kailua Rd.* ☎*808/262–2555* and take them to the Mokulua Islandsfor the day. ⊠*Near Kailua town, turn right on Kailua Rd. at market, cross bridge, then turn left into beach parking lot* ☞*Lifeguard, toilets, showers, picnic tables, grills, playground, parking lot.*

Kualoa Park. Grassy expanses border a long, narrow stretch of beach. While the shallow water is more suited for wading than swimming, the spectacular views of Kāneʻohe Bay and the Koʻolau Mountains make Kualoa one of the island's most beautiful picnic, camping, and beach areas. Dominating the view is an islet called Mokoliʻi, better known as Chinaman's Hat, which rises 206 feet above the water. You can swim in the shallow areas year-round. The one drawback is that it's usually windy, but the wide-open spaces are ideal for kite-flying. ⊠*North of Waiāhole, on Kamehameha Hwy.* ☞*Toilets, showers, picnic tables, grills.*

☾ **Kahana Bay Beach Park.** Local parents often bring their children here to wade in safety in the very shallow, protected waters. This pretty beach cove, surrounded by mountains, has a long arc of sand that is great for walking and a cool, shady grove of tall ironwood and pandanus trees that is ideal for a picnic. An ancient Hawaiian fishpond, which was in use until the 1920s, is visible nearby. The water here is not generally a clear blue due to the runoff from heavy rains in the valley. ⊠*North of Kualoa Park on Kamehameha Hwy.* ☞*Toilets, showers, picnic tables.*

NORTH SHORE

"North Shore, where the waves are mean, just like a washing machine," sing the Kaʻau Crater Boys about this legendary side of the island. And in winter they are absolutely right. At times the waves overtake the road, stranding tourists and locals alike. When the surf is up, there are signs on the beach telling you how far to stay back so that you aren't swept out to sea. The most prestigious big-wave contest in the world, the Eddie Aikau, is held at Waimea Bay on waves the size of a six-story building. The Triple Crown of Surfing roams across three beaches in the winter months.

All this changes come summer when this tiger turns into a kitten, with water smooth enough to water-ski on and ideal for snorkeling. The fierce Banzai Pipeline surf break becomes a great dive area, allowing you to explore the coral heads that, in winter, have claimed so many lives on the ultrashallow but big, hollow tubes created here. Even with the monster surf subsided, this is still a time for caution: Lifeguards are more scarce, and currents don't subside just because the waves do.

That said, it's a place like no other on earth and must be explored. From the turtles at Mokulē'ia to the tunnels at Shark's Cove, you could spend your whole trip on this side and not be disappointed.

Turtle Bay. Now known more for its resort than its magnificent beach, Turtle Bay is mostly passed over on the way to the better-known beaches of Sunset and Waimea. But for the average visitor with the average swimming capabilities, this is the place to be on the North Shore. The crescent-shape beach is protected by a huge sea wall. You can see and hear the fury of the northern swell, while blissfully floating in cool, calm waters. The convenience of this spot is also hard to pass up—there is a concession selling sandwiches and sunblock right on the beach. The resort has free parking for beach guests. At this writing, a planned development near the beach has residents concerned, but plans include parks and public beach access. ⊠ *4 mi north of Kahuku on Kamehameha Hwy.; turn into resort and let guard know where you are going* ☞ *Toilets, showers, food concessions, picnic tables.*

★ **Sunset Beach.** The beach is broad, the sand is soft, the summer waves are gentle, and the winter surf is crashing. Home to the Vans Triple Crown O'Neill World Cup of Surfing, Sunset gets the heaviest surf because it is the exposed point on the northern tip of O'ahu. Many love searching this shore for the puka shells that adorn the necklaces you see everywhere. Carryout truck stands selling shave ice, plate lunches, and sodas usually line the adjacent highway. ✉*1 mi north of 'Ehukai Beach Park on Kamehameha Hwy.* ☞*Lifeguard, toilets, showers, picnic tables.*

'Ehukai Beach Park. What sets 'Ehukai apart is the view of the famous **Banzai Pipeline,** where the winter waves curl into magnificent tubes, making it an experienced wave-rider's dream. It's also an inexperienced swimmer's nightmare, though spring and summer waves are more accommodating to the average swimmer. Except when the surf contests are going on, there's no reason to stay on the central strip. Travel in either direction from the center, and the conditions remain the same but the population thins out, leaving you with a magnificent stretch of sand all to yourself. ✉*Parking lot borders Kamehameha Hwy., 1 mi north of Foodland at Pūpūkea* ☞*Lifeguard, toilets, showers, parking lot.*

GOT A GOZA? For sunbathing, buy a goza, a Japanese beach mat. Everyone knows the frustration of getting out of the ocean and lying down on your beach towel, only to have it quickly become a 20-pound, sand-caked nuisance. The straw gozas keep the sand off your bum without absorbing much water, giving you a cool, comfortable place to recline on the beach. Weighing just ounces and costing just pennies, it may be the best purchase of your trip.

★ **Fodor'sChoice Waimea Bay.** Made popular in that old Beach Boys song "Surfin' U.S.A.," Waimea Bay is a slice of big-wave heaven, home to king-size 25- to 30-foot winter waves. Summer is the time to swim and snorkel in the calm waters. The shore break is great for novice bodysurfers. Due to its popularity, the postage-stamp parking lot is quickly filled, but everyone parks along the side of the road and walks in. ✉*Across from Waimea Valley, 3 mi north of Hale'iwa on Kamehameha Hwy.* ☞*Lifeguard, toilets, showers, picnic tables, parking lot.*

Hale'iwa Ali'i Beach Park. The winter waves are impressive here, but in summer the ocean is like a lake, ideal for family swimming. The beach itself is big and often full of locals. Its broad lawn off the highway invites volleyball and Frisbee games and groups of barbecuers. This is also the opening break for the Triple Crown of Surfing, and the grass is often filled with art festivals or carnivals. Also, the beach park is walking distance from historic Hale'iwa town, a mecca to surfers worldwide who make their pilgrimage here every winter to ride the waves. ⊠*North of Hale'iwa town center and past harbor on Kamehameha Hwy.* ☞*Lifeguard, toilets, showers, picnic tables.*

Mokulē'ia Beach Park. There is a reason why the producers of the TV show *Lost* chose this beach for their set. On the remote northwest point of the island, it is about 10 mi from the closest store or public restroom; you could spend a day here and not see another living soul. And that is precisely its beauty—all the joy of being stranded on a desert island without the trauma of the plane crash. The beach is wide and white, the waters bright blue (but a little choppy) and full of sea turtles and other marine life. Mokulē'ia is a great secret find, just remember to pack supplies and use caution, as there are no lifeguards. ⊠*East of Hale'iwa town center, across from Dillingham Airfield* ☞*No facilities.*

WEST LEEWARD O'AHU

The North Shore may be known as "Country," but the west side is truly the rural area on O'ahu. There are commuters from this side to Honolulu, but many are born, live, and die on this side with scarcely a trip to town. Occasional problems have flared up, mostly due to drug abuse that has ravaged the fringes of the island, but these have generally been car break-ins, not violence. So, in short, lock your car, don't bring valuables, and enjoy the amazing beaches.

The beaches on the west side are expansive and empty. Most O'ahu residents and tourists don't make it to this side simply because of the drive; in traffic it can take almost 90 minutes to make it to Ka'ena Point from Downtown Honolulu. But you'll be hard-pressed to find a better sunset anywhere.

★ **Fodor'sChoice White Plains.** Concealed from the public eye for many years as part of the Barbers Point Naval Air Station, this beach is reminiscent of Waikīkī but without the condos and the crowds. It is a long, sloping beach with numerous surf breaks, but it is also mild enough at shore for older children to play freely. It has views of Pearl Harbor and, over that, Diamond Head. Although the sand lives up to its name, the real joy of this beach comes from its history as part of a military property for the better part of a century, leaving it unchanged. Expansive parking, great restroom facilities, and numerous tree-covered barbecue areas make it a great day-trip spot. As a bonus, a Hawaiian monk seal takes up residence here several months out of the year (seals are rarely seen anywhere in the Islands). ✉*Take Makakilo exit off H1 west, turn left. Follow it into base gates, turn left. Follow blue signs to beach* ☞*Lifeguard, toilets, showers, picnic tables.*

★ **Kō 'Olina.** This is the best spot on the island if you have
☺ small kids. The resort commissioned a series of four man-made lagoons, but, as they are required by law to provide public beach access, you are the winner. Huge rock walls protect the lagoons, making them into perfect spots for the kids to get their first taste of the ocean without getting bowled over. The large expanses of seashore grass and hala trees that surround the semicircle beaches are made-to-order for naptime. A 1½-mi jogging track connects the lagoons. Due to its appeal for *keiki* (children), Kō 'Olina is popular and the parking lot fills up quickly when school is out and on weekends, so try to get there before 10 AM. The biggest parking lot is at the farthest lagoon from the entrance. ✉*23 mi west of Honolulu. Take Kō 'Olina exit off H1 west and proceed to guard shack* ☞*Toilets, showers, food concession.*

Mākaha Beach Park. This beach provides a slice of local life most visitors don't see. Families string up tarps for the day, fire up hibachis, set up lawn chairs, get out the fishing gear, and strum 'ukuleles while they "talk story" (chat). Legendary waterman Buffalo Kaeulana can be found in the shade of the palms playing with his grandkids and spinning yarns of yesteryear. In these waters Buffalo invented some of the most outrageous methods of surfing and raised his world-champion son Rusty. He also made Mākaha the home of the world's first international surf meet in 1954 and still hosts his Big Board Surfing Classic. With its long, slow-building waves, it's a great spot to try out long boarding. The swimming is generally decent in summer, but avoid the big winter waves. ✉*35 mi (1½ hrs) west of Honolulu on H1, then Farrington Hwy.* ☞*Lifeguards, toilets, showers, picnic tables, grills.*

WATER SPORTS & TOURS

There's more to the beach than just lying on it. O'ahu is rife with every type of activity you can imagine. Most of the activities are offered in Waikīkī, right off the beach.

As with all sports, listen to the outfitter's advice—they're not just saying it for fun. Caution is always the best bet when dealing with "mother" ocean. She plays for keeps and forgives no indiscretions. That being said, she offers more entertainment than you can fit into a lifetime, much less a vacation. So try something new and enjoy.

A rule of thumb is that the ocean is much more wily and unpredictable on the north- and west-facing shores, but that's also why those sides have the most famous waves on earth. So plan your activity side according to your skill level.

BOAT TOURS & CHARTERS

Hawai'i Nautical. It's a little out of the way, but the experiences with this local company are worth the drive. Catamaran cruises lead to snorkeling with dolphins, gourmet dinner cruises head out of beautiful Kō'Ōlina harbor, and sailing lessons are available on a 20-foot sailboat and a 50-foot cat. If you're driving out from Waikīkī, you may want to make a day of it, with sailing in the morning then 18 holes on the gorgeous resort course in the afternoon. Three-hour cruise rates with snacks and two drinks begin at $99 per person. ⊠ *Kō'Ōlina Harbor, Kō'Ōlina Marriott Resort, Kapolei* ☎ *808/234–7245.*

★ **Fodor's** Choice **Hawai'i Sailing Adventures.** Looking to escape the "cattle-maran" experience? Then this charter, with its goal of exclusivity and the largest private sailing yacht in the Islands, is for you. They have capacity for up to 50 guests but prefer smaller crowds, and they specialize in dinners catered to your specs. When you want a sail for a romantic occasion or a family reunion unfettered by crowds of people you don't know, try their yacht *Emeraude* and ask for Captain Roger. Two-hour dinner-cruise rates with unlimited super well drinks (drinks made with premium liquors like Tanqueray Ten or Grey Goose) begin at $119 per person. ⊠ *Kewalo Basin, Slip S, Honolulu* ☎ *808/596–9696.*

Sashimi Fun Fishing. A combination trip suits those who aren't quite ready to troll for big game in the open-ocean swells. Sashimi Fun Fishing runs a dinner cruise with fishing and music. They keep close enough to shore to still see O'ahu while jigging for a variety of reef fish. The cruise includes a local barbecue dinner, and you can also cook what you catch. The four-hour dinner-cruise rates with hotel transportation begin at $63 per person. ☎ *808/955–3474.*

Beaches on the leeward side of O'ahu are some of the quietest and most deserted—and have picture-perfect sunsets.

Tradewind Charters. Tradewind specializes in everything from weddings to funerals. They offer half-day private-charter tours for sailing, snorkeling, and whale-watching. Traveling on these luxury yachts not only gets you away from the crowds but also gives you the opportunity to "take the helm" if you wish. The cruise includes snorkeling at an exclusive anchorage as well as hands-on snorkeling and sailing instruction. Charter prices are approximately $495 for up to six passengers. ⊠ *796 Kalanipuu St., Honolulu* ☎ *800/829–4899* ⊕ *www.tradewindcharters.com.*

BOOGIE BOARDING & BODY SURFING

Boogie boarding (or sponging) has become a popular alternative to surfing for a couple of reasons. First, the start-up cost is much less—a usable board can be purchased for $30 to $40 or can be rented on the beach for $5 an hour. Second, it's a whole lot easier to ride a boogie board than to tame a surfboard. For beginner boogie boarding all you must do is paddle out to the waves, turn toward the beach, and kick like crazy when the wave comes.

Most grocery and convenience stores sell boogie boards. Though the boards do not rival what the pros use, you won't notice a difference in their handling on smaller waves. ■ TIP→ Another small investment you'll want to make is surf fins. These smaller, sturdier versions of dive fins sell for $25 to $35 at surf and dive stores, sporting-goods stores, or even

Wal-Mart. Most beach stands do not rent fins with the boards. Though they are not necessary for boogie boarding, fins do give you a tremendous advantage when you are paddling into waves. If you plan to go out in bigger surf, we would also advise you to get fin leashes to prevent loss. For bodysurfing, you definitely want to invest in fins. Check out the same spots as for boogie boarding.

If the direction of the current or dangers of the break are not readily apparent to you, don't hesitate to ask a lifeguard for advice.

BEST SPOTS

Boogie boarding and bodysurfing can be done anywhere there are waves, but, due to a paddling advantage surfers have over spongers, it's usually more fun to go to exclusively boogie-boarding spots.

Kūhiō Beach Park (⊠ *Waikīkī, past Sheraton Moana Surfrider Hotel to Kapahulu Ave. pier*) is an easy spot for the first-timer to check out the action. Try the **Wall,** a break so named for the breakwall in front of the beach. It's a little crowded with kids, but it's close enough to shore to keep you at ease. There are dozens of breaks in Waikīkī, but the Wall is the only one solely occupied by spongers. Start out here to get the hang of it before venturing out to **Canoes** or **Kaiser Bowl's.**

Makapu'u Beach (⊠ *Across from Sea Life Park, 2 mi south of Waimānalo on Kalaniana'ole Hwy.*) on the Windward side is a sponger's dream beach with its extended waves and isolation from surfers. If you're a little more timid, go to the far end of the beach to **Keiki's,** where the waves are mellowed by Makapu'u Point, for an easier, if less thrilling, ride. Although the main break at Makapu'u is much less dangerous than Sandy's, check out the ocean floor—the sands are always shifting, sometimes exposing coral heads and rocks. Also always check the currents: they can get strong. But for the most part, this is the ideal beach for both boogie boarding and bodysurfing.

★ The best spot on the island for advanced boogie boarding is **Sandy Beach** (⊠ *2 mi east of Hanauma Bay on Kalaniana'ole Hwy.*) on the Windward side. It's a short wave that goes right and left, but the barrels here are unparalleled for pure sponging. The ride is intense and breaks so sharply that you actually see the wave suck the bottom dry before it crashes on to it. That's the reason it's also called "Break

Neck Beach." It's awesome for the advanced, but know its danger before enjoying the ride.

EQUIPMENT

There are more than 30 rental spots on Waikīkī Beach, all offering basically the same prices. But if you plan to boogie board for more than just an hour, we would suggest buying a board for $20 to $30 at an ABC convenience store and giving it to a kid when you're preparing to end your vacation. It will be more cost-effective for you and will imbue you with the aloha spirit while making a kid's day.

DEEP-SEA FISHING

The joy of fishing in Hawai'i is that there isn't really a season; it's good year-round. Sure, the bigger yellowfin tuna ('ahi) are generally caught in summer, and the coveted spearfish are more frequent in winter, but you can still catch them any day of the year. You can also find dolphin fish (mahimahi), wahoo (ono), skip jacks, and the king—Pacific blue marlin—ripe for the picking on any given day.

When choosing a fishing boat in the Islands, look for the older, grizzled captains who have been trolling these waters for half a century. All the fancy gizmos in the world can't match an old tar's knowledge of the waters.

The general rule for the catch is an even split with the crew. Unfortunately, there are no "freeze-and-ship" providers in the state, so, unless you plan to eat the fish while you're here, you'll probably want to leave it with the boat. Most boats do offer mounting services for trophy fish; ask your captain.

Besides the gift of fish, a gratuity of 10% to 20% is standard but use your own discretion depending on how you felt about the overall experience.

BOATS & CHARTERS

Hawaii Fishing Adventures. Based out of Kō'Ōlina resort, Captain Jim and his crew try to bring the full Hawaiian experience to their fishing trips. While most fishing boats head straight out to the open ocean, Captain Jim trolls along the Leeward coast giving visitors a nice sense of the island while stalking the fish. They also offer an overnighter to Molokai's Penguin Banks, reputed to be some of Hawai'i's best fishing grounds. The five-hour tour runs $625 with the overnighter booking at $2,400. ☎808/520–4852 ⊕*www.webconsole.net/hifi/index.shtml.*

Inter-Island Sportfishing. The oldest-running sportfishing company on Oʻahu also boasts the largest landed Blue Marlin—more than 1,200 pounds. With two smaller boats and the 53-foot *Maggie Joe* (which can hold up to 25), they can manage any small party with air-conditioned cabins and cutting-edge fishing equipment. They also work with Grey's Taxidermy, the world's largest marine taxidermist, to mount the monster you reel in. Half-day exclusive charter rates for groups of six begin at $700. ☎*808/591–8888* ⊕*www.fish-hawaii.com.*

Magic Sportfishing. The awards Magic has garnered are too many to mention here, but we can tell you their magnificent 50-foot *Pacifica* fishing yacht is built for comfort, whether you're fishing or not. Unfortunately, Magic can accommodate only up to six. Full-day exclusive charter rates begin at $950. ☎*808/596–2998* ⊕*www.magicsportfishing.com.*

JET SKIING, WAKEBOARDING & WATERSKIING

Aloha Parasail/Jet Ski. Jet ski in the immense Keʻehi Lagoon as planes from Honolulu International take off and land right above you. After an instructional safety course, you can try your hand at navigating their buoyed course. They provide free pickup and drop-off from Waikīkī. The Waverunners run about $40 per person for 45 minutes of riding time. ☎*808/521–2446.*

Hawaiʻi Sports Wakeboard and Water Ski Center. Hawaiʻi Sports turns Maunalua Bay into an action water park with activities for all ages. While dad's learning to wakeboard, the kids can hang on for dear life on bumper tubes, and mom can finally get some peace parasailing over the bay with views going to Diamond Head and beyond. There are also banana boats that will ride six, Jet Skis for two, and scuba missions. Half-hour Jet Ski–rental rates begin at $49 per person, and package deals are available. ⊠*Koko Marina Shopping Center, 7192 Kalanianaʻole Hwy., Hawaiʻi Kai* ☎*808/395–3773* ⊕*www.hawaiiwatersportscenter.com.*

KAYAKING

Kayaking is quickly becoming a top choice for visitors to the Islands. Kayaking alone or with a partner on the open ocean provides a vantage point not afforded by swimming and surfing. Even amateurs can travel long distances and keep a lookout on what's going on around them.

This ability to travel long distances can also get you into trouble. ■TIP→Experts agree that rookies should stay on the Windward side. Their reasoning is simple: if you tire, break or lose an oar, or just plain pass out, the onshore winds will eventually blow you back to the beach. The same cannot be said for the offshore breezes of the North Shore and West O'ahu.

Kayaks are specialized: some are better suited for riding waves while others are designed for traveling long distances. Your outfitter can address your needs depending on your activities. Sharing your plans with your outfitter can lead to a more enjoyable experience.

OUTRIGGER CANOES. While everyone is clamoring to learn to surf or to go sailing, no one notices the long, funny-looking boats in front of Duke's that allow you to do both. At $10 for three rides, the price hasn't changed in a decade, and the thrill hasn't changed in centuries. You can get a paddle, but no one expects you to use it—the beach boys negotiate you in and out of the break as they have been doing all their lives. If you think taking off on a wave on a 10-foot board is a rush, wait until your whole family takes off on one in a 30-foot boat!

BEST SPOTS

For something a little different try **Kahana River** (⊠*Empties into Kahana Bay, 8 mi east of Kāne'ohe*), also on the Windward side. The river may not have the blue water of the ocean, but the Ko'olau Mountains, with waterfalls aplenty when it's raining, are magnificent in the background. It's a short jaunt, about 2 mi round-trip, but it is packed with rain-forest foliage and the other rain-forest denizen, mosquitoes. Bring some repellent and enjoy this light workout.

The hands-down winner for kayaking is **Lanikai Beach** (⊠*Past Kailua Beach Park; street parking on Mokulua Dr. for various public-access points to beach*) on the Windward side. This is perfect amateur territory with its still waters and onshore winds. If you're feeling more adventurous, it's a short paddle out to the Mokes. This pair of islands off the coast has beaches, surf breaks on the reef, and great picnicking areas. Due to the distance from shore (about 1 mi), the Mokes usually afford privacy from all but other intrepid kayakers. Lanikai is great year-round,

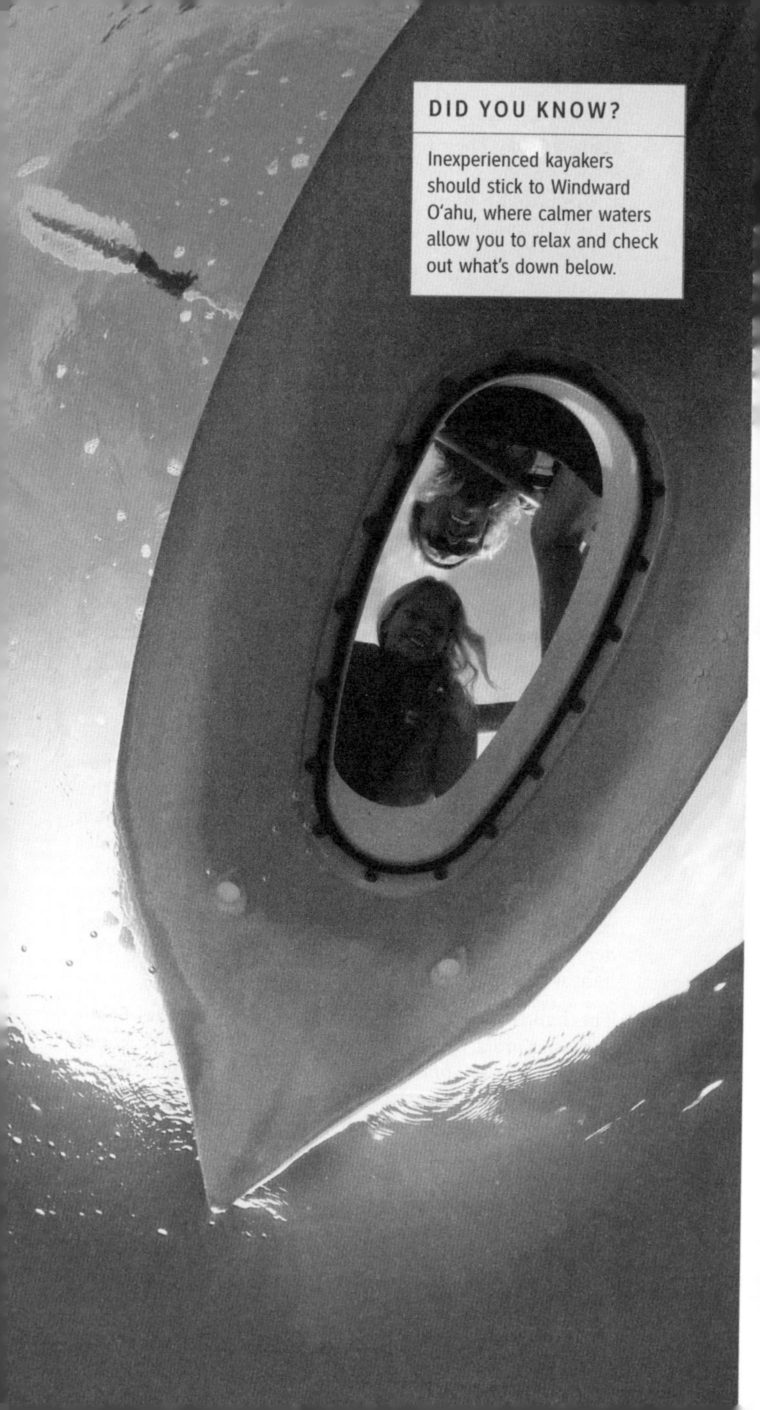

DID YOU KNOW?

Inexperienced kayakers should stick to Windward O'ahu, where calmer waters allow you to relax and check out what's down below.

and most kayak-rental companies have a store right up the street in Kailua.

EQUIPMENT, LESSONS & TOURS

Go Bananas. Staffers make sure that you rent the appropriate kayak for your abilities, and they also outfit the rental car with soft racks to transport the boat to the beach. The store also carries clothing and kayaking accessories. Full-day rates begin at $30 for single kayaks, and $42 for doubles. ✉799 *Kapahulu Ave., Honolulu* ☎808/737–9514.

Twogood Kayaks Hawai'i. The one-stop shopping outfitter for kayaks on the Windward side offers rentals, lessons, guided kayak tours, and even weeklong camps if you want to immerse yourself in the sport. Guides are trained in history, geology, and birdlife of the area. Kayak a full day with a guide for $109; this includes lunch, snorkeling gear, and transportation from Waikīkī. Although their rental prices are about $10 more than average, they do deliver the boats to the water for you and give you a crash course in ocean safety. It's a small price to pay for the convenience and for peace of mind when entering new waters. Full-day rates begin at $49 for single kayaks, and $59 for doubles. ✉345 *Hahani St., Kailua* ☎808/262–5656 ⊕*www.twogoodkayaks.com.*

PARASAILING

Parasailing is the training-wheels approach to extreme sports—you think you want to try something crazy, but you're not ready to step out of an airplane quite yet. Generally you fly about 500 feet off the water, enjoying a bird's-eye view of everything, while also enjoying the silence that envelops you at that height.

Hawai'i X–Treme Parasailing. Reputed to be the highest parasail ride on O'ahu, rides here actually pull people as high as 1,200 feet for 15 minutes. They offer pickups from Waikīkī, making it convenient to try this combo of water skiing and parachuting. Rates run from $45 to $82. ✉*Kewalo Basin Harbor, Honolulu* ☎808/330–8308.

SAILING

For a sailing experience in O'ahu, you need go no farther than the beach in front of your hotel in Waikīkī. Strung along the sand are seven beach catamarans that will provide you with one-hour rides during the day and 90-minute sunset sails. Pricewise look for $12 to $15 for day sails and $15 to $20 for sunset rides. ■TIP→They all have their little perks and they're known for bargaining so feel free to haggle, especially with the smaller boats. Some provide drinks for free, some charge for them, and some let you pack your own, so keep that in mind when pricing the ride.

Mai Tai Catamaran. Taking off from in front of the Sheraton Hotel, this cat is the fastest and sleekest on the beach. If you have a need for speed and enjoy a slightly more upscale experience, this is the boat for you. ☎*808/922–5665.*

Na Hoku II Catamaran. The diametric opposite of Mai'Tai, this is the Animal House of catamarans with reggae music and cheap booze. Their motto is "Cheap drinks, Easy Crew." They're beached right out in front of Duke's Bare-foot Bar at the Outrigger Waikīkī Hotel and sail five times daily. ☎*808/239–3900* ⊕*www.nahokuii.com.*

Pirate Bar Hawaii. A true pirate vacation where the grog is always flowing and your "black jack" is always full (that's a drinking mug to you land lubbers), adventures abound once you set foot on their 80-foot Maxi, the only one of its kind in the Islands. Setting sail out of Kewalo Basin, they will teach you the real meaning of the "No Rules" cruise while sailing into the sunset with their all-pirate crew. It maxes out at 60 people so it's good to get reservations, ask for Captain Rabbit. ☎*808/227–3556.*

SCUBA DIVING

All the great stuff to do atop the water sometimes leads us to forget the real beauty beneath the surface. Although snorkeling and snuba (more on that later) do give you access to this world, nothing gives you the freedom of scuba.

The diving on Oʻahu is comparable with any you might do in the tropics, but its uniqueness comes from the isolated environment of the Islands. There are literally hundreds of species of fish and marine life that you can only find in this chain.

Although instructors certified to license you in scuba are plentiful in the Islands, we suggest that you get your PADI certification before coming as a week of classes may be a bit of a commitment on a short vacation. ■TIP→You can go on introductory dives without the certification, but the best dives require it.

BEST SPOTS

Hanauma Bay (⊠ *7455 Kalaniana'ole Hwy.*) is an underwater state park and a popular dive site in Southeast O'ahu. The shallow inner reef of this volcanic crater bay is filled with snorkelers, but its floor gradually drops from 10 to 70 feet at the outer reef where the big fish prefer the lighter traffic. It's quite a trek down into the crater and out to the water so you may want to consider a dive-tour company to do your heavy lifting. Expect to see butterfly fish, goatfish, parrot fish, surgeonfish, and sea turtles.

The **Mahi Wai'anae**, a 165-foot minesweeper, was sunk in 1982 in the waters just south of Wai'anae on O'ahu's leeward coast to create an artificial reef. It's intact and penetrable, but you'll need a boat to access it. In the front resides an ancient moray eel who is so mellowed that you can pet his barnacled head without fearing for your hand's safety. Goatfish, tame lemon-butterfly fish, and blue-striped snapper hang out here, but the real stars are the patrols of spotted eagle rays that are always cruising by. It can be a longer dive as it's only 90 feet to the hull.

★ **Fodor's**Choice The best shore dive on O'ahu is **Shark's Cove** (⊠ *Across from Foodland in Pūpūkea*) on the North Shore, but unfortunately it's only accessible during the summer months. Novices can drift along the outer wall, watching everything from turtles to eels. Veterans can explore the numerous lava tubes and tunnels where diffused sunlight from above creates a dreamlike effect in spacious caverns. It's 10- to 45-feet deep, ready-made for shore diving with a parking lot right next to the dive spot. **Three Tables** is just west of Shark's Cove, enabling you to have a second dive without moving your car. Follow the three perpendicular rocks that break the surface out to this dive site, where you can find a variety of parrot fish and octopus, plus occasional shark and ray sightings at depths of 30 to 50 feet. It's not as exciting as Shark's Cove, but it is more accessible for the novice diver. Increase your caution the later in the year you come to these sights; the waves pick up strength in fall, and the reef can be turned into a washboard for you and your gear. Both are null and void during the winter surf sessions.

Here in the warm waters off the coast of O'ahu, there's a good chance you'll find yourself swimming alongside a Green Sea Turtle.

EQUIPMENT, LESSONS & TOURS

Captain Bruce's Hawai'i. Captain Bruce's focuses on the west and east shores, covering the *Mahi* and the Corsair. This full-service company has refresher and introductory dives as well as more advanced drift and night dives. No equipment is needed; they provide it all. Most importantly, this is the only boat on O'ahu that offers hot showers onboard. Two-tank boat-dive rates begin at $110 per person. ☎*808/373–3590 or 800/535–2487* ⊕*www.captainbruce.com.*

Reeftrekkers. The owners of the slickest dive Web site in Hawai'i are also the *Scuba Diving* Reader's Choice winners for the past four years. Using the dive descriptions and price quotes on their Web site, you can plan your excursions before ever setting foot on the island. Two-tank boat-dive rates begin at $95 per person. ☎*808/943–0588* ⊕*www. reeftrekkers.com.*

Surf-N-Sea. The North Shore headquarters for all things water-related is great for diving that side as well. There is one interesting perk—the cameraman can shoot a video of you diving. It's hard to see facial expressions under the water, but it still might be fun for those who need documentation of all they do. Two-tank boat-dive rates begin at $110 per person. ☎*808/637–3337* ⊕*www.surfnsea.com.*

SNORKELING

One advantage that snorkeling has over scuba is that you never run out of air. That and the fact that anyone who can swim can also snorkel without any formal training. A favorite pastime in Hawai'i, snorkeling can be done anywhere there's enough water to stick your face in. Each spot will have its great days depending on the weather and time of year, so consult with the purveyor of your gear for tips on where the best viewing is that day. Keep in mind that the North Shore should only be attempted when the waves are calm, namely in the summertime.

■TIP→Think of buying a mask and snorkel as a prerequisite for your trip—they make any beach experience better. Just make sure you put plenty of sunblock on your back because once you start gazing below, your head may not come back up for hours.

BEST SPOTS

As Waimea Bay is to surfing, **Hanauma Bay** (✉*7455 Kalaniana'ole Hwy.*) in Southeast O'ahu is to snorkeling. By midday it can get crowded, but with over a half-million fish to observe, there's plenty to go around. Due to the protection of the narrow mouth of the cove and the prodigious reef, you will be hard-pressed to find a place you will feel safer while snorkeling.

SHARK! "You go in the cage, cage goes in the water, you go in the water, shark's in the water..." You remember this line from *Jaws*, and now you get to play the role of Richard Dreyfus, as **North Shore Shark Adventures** provides you with an interactive experience out of your worst nightmare. The tour allows you to swim and snorkel in a cage as dozens of sharks lurk just feet from you in the open ocean off the North Shore, and all for just $120. ☎*808/228–5900* ⊕*sharktourshawaii.com.*

Directly across from the electric plant outside of Kō'Ōlina resort, **Electric Beach** (✉*1 mi west of Kō'Ōlina*) in West O'ahu has become a haven for tropical fish. The expulsion of hot water from the plant warms the ocean water, attracting all kinds of wildlife. Although the visibility is not always the best, the crowds are thin, and the fish are guaranteed. Just park next to the old train tracks and enjoy this secret spot.

★ **Fodor's**Choice Great shallows right off the shore with huge reef protection make **Shark's Cove** (⊠*Across from Foodland in Pūpūkea*) on the North Shore a great spot for youngsters in the summertime. You can find a plethora of critters from crabs to octopus, in waist-deep or shallower water. The only caveat is that once the winter swell comes, this becomes a human pinball game rather than a peaceful observation spot. Summer only.

EQUIPMENT & TOURS

Ko Olina Kat. The dock in Kō'Ōlina harbor is a little more out of the way, but this is a much more luxurious option than the town snorkel cruises. Three-hour tours of the west side of O'ahu are punctuated with stops for observing dolphins from the boat and a snorkel spot well populated with fish. All gear, snacks, sandwiches, and two alcoholic beverages make for a more complete experience, but also a pricier one (starting at $99.50 per person). ☎808/234–7245.

Snorkel Bob's. We suggest buying your gear, unless it's going to be a one-day affair. Either way, Snorkel Bob's has all the stuff you'll need (and a bunch of stuff you won't) to make your water adventures enjoyable. Also feel free to ask the staff about the good spots at the moment, as the best spots can vary with weather and seasons. ⊠*700 Kapahulu Ave.* ☎808/735–7944.

SNUBA

Snuba, the marriage of scuba and snorkeling, gives the nondiving set their first glimpse into the freedom of scuba. Snuba utilizes a raft with a standard airtank on it and a 20-foot air hose that hooks up to a regulator. Once attached to the hose, you can swim, unfettered by heavy tanks and weights, up to 15 feet down to chase fish and examine reef for as long as you fancy. If you ever get scared or need a rest, the raft is right there, ready to support you. Kids eight years and older can use the equipment. It can be pricey, but, then again, how much is it worth to be able to sit face to face with a 6-foot-long sea turtle and not have to rush to the surface to get another breath? At **Hanauma Bay Snuba Dive** (☎*808/256–8956*), a three-hour outing (with 45 minutes in the water), costs $87.

SUBMARINE TOURS

★ **Atlantis Submarines.** This is the underwater venture for the unadventurous. Not fond of swimming but want to see what you have been missing? Board this 64-passenger vessel for a ride down past ship wrecks, turtle breeding grounds, and coral reefs galore. Unlike a trip to the aquarium, this gives you a chance to see nature at work without the limitations of mankind. The tours, which leave from the pier at the Hilton Hawaiian Village, are available in several languages and run from $84 to $105. ⊠*Hilton Hawaiian Village Beach Resort and Spa, 2005 Kālia Rd., Waikīkī, Honolulu* ☎*808/973–1296.*

SURFING

Perhaps no word is more associated with Hawai'i than surfing. Every year the best of the best gather here to have their Super Bowl: Vans Triple Crown of Surfing. The pros dominate the waves for a month, but the rest of the year belongs to people like us, just trying to have fun and get a little exercise.

O'ahu is unique because it has so many famous spots: Banzai Pipeline, Waimea Bay, Kaiser Bowls, and Sunset Beach resonate in young surfers' hearts the world over. The renown of these spots comes with a price: competition for those waves. As long as you follow the rules of the road and concede waves to local riders, you should not have problems. Just remember that locals view these waves as their property, and everything should be all right.

If you're nervous and don't want to run the risk of a confrontation, try some of the alternate spots listed below. They may not have the name recognition, but the waves can be just as great.

BEST SPOTS

If you like to ride waves in all kinds of craft, try **Mākaha Beach** (⊠*1½ hrs west of Honolulu on H1 and Farrington Hwy.*). It has interminable rights that allow riders to perform all manner of stunts: from six-man canoes with everyone doing headstands to bully boards (oversize boogie boards) with dad's whole family riding with him. Mainly known as a long-boarding spot, it's predominantly local but not overly aggressive to the respectful outsider. The only downside is that it's way out on the west shore. Use caution in the wintertime as the surf can get huge.

If you really need to go somewhere people have heard of, your safest bet on the North Shore is **Sunset Beach** (✉*1 mi north of ʻEhukai Beach Park on Kamehameha Hwy.*). There are several breaks here including **Kammie's** on the west side of the strip and **Sunset Point,** which is inside of the main Sunset break. Both of these tend to be smaller and safer rides for the less experienced. For the daring, Sunset is part of the Triple Crown for a reason. Thick waves and long rides await, but you're going to want to have a thick board and a thicker skull. The main break is very local, so mind your Ps and Qs.

In Waikīkī, try getting out to **Populars,** a break at **Ulukou Beach** (✉*Waikīkī, in front of Royal Hawaiian Hotel*). Nice and easy, Populars never breaks too hard and is friendly to both the rookie and the veteran. The only downside here is the ½-mi paddle out to the break, but no one ever said it was going to be easy, plus the long pull keeps it from getting overcrowded.

White Plains Beach (✉*In former Kalaeloa Military Installation*) is a spot where trouble will not find you. Known among locals as "mini-Waikīkī," it breaks in numerous spots, preventing the logjam that happens with many of Oʻahu's more popular breaks. As part of a military base in West Oʻahu, the beach was closed to the public until a couple of years ago. It's now occupied by mostly novice to intermediate surfers, so egos are at a minimum, though you do have to keep a lookout for loose boards.

EQUIPMENT & LESSONS

C&K Beach Service. To rent a board in Waikīkī, visit the beach fronting the Hilton Hawaiian Village. Rentals cost $10 to $15 per hour, depending on the size of the board, and $18 for two hours. Small-group lessons are $50 per hour with board, and trainers promise to have you riding the waves by lesson's end. ☎*No phone.*

☾ **Hawaiian Fire, Inc.** Off-duty Honolulu firefighters—and some of Hawaiʻi's most knowledgeable water-safety experts— man the boards at one of Hawaiʻi's hottest new surfing schools. Lessons include equipment, safety and surfing instruction, and two hours of surfing time (with lunch break) at a secluded beach near Barbers Point. Transportation is available from Waikīkī. Two-hour group-lesson rates begin at $99 per person, $169 per person for a private lesson. ☎*808/737–3473* ⊕*www.hawaiianfire.com.*

This surfer is doing a stellar job of surfing the infamous Banzai Pipeline on O'ahu's North Shore.

North Shore Eco-Surf Tours. The only prerequisites here are "the ability to swim and the desire to surf." North Shore Eco-Surf has a more relaxed view of lessons, saying that the instruction will last somewhere between 90 minutes and four hours. The group rate begins at $78 per person, $135 for a private lesson. ☎808/638–9503 ⊕*www.ecosurf-hawaii.com.*

WHALE-WATCHING

November is marked by the arrival of snow in much of America, but in Hawai'i it marks the return of the humpback whale. These migrating behemoths move south from their North Pacific homes during the winter months for courtship and calving, and they put on quite a show. Watching males and females alike throwing themselves out of the ocean and into the sunset awes even the saltiest of sailors. Newborn calves riding gently next to their two-ton mothers will stir you to your core. These gentle giants can be seen from the shore as they make a splash, but there is nothing like having your boat rocking beneath you in the wake of a whale's breach.

Hawai'i Sailing Adventures and Hawai'i Nautical both run whale-watching charters during the winter months. At Hawai'i Sailing Adventures, two-hour whale-watching cruise rates with dinner start at $119. At Hawai'i Nauti-

Surf Smart

A few things to remember when surfing in O'ahu:

■ The waves switch with the seasons—they're big in the south in summer, and they loom large in the north in winter. If you're not experienced, it's best to go where the waves are small. There will be fewer crowds, and your chances of injury dramatically decrease.

■ Always wear a leash. It may not look the coolest, but when your board gets swept away from you and you're swimming a half mile after it, you'll remember this advice.

■ Watch where you're going. Take a few minutes and watch the surf from the shore. Observe how big it is, where it's breaking, and how quickly the sets are coming. This knowledge will allow you to get in and out more easily and to spend more time riding waves and less time paddling.

cal, three-hour whale-watching cruise rates with snacks start at $100.

★ **Wild Side Specialty Tours.** Boasting a marine-biologist crew, this west-side tour boat takes you to undisturbed snorkeling areas. Along the way you can view dolphins, turtles, and, in winter, whales. The tours leave early (7 AM) to catch the wildlife still active, so it's important to plan ahead as they're an hour outside Honolulu. Four-hour whale-watching cruise rates with continental breakfast start at $95. ⊠ *Wai'anae Boat Harbor, Slip A11, Wai'anae Boat Harbor* ☎*808/306–7273.*

WINDSURFING & KITEBOARDING

Those who call windsurfing and kiteboarding cheating because they require no paddling have never tried hanging on to a sail or kite. It will turn your arms to spaghetti quicker than paddling ever could, and the speeds you generate...well, there's a reason why these are considered extreme sports.

Windsurfing was born here in the Islands. For amateurs, the Windward side is best because the onshore breezes will bring you back to land even if you don't know what you're doing. The new sport of kite surfing is tougher but more exhilarating as the kite will sometimes take you in the air for hundreds of feet. We suggest only those in top shape try the kites, but windsurfing is fun for all ages.

EQUIPMENT & LESSONS

Kailua Sailboard and Kayaks Company. The appeal here is that they offer both beginner and high-performance gear. They also give lessons, either at $89 for a three-hour group lesson or $109 for a one-hour individual lesson. ■ TIP→ **Since both options are around the same price, we suggest the one-hour individual lesson; then you have the rest of the day to practice what they preach.** Full-day rentals for the more experienced run from $59 for the standard board to $69 for a high-performance board. ✉ *130 Kailua Rd., Kailua* ☎ *808/262–2555* ⊕ *www.kailuasailboards.com.*

Naish Hawai'i. If you like to learn from the best, try out world-champion Robby Naish and his family services. Not only do they build and sell boards, rent equipment, and provide accommodation referrals, but they also offer their windsurfing and kiteboarding expertise. A four-hour package, including 90 minutes of instruction and a four-hour board rental, costs $75. ✉ *155A Hamakua Dr., Kailua* ☎ *808/261–6067* ⊕ *www.naish.com.*

GOLF, HIKING & OTHER OUTDOOR ACTIVITIES

Although much is written about the water surrounding this little rock known as O'ahu, there is as much to be said for the rock itself. It's a wonder of nature, thrust from the ocean floor a hundred millennia ago by a volcanic hot spot that is still spitting out islands today. This is the most remote island chain on earth, and there are creatures and plants that can be seen here and nowhere else. And there are dozens of ways for you to check it all out.

AERIAL TOURS

An aerial tour of the Islands opens up a world of perspective. Looking down from the sky at the outline of the USS *Arizona* where it lays in its final resting place below the waters of Pearl Harbor or getting a glimpse of how Mother Nature carved a vast expanse of volcanic crater are the kinds of views only seen by an "eye in the sky." If you go, don't forget your camera.

★ **Island Seaplane Service.** Harking back to the days of the earliest air visitors to Hawai'i, the seaplane has always had a special spot in island lore. The only seaplane service still operating in Hawai'i takes off from Ke'ehi Lagoon.

Flight options are either a half-hour south and eastern Oʻahu shoreline tour or an hour island circle tour. The *Pan Am Clipper* may be gone, but you can revisit the experience for $125 to $230. ⊠ *85 Lagoon Dr., Honolulu* ☎ *808/836–6273.*

Makani Kai Helicopters. This may be the best way to see the infamous and now closed Sacred Falls park, where a rock slide killed 20 people and injured dozens more; Makani Kai dips their helicopter down to show you one of Hawaiʻi's former favorite hikes. There's also a Waikīkī by Night excursion that soars by the breathtaking Honolulu city lights. Half-hour tour rates begin at $135 per person, and customized private charters are available starting at $1,500 per hour. ⊠ *110 Kapalulu Pl., Honolulu* ☎ *808/834–5813* ⊕ *www.makanikai.com.*

★ **The Original Glider Rides.** "Mr. Bill" has been offering piloted glider (sailplane) rides over the northwest end of Oʻahu's North Shore since 1970. These are piloted scenic rides for one or two passengers in sleek, bubble-top, motorless aircraft. You'll get aerial views of mountains, shoreline, coral pools, windsurfing sails, and, in winter, humpback whales. Reservations are recommended; 10-, 15-, 20-, and 30-minute flights leave every 20 minutes daily 10 to 5. The charge for one passenger is $59 to $129, depending on the length of the flight; two people fly for $138 to $238. ⊠ *Dillingham Airfield, Mokulēʻia* ☎ *808/677–3404.*

BIKING

Oʻahu's coastal roads are flat, well paved, and unfortunately, awash in vehicular traffic. Frankly, biking is no fun in either Waikīkī or Honolulu, but things are a bit better outside the city.

Honolulu City and County Bike Coordinator (☎ *808/768–8335*) can answer all your biking questions concerning trails, permits, and state laws.

BEST SPOTS

★ **Fodor'sChoice** Our favorite ride is in central Oʻahu on the **ʻAiea Loop Trail** (⊠ *Central Oʻahu, just past Keaʻiwa Heiau State Park, at end of ʻAiea Heights Dr.*). There's a little bit of everything you expect to find in Hawaiʻi—wild pigs crossing your path, an ancient Hawaiian *heiau* (holy ground), and the remains of a World War II crashed airplane. Campsites and picnic tables are available along the way and, if you need a snack, strawberry guava trees abound. Enjoy watching the foliage change from bamboo to Norfolk pine in your climb along this 4½-mi track.

If going up a mountain is not your idea of mountain biking, then perhaps **Ka'ena Point Trail** (⊠ *West O'ahu, end of Farrington Hwy.*) is better suited to your needs. A longer ride (10 mi), but much flatter, takes you oceanside around the westernmost point on the island. You pass sea arches and a mini-blowhole then finish up with some motocross jumps right before you turn around. There's no water on this ride either, but at least at the end you have the Yokohama beach showers to cool you off.

Biking the North Shore may sound like a great idea, but the two-lane road is narrow and traffic-heavy. We suggest you try the **West Kaunala Trail** (⊠ *End of Pūpūkea Rd. This road is next to Foodland, the only grocery store on North Shore*). It's a little tricky at times, but with the rain-forest surroundings and beautiful ocean vistas you'll hardly notice your legs burning on the steep ascent at the end. It's about 5½ mi round-trip. Bring water because there's none on the trail unless it comes from the sky.

EQUIPMENT & TOURS

Blue Sky Rentals & Sports Center. Known more for motorcycles than for man-powered bikes, Blue Sky does have bicycles for $25 for 8 hours, $30 for a day, and $75 per week—no deposit is required. The prices include a bike, a helmet, and a lock. ⊠ *1920 Ala Moana Blvd., across from Hilton Hawaiian Village, Waikīkī, Honolulu* ☎808/947–0101.

Boca Hawai'i LLC. This is your first stop if you want to do intense riding. The triathlon shop, owned and operated by top athletes, has full-suspension Trek 4500s for mountain bikes or Trek 1000 for street bikes, both for $35 a day but that drops to $25 a day if you rent it for more than one day. Call ahead and reserve a bike as supplies are limited. ⊠ *330 Cooke St., next to Bike Factory, Kaka'ako, Honolulu* ☎808/591–9839.

Hawai'i Bicycling League. Not much for riding by yourself? Visit this shop online, and you can get connected with rides and contests. ⊡ *Box 4403, Honolulu 96813* ☎808/735–5756 ⊕*www.hbl.org*.

DID YOU KNOW?

Windsurfing is a sport some say was born on the Hawaiian Islands. Newbies looking for gentle breezes can give it a shot on the Windward side of O'ahu.

CAMPING

Camping has always been the choice of cost-conscious travelers who want to be vacationing for a while without spending a lot of money. But now, with the growth of eco-tourism and the skyrocketing cost of gas, it has become more popular than ever. Whatever your reasons for getting back to nature, O'ahu has plenty to offer year-round.

■TIP→ **Camping here is not as highly organized as it is on the Mainland: expect few marked sites, scarce electrical outlets, and nary a ranger station.** What you find instead are unblemished spots in the woods and on the beach. With price tags ranging from free to $5, it's hard to complain about the lack of amenities.

STATE PARKS

There are four state recreation areas at which you can camp, one in the mountains and three on the beach. All state parks require 30 days' advance notice and a $5 fee a day. To obtain a camping permit as well as rules and regulations for state parks, write to the **Department of Land and Natural Resources, State Parks Division** (⌂Box 621, Honolulu 96809 ☎808/587–0300 ⊕www.state.hi.us/dlnr/dsp).

Keaīwa Heiau State Recreation Area (⊠End of Aiea Heights Rd.☎808/483–2511), the mountain option, consists of nearly 400 acres of forests and hiking trails in the foothills of the Ko'olaus. The park is centered around an ancient Hawaiian holy site, known as a heiau, that is believed to be the site of many healings. Proper respect is asked of campers in the area.

Of the beach sites, **Kahana Valley State Park** (⊠Kamehameha Hwy. near Kahana Bay) is the choice for a true Hawaiian experience. You camp alongside a beautiful Windward bay, a short walk away from the Huilua Fishpond, a national historic landmark. There are rain-forest hikes chock-full of local fruit trees, a public hunting area for pigs, and a coconut grove for picnicking. The water is suitable for swimming and body surfing, though it's a little cloudy for snorkeling. Camping here gives you a true taste of old Hawai'i, as they lived it.

COUNTY CAMPSITES

As for the county spots, there are 15 currently available and they all do require a permit. The good news is that the permits are free and are easy to obtain. Contact the **Department of Parks and Recreation** (⊠650 S. King St., Honolulu

☏808/768–3440), or any of the satellite city halls (Ala Moana Mall, Fort St. Mall, and Kapolei Hale), for permits and rules and regulations.

★ **Fodor's**Choice For beach camping we suggest Bellows and Kualoa. **Bellows Field Beach Park** (✉220 Tinker Rd. ☏808/259–8080) has the superior beach as well as excellent cover in the grove of ironwood trees. The Windward beach is more than 3 mi long, and both pole fishing and campfires in designated areas are allowed here. You can feel secure with the kids as there are lifeguards and public phones. The only downside is that camping is only permitted on the weekends.

The beach at **Kualoa Regional Park** (✉49-479 Kamehameha Hwy. ☏808/237–8525) isn't the magnificent giant that Bellows is, but the vistas are both magnificent and historic. Near Chinaman's Hat (Mokoli'i Island) at the northern end of Kāne'ohe Bay, the park is listed on the National Registry of Historic Places due to its significance to the Hawaiians. The park is expansive, with large grassy areas, picnic tables, and comfort stations. Although the beach is just a bit of a sandy strip, the swimming and snorkeling are excellent.

Camping is not just all about the beach, however. Nestled in the foothills of the Ko'olaus is the serene **Hoomaluhia Botanical Garden** (✉End of Luluku Rd. in Kāne'ohe ☏808/233–7323). The 400-acre preserve has catch-and-release fishing, extensive hiking trails, and a large selection of tropical shrubs and trees. There are five fire circles. Though it is a beautiful area, they do caution campers to be prepared for rain, mud, and mosquitoes.

GOLF

Unlike on the Neighbor Islands, the majority of O'ahu's golf courses are not associated with hotels and resorts. In fact, of the island's three-dozen-plus courses, only five are tied to lodging and none of them are in the tourist hub of Waikīkī.

Green fees listed here are the highest course rates per round on weekdays and weekends for U.S. residents. (Some courses charge non-U.S. residents higher prices.) Discounts are often available for resort guests and for those who book tee times on the Web. Twilight fees are usually offered, call individual courses for information.

WAIKĪKĪ

Ala Wai Municipal Golf Course. Just across the Ala Wai Canal from Waikīkī, Ala Wai is said to host more rounds than any other U.S. course. Not that it's a great course, just really convenient, being Honolulu's only public "city course." Although residents can obtain a city golf card that allows automated tee-time reservations over the phone, the best bet for a visitor is to show up and expect to wait at least an hour. The course itself is flat. Robin Nelson did some redesign work in the 1990s, adding mounding, trees, and a lake. The Ala Wai Canal comes into play on several holes on the back nine, including the treacherous 18th. ⊠ *404 Kapahulu Ave., Waikīkī, Honolulu* ☎ *808/733-7387, 808/739-1900 golf shop* 🏌 *18 holes. 5861 yds. Par 70. Green Fee: $42* ☞ *Facilities: Driving range, putting green, golf carts, pull carts, rental clubs, pro shop, lessons, restaurant, bar.*

SOUTHEAST O'AHU

Hawai'i Kai Golf Course. The **Championship Golf Course** (William F. Bell, 1973) winds through a Honolulu suburb at the foot of Koko Crater. Homes (and the liability of a broken window) come into play on many holes, but that is offset by views of the nearby Pacific and a crafty routing of holes. With several lakes, lots of trees, and bunkers in all the wrong places, Hawai'i Kai really is a "championship" golf course, especially when the trade winds howl. The **Executive Course** (1962), a par-55 track, is the first of only three courses in Hawai'i built by Robert Trent Jones Sr. Although a few changes have been made to his original design, you can find the usual Jones attributes, including raised greens and lots of risk-reward options. ⊠ *8902 Kalaniana'ole Hwy., Hawai'i Kai* ☎ *808/395-2358* ⊕ *www.hawaiikaigolf.com* 🏌 *Championship Course: 18 holes. 6222 yds. Par 72. Green Fee: $90/$100. Executive Course: 18 holes. 2223 yds. Par 54. Green Fee: $37/$42* ☞ *Facilities: Driving range, putting green, golf carts, pull carts, rental clubs, pro shop, lessons, restaurant, bar.*

WINDWARD O'AHU

Ko'olau Golf Club. Ko'olau Golf Club is marketed as the toughest golf course in Hawai'i and one of the most challenging in the country. Dick Nugent and Jack Tuthill (1992) routed 10 holes over jungle ravines that require at least a 110-yard carry. The par-4 18th may be the most difficult closing hole in golf. The tee shot from the regular tees must carry 200 yards of ravine, 250 from the blue tees. The approach shot is back across the ravine, 200 yards to a well-bunkered green. Set at the Windward base of the Koʻolau Mountains, the course is as much beauty as beast. Kāneʻohe Bay is visible from most holes, orchids and yellow ginger bloom, the shama thrush (Hawaiʻi's best singer since Don Ho) chirrups, and waterfalls flute down the sheer, green mountains above. ✉ *45-550 Kionaole Rd., Kāneʻohe* 📞 *808/236–4653* ⊕ *www.koolaugolfclub.com* ⛳ *18 holes. 7310 yds. Par 72. Green Fee: $135* ⛳ *Facilities: Driving range, putting green, golf carts, rental clubs, pro shop, golf academy, restaurant, bar.*

★ **Fodor's Choice Luana Hills Country Club.** In the cool, lush Maunawili Valley, Pete and Perry Dye created what can only be called target jungle golf. In other words, the rough is usually dense jungle, and you may not hit driver on three of the four par-5s, or several par-4s, including the perilous 18th that plays off a cliff to a narrow green protected by a creek. Mt. Olomana's twin peaks tower over Luana Hills. ∎TIP➔ **The back nine wanders deep into the valley, and includes an island green (par-3 11th) and perhaps the loveliest inland hole in Hawaiʻi (par-4 12th).** ✉ *770 Auloa Rd., Kailua* 📞 *808/262–2139* ⊕ *www.luanahills.com* ⛳ *18 holes. 6164 yds. Par 72. Green Fee: $125* ⛳ *Facilities: Driving range, putting green, golf carts, rental clubs, pro shop, restaurant, bar.*

★ **Olomana Golf Links.** Bob and Robert L. Baldock are the architects of record for this layout, but so much has changed since it opened in 1969 that they would recognize little of it. A turf specialist was brought in to improve fairways and greens, tees were rebuilt, new bunkers added, and mangroves cut back to make better use of natural wetlands. But what really puts Olomana on the map is that this is where wunderkind Michelle Wie learned the game. ✉ *41-1801 Kalanianaʻole Hwy., Waimānalo* 📞 *808/259–7926* ⊕ *www.olomanagolflinks.com* ⛳ *18 holes. 6326 yds. Par 72. Green Fee: $80* ⛳ *Facilities: Driving range, putting green, golf carts, pull carts, rental clubs, pro shop, lessons, restaurant, bar.*

NORTH SHORE

Turtle Bay Resort & Spa. When the Lazarus of golf courses, the **Fazio Course** at Turtle Bay (George Fazio, 1971), rose from the dead in 2002, Turtle Bay on Oʻahu's rugged North Shore became a premier golf destination. Two holes had been plowed under when the **Palmer Course** at Turtle Bay (Arnold Palmer and Ed Seay, 1992) was built, while the

DID YOU KNOW?

The North Shore's Turtle Bay Resort attracts golfers who come for the prized Palmer Course.

other seven lay fallow, and the front nine remained open. Then new owners came along and re-created holes 13 and 14 using Fazio's original plans, and the Fazio became whole again. It's a terrific track with 90 bunkers. The gem at Turtle Bay, though, is the Palmer Course. The front nine is mostly open as it skirts Punaho'olapa Marsh, a nature sanctuary, while the back nine plunges into the wetlands and winds along the coast. The short par-4 17th runs along the rocky shore, with a diabolical string of bunkers cutting diagonally across the fairway from tee to green. ⊠ *57-049 Kuilima Dr., Kahuku* ☎ *808/293–8574* ⊕ *www.turtlebayresort.com* ↳ *Fazio Course: 18 holes. 6535 yds. Par 72. Green Fee: $160. Palmer Course: 18 holes. 7199 yds. Par 72. Green Fee: $185* ☞ *Facilities: Driving range, putting green, golf carts, rental clubs, pro shop, lessons, restaurant, bar.*

WEST (LEEWARD) & CENTRAL OAHU

★ **Coral Creek Golf Course.** On the 'Ewa Plain, 4 mi inland, Coral Creek is cut from ancient coral—left from when this area was still under water. Robin Nelson (1999) does some of his best work in making use of the coral, and of some dynamite, blasting out portions to create dramatic lakes and tee and green sites. They could just as easily call it Coral Cliffs, thanks to the 30- to 40-foot cliffs Nelson created. These include the par-3 10th green's grotto and waterfall, and the vertical drop-off on the right side of the par-4 18th green. An ancient creek meanders across the course, but there's not much water, just enough to be a babbling nuisance. ⊠ *91-1111 Geiger Rd., 'Ewa Beach* ☎ *808/441–4653* ⊕ *www.coralcreekgolfhawaii.com* ↳ *18 holes. 6818 yds. Par 72. Green Fee: $130* ☞ *Facilities: Driving range, putting green, golf carts, rental clubs, pro shop, lessons, restaurant, bar.*

Kō'Ōlina Golf Club. Hawai'i's golden age of golf-course architecture came to O'ahu when Kō'Ōlina Golf Club opened in 1989. Ted Robinson, king of the water features, went splash-happy here, creating nine lakes that come into play on eight holes, including the par-3 12th, where you reach the tee by driving behind a Disney-like waterfall. Tactically, though, the most dramatic is the par-4 18th, where the approach is a minimum 120 yards across a lake to a two-tiered green guarded on the left by a cascading waterfall. Today, Kō'Ōlina, affiliated with the adjacent 'Ihilani Resort and Spa (guests receive discounted rates), has matured into one of Hawai'i's top courses. You can niggle about routing issues—the first three holes play into the trade winds (and the morning sun), and two consecutive par-5s on the back nine play into the trades—but Robinson does enough solid design to make those of passing concern. ✉ *92-1220 Ali'inui Dr., Kapolei* ☎ *808/676–5300* ⊕ *www.koolina golf.com* ⚑ *18 holes. 6867 yds. Par 72. Green Fee: $170* ☞ *Facilities: Driving range, putting green, golf carts, rental clubs, pro shop, golf academy, restaurant, bar.*

Royal Kunia Country Club. At one time the PGA Tour considered buying Royal Kunia Country Club and hosting the Sony Open there. It's that good. ■TIP→ **Every hole offers fabulous views from Diamond Head to Pearl Harbor to the nearby Wai'anae Mountains.** Robin Nelson's eye for natural sight lines and dexterity with water features adds to the visual pleasure. ✉ *94-1509 Anonui St., Waipahu* ☎ *808/688–9222* ⊕ *www.royalkuniacc.com* ⚑ *18 holes. 7007 yds. Par 72. Green Fee: $135* ☞ *Facilities: Driving range, putting green, golf carts, rental clubs, pro shop, restaurant.*

Waikele Golf Course. Outlet stores are not the only bargain at Waikele. The adjacent golf course is a daily-fee course that offers a private clublike atmosphere and a terrific Ted Robinson (1992) layout. The target off the tee is Diamond Head, with Pearl Harbor to the right. Robinson's water features are less distinctive here, but define the short par-4 4th hole, with a lake running down the left side of the fairway and guarding the green; and the par-3 17th, which plays across a lake. The par-4 18th is a terrific closing hole, with a lake lurking on the right side of the green. ✉ *94-200 Paioa Pl., Waipahu* ☎ *808/676–9000* ⊕ *www. golfwaikele.com* ⚑ *18 holes. 6261 yds. Par 72. Green Fee: $125* ☞ *Facilities: Driving range, putting green, golf carts, rental clubs, pro shop, lessons, restaurant, bar.*

HIKING

The trails of O'ahu cover a full spectrum of environments: desert walks through cactus, slippery paths through bamboo-filled rain forest, and scrambling rock climbs up ancient volcanic calderas. The only thing you won't find is an overnighter as even the longest of hikes won't take you more than half a day. In addition to being short in length, many of the prime hikes are within 10 minutes of downtown Waikīkī, meaning that you won't have to spend your whole day getting back to nature.

ON THE TRAIL. To obtain an O'ahu recreation map that outlines the island's 33 major trails for $3.95, contact the **Hawai'i State Department of Land and Natural Resources** (✉ *1151 Punchbowl St., Room 130, Honolulu* ☎ *808/587–0300* ⊕ *www.hawaii.gov*). Contact the City and County of Honolulu **Trails and Access Manager** (☎ *808/973–9782*) for a free hiking-safety guide. Ask for a copy of *Hiking on O'ahu: The Official Guide*.

BEST SPOTS

Every vacation has requirements that must be fulfilled so that when your neighbors ask, you can say, "Yeah, did it." **Diamond Head Crater** is high on that list of things to do on O'ahu. It's a hike easy enough that even grandma can do it, as long as she takes a water bottle because it's hot and dry. Only a mile up, a clearly marked trail with handrails scales the inside of this extinct volcano. At the top, the fabled 99 steps take you up to the pill box overlooking the Pacific Ocean and Honolulu. It's a breathtaking view and a lot cheaper than taking a helicopter ride for the same photo op. ✉ *Diamond Head Rd. at 18th Ave. Enter on east of crater; there's limited parking inside, most park on street and walk in.*

★ **Fodor's Choice** Travel up into the valley beyond Honolulu to make the **Mānoa Falls** hike. Though only a mile long, this path passes through so many different ecosystems that you feel as if you're in an arboretum. Walk among the elephant ear ape plants, ruddy fir trees, and a bamboo forest straight out of China. At the top are 150-foot falls with a small pool not quite suited for swimming but good for wading. This hike is more about the journey than the destination. Make sure you bring some mosquito repellent because they grow 'em big up here. ⊹ *Behind Mānoa Valley in Paradise Park. Take West Mānoa Rd. to end, park on side of road, and follow trail signs in.*

For the less adventurous hiker and anyone looking for a great view, there is the **Makapu'u Lighthouse Trail.** The paved trail runs up the side of Makapu'u Point in Southeast O'ahu. Early on, the trail is surrounded by lava rock, but, as you ascend, foliage—the tiny white koa haole flower and the cream-tinged spikes of the kiawe—begins to take over the barren rock. Once atop the point, you begin to understand how alone these Islands are in the Pacific. The easternmost tip of O'ahu, this is where the island divides the sea, giving you a spectacular view of the cobalt ocean meeting the land in a cacophony of white caps. To the south are several tide pools and the lighthouse. The eastern view looks down upon Rabbit and Kāohikaipu Islands, two bird sanctuaries just off the coast. The 2-mi round-trip hike is a great break on a circle-island trip. ⊹ *Take Kalaniana'ole Hwy. to base of Makapu'u Pt. Look forasphalt strip snaking up mountain.*

★ **Fodor's Choice Ka'ena Point** trail is a little longer (at 5 mi round-trip) and hotter than Makapu'u Point, but it is right next to the beach, and there are spots where you can get in and cool off. Sea-carved cliffs give way to lava-rock beaches and sea arches. Halfway to the point, there is a double blow hole, which is a good indicator of sea conditions. If it is blowing good, stay out of the water. Though the area is hot and dry, there is still much wildlife here, as it is the only nesting ground for many rare sea birds. ■TIP→**Keep a lookout for the Laysan albatrosses; these enormous birds have recently returned to the area. Don't be surprised if they come in for a closer look at you, too.** There has been a cave-in of an old lava tube, so be careful when crossing it, but enjoy the view in its enormous mouth. ⊹ *Take Farrington Hwy. to its end at Yokohamas. Hike in on old 4WD trail.*

GOING WITH A GUIDE

Hawai'i Nature Center. A good choice for families, the center in upper Makīkī Valley conducts a number of programs for both adults and children. There are guided hikes into tropical settings that reveal hidden waterfalls and protected forest reserves. They don't run tours every day so it is good to get advance reservations. ⊠ *2131 Makīkī Heights Dr., Makīkī Heights* ☎ *808/955–0100.*

O'ahu Nature Tours. Guides explain the native flora and fauna that is your companion on glorious sunrise, hidden-waterfall, mountain-forest, rain-forest, and volcanic walking tours. ☎ *808/924–2473* ⊕ *www.oahunaturetours.com.*

HORSEBACK RIDING

★ **Happy Trails Hawai'i.** Take a guided horseback ride through the verdant Waimea Valley on the North Shore along trails that offer panoramic views from Ka'ena Point to the famous surfing spots. Rates for a 90-minute trail ride begin at $55. ⊠ *1 mi mauka up Pupakea Rd. on right, Pupakea* ☎ *808/638–7433.*

Kualoa Ranch. This ranch across from Kualoa Beach Park on the Windward side leads trail rides in the Ka'a'awa Valley. Rates for a one-hour trail ride begin at $59. Kualoa has other activities such as bus and Jeep tours, all-terrain-vehicle trail rides, and children's activities, which may be combined for half- or full-day package rates. ✉ *49-560 Kamehameha Hwy., Ka'a'awa* ☎ *808/237–8515* ⊕ *www.kualoa.com.*

Turtle Bay Stables. This is the only spot on the island where you can take the horses on the beach. The stables here are part of the North Shore resort, but can be utilized by nonguests. The sunset ride is a definite must if you are a friend of our four-legged friends. Rates for a 45-minute trail ride begin at $50. ✉ *4 mi north of Kahuku in the Turtle Bay Resort* ☎ *808/293–8811.*

TENNIS

O'ahu has 181 public tennis courts that are free and open for play on a first-come, first-served basis; you're limited to 45 minutes of court time if others are waiting to play. A complete listing is free of charge from the **Department of Parks and Recreation** (✉ *Tennis Unit, 650 S. King St., Honolulu* ☎ *808/971–7150* ⊕ *www.co.honolulu.hi.us*).

Kapi'olani Park, on the Diamond Head end of Waikīkī, has two tennis locations. The **Diamond Head Tennis Center** (✉ *3908 Pākī Ave.* ☎ *808/971–7150*), near Kapi'olani Park, has nine courts open to the public. There are more than a dozen courts for play at **Kapi'olani Tennis Courts** (✉ *2748 Kalākaua Ave.* ☎ *808/971–2510*). The closest public courts to the 'Ewa end of Waikīkī are in **Ala Moana Park** (✉ *Ala Moana Blvd.* ☎ *808/592–7031*).

The **Pacific Beach Hotel** (✉ *2490 Kalākaua Ave., Waikīkī, Honolulu* ☎ *808/922–1233*)has rooftop tennis courts that are open to nonguests for a fee.

Shops & Spas

WORD OF MOUTH

"Aaaah as a super shopper, I would go to O'ahu to shop. Assuming you are staying in Waikiki or the Ala Moana area, you could easily do two or three days with shopping and sightseeing."

—MelissaHI

By Chad
Pata

EASTERN AND WESTERN TRADITIONS MEET ON O'AHU,
where savvy shoppers find luxury goods at high-end malls
and scout tiny boutiques and galleries filled with pottery,
blown glass, woodwork, and Hawaiian-print clothing by
local artists. This blend of cultures is pervasive in the wide
selection of spas as well. Hawaiian lomilomi and hot-stone
massages are as omnipresent as the orchid and plumeria
flowers decorating every treatment room.

SHOPS

You'll find that shops stay open fairly late in Waikīkī.
Stores open at around 9 AM and many don't close until 10
or even 11 PM.

WAIKĪKĪ

Most hotels and shops are clustered along a relatively short
strip in Waikīkī, which can be convenient or overwhelming,
depending on one's sensibilities.

SHOPPING CENTERS

2100 Kalākaua. Tenants of this elegant, town-house-style
center include Chanel, Coach, Tiffany & Co., Yves Saint
Laurent, Gucci, and Tod's. ⊠*2100 Kalākaua Ave., Waikīkī*
☎*808/550–4449.*

DFS Galleria Waikīkī. Hermès, Cartier, and Calvin Klein are
among the shops at this enclosed mall, as well as Hawai'i's
largest beauty and cosmetics store. An exclusive boutique floor caters to duty-free shoppers only. Amusing
and authentic Hawaiian-style shell necklaces, soaps, and
printed wraps are rewards for anyone willing to wade
through the pervasive tourist schlock along the Waikīkī
Beach Walk, an area of fashions, arts and crafts, and gifts.
The Kālia Grill and Starbucks offer a respite for weary
shoppers. ⊠*Kalākaua and Royal Hawaiian Aves., Waikīkī*
☎*808/931–2655.*

King Kalākaua Plaza. Banana Republic and Niketown—both
two stories high and stocked with the latest fashions—
anchor the King Kalākaua Plaza. ⊠*2080 Kalākaua Ave.,
Waikīkī* ☎*808/955–2878.*

Royal Hawaiian Shopping Center. Completely renovated in
2006 with a more open and inviting facade, this three-
block-long center may still be in flux in 2008. The final
tenant mix has more than 100 stores, including Hawaiian

Heirloom Jewelry Collection by Phillip Rickard, which also has a museum with Victorian pieces. Bike buffs can check out the Harley-Davidson Motor Clothes and Collectibles Boutique, and the Ukelele House may inspire musicians to learn a new instrument. There are restaurants and even a post office. ⊠ *2201 Kalākaua Ave., Waikīkī* ☎ *808/922–0588*

CLOTHING

Cinnamon Girl. Adorable matching mother–daughter dresses in subtle tropical prints, flower-adorned rubber slippers, and fun accessories. Shops also located in Ala Moana Center and Ward Warehouse. ⊠ *Westin Moana Surfrider, 2365 Kalākaua Ave.* ☎ *808/922–5536* ⊕ *www.cinnamongirl.com.*

Moonbow Tropics. An elegant selection of silk Tommy Bahama Aloha shirts, as well as tropical styles for women. ⊠ *Westin Moana Surfrider, 2365 Kalākaua Ave., Waikīkī* ☎ *808/924–1496*

Reyn's. Reyn's is a good place to buy the aloha-print fashions residents wear. This company manufacturers its own label in the Islands; has 13 locations statewide; and offers styles for men, women, and children. ⊠ *Sheraton Waikīkī, 2255 Kalākaua Ave., Waikīkī* ☎ *808/923–0331.*

GALLERIES

Gallery Tokusa. *Netsuke* is a toggle used to fasten small containers to obi belts on a kimono. Gallery Tokusa specializes in intricately carved netsuke, both antique and contemporary, and one-of-a-kind necklaces. ⊠ *Halekūlani, 2199 Kālia Rd., Waikīkī* ☎ *808/923–2311.*

Norma Kress Gallery. Emerging native Hawaiian and Pacific Island artists show their work at this hotel gallery, highlighted with pottery, sculpture, paintings, drawings, and photography. ⊠ *Hawai'i Prince Hotel, 100 Holomana St., Waikīkī* ☎ *808/952–4761.*

GIFTS

★ **Sand People.** This little shop stocks easy-to-carry gifts, such as fish-shape Christmas ornaments, Hawaiian-style notepads, charms in the shape of flip-flops (known locally as "slippers"), soaps, and ceramic clocks. Also located in Kailua. ⊠ *Westin Moana Surfrider, 2369 Kalākaua, Waikīkī* ☎ *808/924–6773*

Buying Tropical Flowers & Fruit

Bring home fresh pineapple, papaya, or coconut to share with friends and family. Orchids also will brighten your home and remind you of your trip to the Islands. By law, all fresh-fruit and plant products must be inspected by the Department of Agriculture before export. Be sure to inquire at the shop about the Department of Agriculture rules so a surprise confiscation doesn't spoil your departure. In most cases, shipping to your home is best.

Kawamoto Nursery. Kawamoto grows all flowers on its three-acre orchid farm near downtown Honolulu. Their specialty is the Cattleylea, a favorite for Mother's Day, and they have decades of experience shipping temperamental orchids to the Mainland. ⊠ *2630 Waiomao Rd.* ☎ *808/732-5808* ⊕ *www.kawamotoorchids.com.*

Tropical Fruits Distributors of Hawai'i. Avoid the hassle of airport inspections. This company specializes in packing inspected pineapple and papaya; they will deliver to your hotel and to the airport check-in counter, or ship to the mainland United States and Canada. Think about ordering on the Web, unless you are planning a trip to the North Shore. ⊘ *64-1551 Kamehameha Hwy.* ☎ *808/847-3234* ⊘ *Ilalo St., Wahiawa* ☎ *800/697-9100* ⊕ *www.dolefruithawaii.com.*

JEWELRY

Philip Rickard. The heirloom design collection of this famed jeweler features custom Hawaiian wedding jewelry. ⊠ *Royal Hawaiian Shopping Center, 2201 Kalākaua Ave., Waikīkī* ☎ *808/924–7972.*

DOWNTOWN HONOLULU & CHINATOWN

SHOPPING CENTERS

Getting to the Ala Moana shopping centers from Waikīkī is quick and inexpensive thanks to **TheBus** and the **Waikīkī Trolley.**

Ala Moana Shopping Center. One of the nation's largest open-air malls is five minutes from Waikīkī by bus. Designer shops in residence include Gucci, Louis Vuitton, Gianni Versace, and Emporio Armani. All of Hawai'i's major department stores are here, including Neiman Marcus, Sears, and Macy's. More than 240 stores and 60 restaurants make up this 50-acre complex. One of the most interesting shops is Shanghai Tang. First opened in Hong Kong, the store imports silks and other fine fabrics, and upholds the tradition of old-style Shanghai tailoring. To get to the mall from Waikīkī, catch TheBus lines 8, 19, or 20; a one-way ride is $2. Or hop aboard the Waikīkī Trolley's pink line, which comes through the area every half hour. ⊠*1450 Ala Moana Blvd., Ala Moana* ☎*808/955–9517 special events and shuttle service.*

Aloha Tower Marketplace. Billing itself as a festival marketplace, Aloha Tower cozies up to Honolulu Harbor. Along with restaurants and entertainment venues, it has 80 shops and kiosks selling mostly visitor-oriented merchandise, from expensive sunglasses to exceptional local artwork to souvenir refrigerator magnets. Don't miss the aloha shirts and fancy hats for dogs at Pet Gear, and the curious mix of furniture, stationery, and clothing in Urban Rejuvenation. To get there from Waikīkī take the E-Transit Bus, which goes along TheBus routes every 15 minutes. ⊠*1 Aloha Tower Dr., at Piers 8, 9, and 10, Downtown Honolulu* ☎*808/566–2337* ⊕*www.alohatower.com.*

Ward Centers. Heading west from Waikīkī toward Downtown Honolulu, you'll run into a section of town with five distinct shopping-complex areas; there are more than 120 specialty shops and 20 restaurants here. The Entertainment Complex features 16 movie theaters. ■TIP➔**A "shopping concierge" can assist you in navigating your way through the center, which spans four city blocks**. For distinctive Hawaiian gift stores, visit Nohea Gallery and Native Books/Na Mea Hawaii, carrying quality work from Hawai'i artists, including mu'umu'u, lauhala products, and unparalleled Niihau shell necklaces. Island Soap and Candle Works (808/591–0533) makes all of its candles and soaps on-site with Hawaiian flower scents. Take TheBus routes 19 or 20; fare is $2 one-way. Or follow the Waikīkī Trolley yellow line, which comes through the area every 45 minutes. ⊠*1050–1200 Ala Moana Blvd., Ala Moana.*

BOOKS

Bestsellers. Hawai'i's largest independent bookstore has its flagship shop in Downtown Honolulu on Bishop Square. They carry books by both local and national authors. There are also locations of Bestsellers at the Honolulu International Airport and in Waikīkī at the Hilton Hawaiian Village. ⊠*1003 Bishop St., Downtown Honolulu* ☎*808/528–2378.*

KONA KEEPSAKES. Items handcrafted from native Hawaiian wood make beautiful gifts. Koa and milo have a distinct color and grain. The scarcity of koa forests makes the wood extremely valuable. That's why you'll notice a large price gap between koa wood veneer products and the real thing.

Borders Books. Borders stocks more than 200 books in its Hawaiian section; learn about Hawaiian plants, hula, or surfing. This two-story location has books, music, movies, and a café. ⊠*Ward Centre, 1200 Ala Moana Blvd.* ☎*808/591–8995.*

★ **Native Books/Na Mea Hawai'i.** In addition to clothing for adults and children and unusual artwork such as Niihau shell necklaces, this boutique's book selection covers Hawaiian history and language, and offers children's books set in the Islands. ⊠*Ward Warehouse, 1050 Ala Moana Blvd.* ☎*808/596–8885.*

CLOTHING

★ **Anne Namba Designs.** Anne Namba brings the beauty of classic kimonos to contemporary fashions. In addition to women's apparel, she's also designed a men's line and a wedding couture line. ⊠*324 Kamani St., Downtown Honolulu* ☎*808/589–1135.*

Hilo Hattie. Busloads of visitors pour in through the front doors of the world's largest manufacturer of Hawaiian and tropical aloha wear. Once shunned by Honolulu residents for its three-shades-too-bright tourist-wear, it has become a favorite source for Island gifts, macadamia nut and chocolate packages, and clothing for elegant Island functions. Free shuttle service is available from Waikīkī. ⊠*700 N. Nimitz Hwy., Iwilei* ☎*808/535–6500.*

Reyn's. Reyn's is a good place to buy the aloha-print fashions residents wear. Look for the limited-edition Christmas shirt, a collector's item manufactured each holiday season. Reyn's has 13 locations statewide and offers styles for men, women, and children. ⊠*Ala Moana Shopping Center, 1450 Ala Moana Blvd., Ala Moana* ☎*808/949–5929* ⊠*Kāhala Mall, 4211 Wai'alae Ave., Kāhala* ☎*808/737–8313.*

★ **Shanghai Tang.** First opened in Hong Kong, Shanghai Tang now has its 11th branch at Ala Moana. An emphasis on workmanship and the luxury of fine fabrics upholds the tradition of old-Shanghai tailoring. They do custom work for men, women, and children. ⊠*Ala Moana Shopping Center, Ala Moana* ☎*808/942–9800.*

FOOD SPECIALTIES

Honolulu Chocolate Company. To really impress those back home, pick up a box of gourmet chocolates here. They dip the flavors of Hawai'i, from Kona coffee to macadamia nuts, in fine chocolate. ⊠*Ward Centre, 1200 Ala Moana Blvd., Ala Moana* ☎*808/591–2997.*

Longs Drugs. For gift items in bulk, try one of the many outposts of Longs, the perfect place to stock up on chocolate-covered macadamia nuts—at reasonable prices—to carry home. ⊠*Ala Moana Shopping Center, 1450 Ala Moana Blvd., 2nd level, Ala Moana* ☎*808/941–4433* ⊠*Kāhala Mall, 4211 Wai'alae Ave., Kāhala* ☎*808/732–0784.*

GALLERIES

Louis Pohl Gallery. Modern works from some of Hawai'i's finest artists. ⊠*1111 Nu'uanu Ave., Downtown Honolulu* ☎*808/521–1812*

★ **Nohea Gallery.** These shops are really galleries representing more than 450 artists who specialize in koa furniture, bowls, and boxes, as well as art glass and ceramics. Original paintings and prints—all with an Island theme—add to the selection. They also carry unique handmade Hawaiian jewelry with ti leaf, maile, and coconut-weave designs. ■TIP→**The koa photo albums in these stores are easy to carry home and make wonderful gifts.** ⊠*Ward Warehouse, 1050 Ala Moana Blvd., Ala Moana* ☎*808/596–0074* .

HAWAIIAN ARTS & CRAFTS

Hawaiian Quilt Collection. Traditional Island comforters, wall hangings, pillows, and other Hawaiian-print quilt items are the specialty here. ⊠*Ala Moana Center, 1450 Ala Moana Blvd., Ala Moana* ☎*808/946–2233.*

My Little Secret. The word is out that this is a wonderful selection of Hawaiian arts, crafts, and children's toys. ⊠*Ward Warehouse, 1050 Ala Moana Blvd., Ala Moana* ☎*808/596–2990.*

Na Hoku. If you look at the wrists of kama'aina (local) women, you're apt to see Hawaiian heirloom bracelets fashioned in either gold or silver in a number of Island-inspired designs. Na Hoku sells jewelry in designs that capture the heart of the Hawaiian lifestyle in all its elegant diversity.

✉*Ala Moana Center, 1450 Ala Moana Blvd., Ala Moana* ☎*808/946–2100.*

HONOLULU: EAST

KAPAHULU

Bailey's Antiques & Aloha Shirts. Vintage aloha shirts are the specialty at this kitschy store. Prices start at $3.99 for the 10,000 shirts in stock, and the tight space and musty smell are part of the thrift-shop atmosphere. ■TIP➔**Antiques hunters can also buy old-fashioned postcards, authentic military clothing, funky hats, and denim jeans from the 1950s.** ✉*517 Kapahulu Ave., Kapahulu* ☎*808/734–7628.*

KĀHALA & HAWAI'I KAI

Island Treasures. Local residents come here to shop for gifts that are both unique and within reach of almost every budget, ranging in price from $1 to $5,000. Located next to Zippy's and overlooking the ocean, the store has hand-bags, toys, jewelry, home accessories, soaps and lotions, and locally made original artwork. Certainly the most interesting shop in Hawai'i Kai's suburban mall atmosphere, this store is also a good place to purchase CDs of some of the best Hawaiian music. ✉*Koko Marina Center, 7192 Kalaniana'ole Hwy., Hawai'i Kai* ☎*808/396–8827.*

Kāhala Mall. The only shopping of note in the area is located at the indoor mall, which has 90 stores, including Macy's, Gap, Reyn's Aloha Wear, and Barnes & Noble. Don't miss fashionable boutiques such as **Ohelo Road** (☎*808/735–5525*), where contemporary clothing for all occasions fills the racks. Eight movie theaters (☎*808/593–3000*) provide postshopping entertainment. ✉*4211 Wai'alae Ave., Kāhala* ☎*808/732–7736.*

WINDWARD O'AHU

Shopping on the Windward side is one of O'ahu's best-kept secrets. A half hour by car or about an hour on TheBus, it's definitely a shopping/activity destination. At Windward Mall in Kāne'ohe, stop by the Lomi Shop for authentic Tahitian oils and a 10-minute foot massage in the entrance built to resemble a voyaging canoe. The real treats, however, lie in the small boutiques and galleries in the heart of Kailua—the perfect place to gather unique gifts. After shopping, enjoy the outdoors in one of the most beautiful beach towns in the world. Kailua is the best place to rent kayaks and paddle out to the Mokulua Islands with a guide, take a windsurfing lesson, or watch the expert kiteboarders sailing across the bay. ■TIP➜ **Stop by Kalapawai Market in Lanikai—the only shop in Lanikai, which is right next to Kailua—for sandwiches and cold drinks and souvenirs, and finish the day relaxing on a sparsely populated white-sand beach.** The surf here is minimal, making it a perfect picnic spot with the kids, but not the place to learn to ride waves. Save that for Waikīkī.

The Balcony Gallery. Known almost exclusively to Kailua residents, this small, out-of-the-way gallery features contemporary paintings, photographs, glass, woodwork, ceramics, and jewelry from artists in the Islands. ■TIP➜ **Join them from 2 to 5 PM on the second Sunday of every month for a tour of 15 art venues in the area.** Gallery hours are limited; call before you go. ⊠*442A Uluniu St., Kailua* ☎*808/263–4434* ⊙*Closed Sun. and Mon.*

Bookends. The perfect place to shop for gifts, or just take a break with the family, this bookstore feels more like a small-town library, welcoming browsers to linger for hours. The large children's section is filled with toys and books to read. ⊠*600 Kailua Rd., Kailua* ☎*808/261–1996.*

★ **Fodor'sChoice Global Village.** Tucked into a tiny strip mall near Maui Tacos, this boutique features contemporary apparel for women, Hawaiian-style children's clothing, and unusual jewelry and gifts from all over the world. Look for Kula Cushions eye pillows (made with lavender grown on Maui), coasters in the shape of flip-flops, a wooden key holder shaped like a surfboard, and placemats made from lauhala and other natural fibers, plus accessories you won't find anywhere else. ⊠*Kailua Village Shops, 539 Kailua Rd., Kailua* ☎*808/262–8183*

★ **Fodor'sChoice Jeff Chang Pottery & Fine Crafts.** With store locations downtown and in Waikīkī, Jeff Chang has become synonymous with excellent craftsmanship and originality in Raku pottery, blown glass, and koa wood. Gift ideas include petroglyph stoneware coasters, photo albums covered in Hawaiian-print fabric, blown-glass penholders and business-card holders, and Japanese Aeto chimes. The owners choose work from 300 different local and national artists. ⊠*Kailua Village Shops, 539 Kailua Rd., Kailua* ☎*808/262–4060.*

★ **Fodor'sChoice Under a Hula Moon.** Exclusive tabletop items and Pacific home decor, such as shell wreaths, shell night lights,

Hawaiian-print kitchen towels, and Asian silk clothing, define this eclectic shop. ⊠*Kailua Shopping Center, 600 Kailua Rd., Kailua* ☎*808/261–4252*

NORTH SHORE

A drive to the North Shore takes about one hour from Waikīkī, but allot a full day to explore the beaches and Hale'iwa, a burgeoning attraction that has managed to retain its surf-town charm. The occasional makeshift stand selling delicious fruit or shrimp beside the road adds character to the beach, farm, and artist colony atmosphere. Eclectic shops are the best place to find skin-care products made on the North Shore, Hawaiian music CDs, sea glass and shell mobiles, coffee grown in the Islands, and clothing items unavailable elsewhere. Be sure to chat with the owners in each shop. North Shore residents are an animated, friendly bunch with multiple talents. Stop in for coffee and the shop's owner might reveal a little about his or her passion for creating distinguished pieces of artwork.

★ **The Growing Keiki.** Frequent visitors return to this store year after year. They know they'll find a fresh supply of original, handpicked, Hawaiian-style clothing for youngsters. ⊠*66-051 Kamehameha Hwy., Hale'iwa* ☎*808/637–4544.*

Matsumoto Shave Ice. Actor Tom Hanks, sumo wrestler Konishiki, and ice skater Kristi Yamaguchi have all stopped in for a cold flavored cone at Matsumoto's. If you're going to the North Shore, it's a must to stop by this legendary shack established in 1951. On average, they produce 1,000 shave ices a day. For something different, order a shave ice with adzuki beans—the red beans are boiled until soft, mixed with sugar, and then placed in the cone with the ice on top. Matsumoto's also has T-shirts and souvenirs. ⊠*66-087 Kamehameha Hwy., Hale'iwa* ☎*808/637–4827.*

★ **Fodor'sChoice** **Silver Moon Emporium.** This small boutique carries everything from Brighton accessories and fashionable T-shirts to Betsy Johnson formal wear, and provides attentive yet casual personalized service. Their stock changes frequently, and there's always something wonderful on sale. No matter what your taste, you'll find something for everyday wear or special occasions. ⊠*North Shore Marketplace, 66-250 Kamehameha Hwy., Hale'iwa* ☎*808/637–7710.*

★ **Outrigger Trading Company.** Though this shop has been in business since 1982, its upstairs location in the North Shore Marketplace often gets bypassed when it shouldn't. Look for Jam's World patchwork tablecloths with an aloha flair, shell boxes, mobiles made of ceramic fish and driftwood, stained-glass ornaments, and beach-glass wind chimes. Other novelties include hula-girl and bamboo lamps and silk-screened table runners. ⊠*North Shore Marketplace, 66-250 Kamehameha Hwy., Hale'iwa.*

WEST O'AHU

Shopping on this part of the island is at two extremes— an outdoor market that literally sells everything under the sun, and a high-end shopping outlet with all the big designer names.

Aloha Stadium Swap Meet. This thrice-weekly outdoor bazaar attracts hundreds of vendors and even more bargain hunters. Every Hawaiian souvenir imaginable can be found here, from coral-shell necklaces to bikinis, as well as a variety of ethnic wares, from Chinese brocade dresses to Japanese pottery. There are also ethnic foods, silk flowers, and luggage in aloha-floral prints. Shoppers must wade through the typical sprinkling of used goods to find value. Wear comfortable shoes, use sunscreen, and bring bottled water. The flea market takes place in the Aloha Stadium parking lot Wednesday and weekends from 6 to 3. Admission is 50¢. Several shuttle companies serve Aloha Stadium for the swap meet, including VIP Shuttle ☎*808/839–0911*; Rabbi Shuttle ☎*808/922–4900*; Reliable Shuttle ☎*808/924–9292*; and Hawaii Supertransit: ☎*808/841–2928.* The average cost is $9 per person, round-trip. For a cheaper but slower ride, take TheBus. Check routes at ⊕*www.thebus.org.* ⊠*99-500 Salt Lake Blvd., 'Aiea* ☎*808/486–6704.*

Waikele Premium Outlets. Anne Klein Factory, Donna Karan Company Store, Kenneth Cole, and Saks Fifth Avenue Outlet anchor this discount destination. You can take a shuttle to the outlets, but the companies do change over frequently. One to try: Moha Shuttle ☎*808/216–8006*; $10 round-trip. ⊠*H1, 30 mins west of Downtown Honolulu, Waikele* ☎*808/676–5656.*

Creative artisans weave flowers, ferns, vines, and seeds into gorgeous leis that brighten every occasion in Hawai'i, from birthdays to bar mitzvahs to baptisms.

SPAS

Day spas provide additional options to the self-indulgent services offered in almost every major hotel on the island.

Ampy's European Facials and Body Spa. This 30-year-old spa has kept its prices reasonable over the years thanks to their "no frills" way of doing business. All of Ampy's facials are 75 minutes, and the spa has become famous for custom aromatherapy treatments. Call at least a week in advance because the appointment book fills up quickly here. It's in the Ala Moana Building, adjacent to the Ala Moana Shopping Center. ✉ *1441 Kapi'olani Blvd., Suite 377, Ala Moana* ☎ *808/946–3838* ☞ *$70, 60-min lomilomi massage. Sauna. Services: massage, body treatments, facials, hand and foot care.*

Hawaiian Rainforest Salon and Spa. The most popular treatment at this spa uses pressure and heat from natural Hawaiian lava rocks to massage your pain away. They also have Vichy showers, aromatherapy whirlpool baths, a Korean-style Akasuri body polish, and a wide selection of packages. If you're sleepy from the long flight, try the jet-lag remedy, a 25-minute treatment that includes a neck massage and scalp rub. ✉ *Pacific Beach Hotel, 5th fl., 2490 Kalākaua Ave., Waikīkī* ☎ *808/441–4890* ⊕ *www.*

hawaiianrainforest.com ☞ *$90, 50-min lomilomi massage. Hair salon, hot tubs, sauna. Services: massage, body wraps, body care, facials, makeup.*

★ Fodor'sChoice **J. W. Marriott 'Ihilani Resort & Spa.** Soak in warm seawater among velvety orchid blossoms at this unique Hawaiian hydrotherapy spa. Thalassotherapy treatments combine underwater jet massage with color therapy and essential oils. Specially designed treatment rooms have a hydrotherapy tub, a Vichy-style shower, and a needle shower with 12 heads. The spa's Pua Kai line of natural aromatherapy products includes massage and body oil, bath crystals and body butter, which combine ingredients such as ginger, jasmine, rose petals, and coconut and grapeseed oil. ✉ *J. W. Marriott 'Ihilani Resort & Spa, 92-1001 'Ōlani St., Kapolei* ☎ *808/679–0079* ⊕ *www.ihilani.com* ☞ *$174, 50-min lomilomi massage. Hair salon, hot tubs (indoor and outdoor), sauna, steam room. Gym with: cardiovascular machines, free weights, weight-training equipment. Services: aromatherapy, body wraps and scrubs, facials, massage, thalassotherapy. Classes and programs: aerobics, body sculpting, dance classes, fitness analysis, guided walks, personal training, Pilates, tai chi, yoga.*

Mandara Spa at the Hilton Hawaiian Village Beach Resort & Spa. From its perch in the Kalia Tower, Mandara Spa, an outpost of the chain that originated in Bali, overlooks the mountains, ocean, and downtown Honolulu. Fresh Hawaiian ingredients and traditional techniques headline an array of treatments. Try an exotic upgrade, such as eye treatments using Asian silk protein and reflexology. The delicately scented, candlelit foyer can fill up quickly with robe-clad conventioneers, so be sure to make a reservation. There are spa suites for couples, a private infinity pool, and a café. ✉ *Hilton Hawaiian Village Beach Resort and Spa, 2005 Kālia Rd., Waikīkī* ☎ *808/949–4321* ⊕ *www.hilton hawaiianvillage.com* ☞ *$115, 50-min lomilomi massage. Hair salon, hot tubs (indoor and outdoor), sauna, steam room. Gym with: cardiovascular machines, free weights, weight-training equipment. Services: aromatherapy, body wraps and scrubs, facials, massages.*

Nā Hō'ola at the Hyatt Regency Waikīkī Resort & Spa. Nā Hō'ola is the largest spa in Waikīkī, sprawling across the fifth and sixth floors of the Hyatt, with 19 treatment rooms, jet baths, and Vichy showers. Arrive early for your treatment to enjoy the postcard views of Waikīkī Beach. Four packages identified by Hawai'i's native healing plants—noni, kukui, awa, and kalo—combine various body, face, and hair treatments and span 2½ to 4 hours. The Champagne of the Sea body treatment employs a self-heating mud wrap to release tension and stress. The small exercise room is for use by hotel guests only. ⊠*Hyatt Regency Waikīkī Resort and Spa, 2424 Kalākaua Ave., Waikīkī* ☎*808/921–6097* ⊕*www.waikiki.hyatt.com* ☞*$130, 50-min lomilomi massage. Sauna, showers. Gym with: cardiovascular machines. Services: aromatherapy, body scrubs and wraps, facials, hydrotherapy, massage.*

★ **Fodor'sChoice SpaHalekulani.** SpaHalekulani mines the traditions and cultures of the Pacific Islands with massages, body, and facial therapies. Try the Polynesian Nonu, which uses warm stones and healing nonu gel. The invigorating Japanese Ton Ton Amma massage is another popular choice. The exclusive line of bath and body products is scented by maile, lavender orchid, hibiscus, coconut passion, or Manoa mint. ⊠*Halekūlani Hotel, 2199 Kālia Rd., Waikīkī* ☎*808/931–5322* ⊕*www.halekulani.com* ☞*$220, 75-min lomilomi massage. Use of facilities is specific to treatment but may include Japanese furo bath, steam shower, or whirlpool tub. Services: hair salon, nail care, massage, facials, body treatments.*

The Spa Luana at Turtle Bay Resort. Luxuriate at the ocean's edge in this serene spa. Don't miss the tropical Pineapple Pedicure ($65), administered outdoors overlooking the North Shore. Tired feet soak in a bamboo bowl filled with coconut milk before the pampering really begins with Hawaiian algae salt, Island bee honey, kukui nut oil, and crushed pineapple. There are private spa suites, an outdoor treatment cabana that overlooks the surf, an outdoor exercise studio, and a lounge area and juice bar. ⊠*Turtle Bay Resort, 57-091 Kamehameha Hwy., North Shore* ☎*808/447–6868* ⊕*www.turtlebayresort.com* ☞*$105, 50-min lomilomi massage. Hair and nail salon, showers, steam room, outdoor whirlpool. Gym with: free weights, cardio and weight-training machines. Services: facials, massages, body treatments, waxing. Classes and programs: hula aerobics, Pilates, yoga.*

Entertainment & Nightlife

WORD OF MOUTH

"My husband and I spent a week of our honeymoon on O'ahu last year. We like lively places, and there is plenty of nightlife in Waikīkī."

—optimystic

By Chad
Pata
MANY FIRST-TIME VISITORS ARRIVE IN THE ISLANDS expecting to see scenic beauty and sandy beaches but not much at night. That might be true on some of the other Islands, but not in Oʻahu. Honolulu sunsets herald the onset of the best nightlife scene in the Islands.

Local artists perform every night of the week along Waikīkī's Kalākaua and Kūhiō avenues and in Downtown Honolulu; the clubs dance to every beat from Top 40 to alternative to '80s.

The arts also thrive alongside the tourist industry. Oʻahu has an established symphony, a thriving opera company, chamber-music groups, and community theaters. Major Broadway shows, dance companies, and rock stars also make their way to Honolulu. Check the local newspapers— *MidWeek*, the *Honolulu Advertiser*, the *Honolulu Star-Bulletin*, or the *Honolulu Weekly*—for the latest events.

Whether you make it an early night or stay up to watch that spectacular tropical sunrise, there's lots to do in paradise.

ENTERTAINMENT

DINNER CRUISES & SHOWS
Dinner cruises depart either from the piers adjacent to the Aloha Tower Marketplace in Downtown Honolulu or from Kewalo Basin, near Ala Moana Beach Park, and head along the coast toward Diamond Head. There's usually a buffet-style dinner with a local accent, dancing, drinks, and a sensational sunset. Except as noted, dinner cruises cost approximately $40 to $110, cocktail cruises $25 to $40. Most major credit cards are accepted. In all cases, reservations are essential.

Aliʻi Kai Catamaran. Patterned after an ancient Polynesian vessel, this huge catamaran casts off from Aloha Tower with 1,000 passengers. The deluxe dinner cruise has two bars, a huge dinner, and an authentic Polynesian show with colorful hula music. The food is good, the after-dinner show loud and fun, and everyone dances on the way back to shore. Rates begin at $66 and include round-trip transportation, the dinner buffet, and one drink. ⊠*Pier 5, street level, Honolulu* ☎*808/539–9400 Ext. 5.*

★ **Atlantis Cruises.** The sleekly high-tech *Navatek,* a revolutionary craft designed to sail smoothly in rough waters, powers farther along Waikīkī's coastline than its com-petitors, sometimes making it past Diamond Head and all the way to Hanauma Bay. Choose from sunset dinner or moonlight cruises aboard the 300-passenger boat where you can feast on beef tenderloin and whole lobster or opt for the downstairs buffet. There's also the option of humpback whale–watching cruises December–mid-April. Tours leave from Pier 6, next to Aloha Tower Marketplace. Rates begin at $75 for the buffet, including one drink; the sit-down dinner, which includes three drinks, starts at $105. ⊠*Honolulu Harbor* ☎808/973–1311 ⊕*www. atlantisadventures.com.*

Creation: A Polynesian Journey. A daring Samoan fire-knife dancer is the highlight of this show that traces Hawai'i's cul-ture and history, from its origins to statehood. ⊠*'Āinahau Showroom, Sheraton Princess Ka'iulani Hotel, 120 Ka'iulani Ave., Waikīkī* ☎808/931–4660 ☉*Dinner shows Tues.–Sun. at 6.*

★ **Magic of Polynesia.** Hawai'i's top illusionist, John Hirokawa, displays mystifying sleight of hand in this highly entertain-ing show, which incorporates contemporary hula and island music into its acts. ⊠*Waikīkī Beachcomber Hotel, 2300 Kalākaua Ave., Waikīkī* ☎808/971–4321 ☉*Nightly at 8.*

Paradise Cruises. Prices vary depending on which deck you choose on the 1,600-passenger, four-deck *Star of Hono-lulu.* For instance, a seven-course French-style dinner and live jazz on the top deck starts at $165. A steak-and-crab feast on level two starts at $78. This ship also features daily Hawaiiana Lunch cruises that offer lei-making and 'ukulele and hula lessons starting at $52. Evening excursions also take place on the 340-passenger *Starlet I* and 230-passenger *Starlet II,* which offer three-course dinners beginning at $43. You can bring your bathing suits for a morning cruise for $63 complete with ocean fun on a water trampoline and slide, and feast on a BBQ lunch before heading back to shore. ⊠*1540 S. King St., Honolulu* ☎808/983–7827 ⊕*www.paradisecruises.com.*

☘ **Polynesian Cultural Center.** Easily one of the best on the Islands, this show has soaring moments and an "erupting volcano." The performers are students from Brigham Young University's Hawai'i campus. ⊠*55-370 Kamehameha Hwy., Lā'ie* ☎808/293–3333 or 800/367–7060 ⊕*www.polynesia. com* ☉*Mon.–Sat. 12:30–9:30.*

Society of Seven. This lively, popular septet has great staying power and, after more than 25 years, continues to put on one of the best shows in Waikīkī. They sing, dance, do impersonations, play instruments, and, above all, entertain with their contemporary sound. ⊠*Outrigger Waikīkī on the Beach, 2335 Kalākaua Ave., Waikīkī* ☎*808/922–6408* ⊕*www.outrigger.com* ☉*Tues.–Sat. at 8:30.*

LŪʻAU

The lūʻau is an experience that everyone, both local and tourist, should have. Today's lūʻau still adhere to traditional foods and entertainment, but there's also a fun, contemporary flair. With most, you can even watch the roasted pig being carried out of its *ʻimu,* a hole in the ground used for cooking meat with heated stones.

Lūʻau cost anywhere from $56 to $195. Most that are held outside of Waikīkī offer shuttle service so you don't have to drive. Reservations are essential.

Germaine's Lūʻau. Widely regarded as the most folksy and local, this lūʻau is held in Kalaeloa in Leeward Oʻahu. The food is the usual multicourse, all-you-can-eat buffet, but it's very tasty. It's a good lūʻau for first-timers and at a reasonable price. Expect a lively crowd on the 35-minute bus ride from Waikīkī. Admission includes buffet, Polynesian show, and shuttle transport from Waikīkī. ☎*808/949–6626 or 800/367–5655* ⊕*www.germainesluau.com* ⊠*$65* ☉*Daily at 6.*

PŪPŪ. Entertaining Hawaiian style means having a lot of pūpū—the local term for appetizers or hors d'oeuvres. Locals eat these small portions of food mostly as they wind down from their work day, relax, and enjoy a couple of beers. Popular pūpū include sushi, tempura, teriyaki chicken skewers, BBQ meat, and our favorite: poke (pronounced "po-keh"), or raw fish, seasoned with seaweed, shoyu, and other flavorings.

★ **Paradise Cove Lūʻau.** The scenery is the best here—the sunsets are unbelievable. Watch Mother Nature's special-effects show in Kapolei/Ko Olina Resort in Leeward Oʻahu, a good 27 mi from the bustle of Waikīkī. The party-hearty atmosphere is kid-friendly with Hawaiian games, canoe rides in the cove, and lots of predinner activities. The stage show includes a fire-knife dancer, singing emcee, and both traditional and contemporary hula. Basic admission includes buffet, activities, and the show. Shuttle transport from

DID YOU KNOW?

The ancient art of hula is taught to many keiki (children) on O'ahu from a very young age. Catch a performance here, at Kapi'olani Park.

Waikīkī is $8. You pay extra for table service and box seating. ☎808/842–5911 ⊕*www.paradisecovehawaii.com* ✉*$65–$115* ⊘*Daily at 5:30, doors open at 5.*

★ Fodor'sChoice **Polynesian Cultural Center Ali'i Lū'au.** This elaborate lū'au has the sharpest production values but no booze (it's a Mormon-owned facility). It's held amid the seven re-created villages at the Polynesian Cultural Center in the North Shore town of Lā'ie, about an hour's drive from Honolulu. The lū'au includes tours of the park with shows and activities. Package rates vary depending on activities and amenities (personalized tours, reserved seats, buffet vs. dinner service, backstage tour, etc.). Waikīkī transport is available, call for prices. ☎*808/293–3333 or 800/367–7060* ⊕*www.polynesia.com* ✉*$83–$215* ⊘*Mon.–Sat. center opens at noon; lū'au starts at 5.*

FILM

Hawai'i International Film Festival. It may not be Cannes, but this festival is unique and exciting. During the week-long event from the end of November to early December, top films from the United States, Asia, and the Pacific are screened day and night at several theaters on O'ahu to packed crowds. It's a must-see for film adventurers. ☎*808/528–3456* ⊕*www.hiff.org.*

★ **Sunset on the Beach.** It's like watching a movie at the drive-in, minus the car and the impossible speaker box. Think romantic and cozy; bring a blanket and find a spot on the sand to enjoy live entertainment, food from top local restaurants, and a movie feature on a 40-foot screen. Held twice a month on Waikīki iki's Queen's Surf Beach across from the Honolulu Zoo, Sunset on the Beach is a favorite event for both locals and tourists. If the weather is blustery, beware of flying sand. ☎*808/923–1094* ⊕*www.waikiki improvement.com.*

MUSIC

Hawai'i Opera Theater. Better known as "HOT," the Hawai'i Opera Theater has been known to turn the opera-challenged into opera lovers. All operas are sung in their original language with projected English translation. Tickets range from $29 to $120. ✉*Neil Blaisdell Center Concert Hall, Ward Ave. and King St., Downtown Honolulu* ☎*808/596–7858* ⊕*www.hawaiiopera.org.*

Honolulu Symphony Orchestra. In recent years, the Honolulu Symphony has worked hard to increase its appeal to all

CLOSE UP

Island Sounds

Hawaii has a vigorous music scene largely invisible outside the state but central to its cultural identity. The Grammy Awards only got around to recognizing Hawaiian music with an award in 2005, but local artists sell thousands of albums and regularly tour island conclaves on the mainland, even playing Carnegie Hall. Like country, Hawaiian music has several subcategories: indigenous chant; early Western-style choral music; "traditional" songs that span the 20th century; contemporary Hawaiian, which melds all of the above with rock, pop, and even folk; instrumental slack key guitar and 'ukulele music; reggae and rap mixes. Most islands boast at least one Hawaiian music station—often two; one for classic Hawaiian, one for more contemporary stuff. Performers to listen for include the Cazimero Brothers, Keali'i Reichel, and Israel Kamakawiwo'ole (just say "Iz"). Or you might get a kick out of Don Tiki's revival of the '60s-era xylophone-and-birdcall school of island music.

5

ages. The orchestra performs at the Neil Blaisdell Concert Hall under the direction of the young, dynamic Samuel Wong. The Honolulu Pops series, with performances under the summer stars at the Waikīkī Shell, features top local and national artists under the direction of talented conductor-composer Matt Cattingub. Tickets are $17 to $59. ⊠*Dole Cannery, 650 Iwilei Rd., Suite 202, Iwilei* ☎*808/792–2000* ⊕*www.honolulusymphony.com.*

Honolulu Zoo Concerts. For almost two decades, the Honolulu Zoo Society has sponsored Wednesday-evening concerts from June to August on the zoo's stage lawn. Listen to local legends play everything from Hawaiian to jazz to Latin music. ■TIP→ **At just $1 admission, this is one of the best deals in town.** Take a brisk walk through the zoo exhibits before they close at 5:30 PM or join in the family activities; bring your own picnic for the concert, which starts at 6 PM. It's an alcohol-free event, and there's a food concession for those who come unprepared. ⊠*151 Kapahulu Ave., Waikīkī* ☎*808/926–3191* ⊕*www.honoluluzoo.org* ⊿*$1* ☉*Gates open at 4:30.*

THEATER

Army Community Theatre. This is a favorite for its revivals of musical theater classics presented in an 800-seat house. The casts are talented, and the fare is great for families. ✉*Richardson Theater, Fort Shafter, Downtown Honolulu* ☎*808/438–4480* 🖃*$14–$20.*

NIGHTLIFE

O'ahu is the best of all the Islands for nightlife. The locals call it *pau hana* but you might call it "off the clock and ready for a cocktail." The literal translation of the Hawaiian phrase means "done with work." On weeknights, it's likely that you'll find the working crowd still in their casual business attire sipping a few gin and tonics even before the sun goes down. Those who don't have to wake up in the early morning change into a fresh outfit and start the evening closer to 10 PM.

You can find a bar in just about any area on O'ahu. Most of the clubs, however, are in Waikīkī, Ala Moana, and Downtown Honolulu. The drinking age is 21 on O'ahu and throughout Hawai'i. Many bars will admit younger people but will not serve them alcohol. By law, all establishments that serve alcoholic beverages must close by 2 AM. The only exceptions are those with a cabaret license, which have a 4 AM curfew. ■TIP➔ Most places have a cover charge of $5 to $10, but with some establishments, getting there early means you don't have to pay.

WAIKĪKĪ

BARS

Banyan Veranda. The Banyan Veranda is steeped in history. From this location the radio program *Hawai'i Calls* first broadcast the sounds of Hawaiian music and the rolling surf to a U.S. mainland audience in 1935. Today, a variety of Hawaiian entertainment continues to provide the perfect accompaniment to the sounds of the waves. ✉*Sheraton Moana Surfrider, 2365 Kalākaua Ave., Waikīkī* ☎*808/922–3111.*

★ **Cobalt Lounge.** Take the glass elevator up 30 stories to enjoy the sunset. Floor-to-ceiling windows offer breathtaking views of Diamond Head and the Waikīkī shoreline. Leather sofas and cobalt-blue lighting set the "blue" Hawai'i mood. After darkness falls, you can find soft lights, starlight, and dancing in this lounge in the center of the Hanohano Room. ⊠*Sheraton Waikīkī, 2255 Kalākaua Ave., Waikīkī* ☎*808/922–4422* ⊙*1st and 3rd Sat. of month.*

★ **Duke's Canoe Club.** Making the most of its oceanfront spot on Waikīkī Beach, Duke's presents "Concerts on the Beach" every Friday, Saturday, and Sunday with contemporary Hawaiian musicians like Henry Kapono. National musicians like Jimmy Buffett have also performed here. At Duke's Barefoot Bar, solo Hawaiian musicians take the stage nightly, and it's not unusual for surfers to leave their boards outside to step in for a casual drink after a long day on the waves. ⊠*Outrigger Waikīkī, 2335 Kalākaua Ave., Waikīkī* ☎*808/922–2268.*

★ **Mai Tai Bar at the Royal Hawaiian.** The bartenders sure know how to make one killer mai tai—just one could do the trick. This is, after all, the establishment that came up with the famous drink in the first place. The pink, umbrella-covered tables at the outdoor bar are front-row seating for Waikīkī sunsets and an unobstructed view of Diamond Head. Contemporary Hawaiian music is usually on stage, and the staff is extremely friendly. ⊠*Royal Hawaiian Hotel, 2259 Kalākaua Ave., Waikīkī* ☎*808/923–7311.*

★ Fodor's Choice **Moana Terrace.** Three floors up from Waikīkī Beach, this open-air terrace is the home of Aunty Genoa Keawe, the "First Lady of Hawaiian Music." Her falsetto sessions include jams with the finest of Hawai'i's musicians. ⊠*Waikīkī Beach Marriott Resort, 2552 Kalākaua Ave., Waikīkī* ☎*808/922–6611.*

Shore Bird Oceanside Bar and Grill. This Waikīkī beachfront bar spills right out onto the sand. Local bands play nightly until 1 AM. ⊠*Outrigger Reef on the Beach hotel, 2169 Kālia Rd., Waikīkī* ☎*808/922–2887.*

Tiki's Grill and Bar. Get in touch with your primal side at this restaurant–bar overlooking Kūhiō Beach. Tiki torches, tiki statues, and other South Pacific art set the mood. A twentysomething mix of locals and tourists comes on the weekends to get their fill of kitschy-cool. There's nightly entertainment featuring contemporary Hawaiian musicians. Don't leave without sipping on a "lava flow." It's served in a whole coconut, which is yours to keep at the end of the night. ⊠*Aston Waikīkī Beach Hotel, 2570 Kalākaua Ave., Waikīkī* ☎*808/923–8454.*

Hula has been called "the heartbeat of the Hawaiian people." But hula isn't just dance; it is storytelling.

CLUBS

Hula's Bar and Lei Stand. Hawai'i's oldest and best-known gay-friendly nightspot offers calming panoramic outdoor views of Diamond Head and the Pacific Ocean by day and a high-energy club scene by night. Check out the sound-proof, glassed-in dance floor. ⊠ *Waikīkī Grand Hotel, 134 Kapahulu Ave., 2nd fl., Waikīkī* ☎808/923–0669.

Nashville Waikīkī. Country music in the tropics? You bet! Put on your *paniolo* (Hawaiian cowboy) duds and mosey on out to the giant dance floor. There are pool tables, dartboards, line dancing, and free dance lessons (Wednesday at 6:30 PM) to boot. Look for wall-to-wall crowds on the weekend. ⊠ *Ohana Waikīkī West Hotel, 2330 Kūhiō Ave., Waikīkī* ☎808/926–7911.

The W. The Diamond Head Grill restaurant is also an after-hours nightclub, full of hip, young professionals who enjoy martinis and the chance to do some not-so-serious networking. Look for a younger group on Saturday. Enjoy some fantastic (though pricey) eats until midnight, and keep dancing until 2 AM. ⊠ *2885 Kalākaua Ave., Waikīkī* ☎808/922–1700 ◷ *Fri. and Sat. at 9 PM.*

Zanzabar. Traverse a winding staircase and make an entrance at Zanzabar where DJs spin top hits, from hip-hop to soul and techno to trance. It's easy to find a drink at this high-energy nightspot with its three bars. Not exactly sure how to get your groove on? Zanzabar offers free Latin dance lessons every Tuesday at 8 PM. Most nights are 21 and over, Sunday, Tuesday, Wednesday, and Thursday allow 18 and over in for $15. ⊠ *Waikīkī Trade Center, 2255 Kūhiō Ave., Waikīkī* ☎ *808/924–3939.*

ELSEWHERE IN HONOLULU

BARS

Anna Bannana's. Generations of Hawai'i college students have spent more than an evening or two at this legendary two-story, smoky dive near the University of Hawai'i campus. A living-room atmosphere makes it a comfortable place to hang out. Here, the music is fresh, loud, and sometimes experimental. Live music happens Friday and Saturday, starting at 9 PM. There's also open-mike night for amateurs on Monday. ⊠ *2440 S. Beretania St., Mō'ili'ili* ☎ *808/946–5190.*

Don Ho's Grill. This popular waterfront restaurant in the Aloha Tower Marketplace houses the Tiny Bubbles Bar, famous for its "suck 'em up" mai tai, a Don Ho classic. The dinner hour features Hawaiian musicians like Jerry Santos and Robert Cazimero. On the weekend, live bands play reggae music from 10 PM to 2 AM. ⊠ *Aloha Tower Marketplace, 1 Aloha Tower Dr., Downtown Honolulu* ☎ *808/528–0807.*

★ Fodor'sChoice **Mai Tai Bar at Ala Moana Center.** After a long day of shopping, the Mai Tai Bar on the third floor of Ala Moana Center is a perfect spot to relax. There's live entertainment and two nightly happy hours: one for food items and another strictly for specialty drinks. There's never a cover charge and no dress code, but to avoid waiting in line, get there before 9 PM. ⊠ *1450 Ala Moana Blvd., Ala Moana* ☎ *808/947–2900.*

Opium Den & Champagne Bar at Indigo's. This bar at the edge of Chinatown resembles a joint right out of a film noir. Jazz plays early in the evening on Tuesday; late-night DJs spin trance, Top 40, funk, disco, and rock on weekends. In addition to champagne, happy hour features sake martinis and complimentary pūpū buffet. ⊠ *Indigo Euroasian Cuisine, 1121 Nu'uanu Ave., Downtown Honolulu* ☎ *808/521–2900.*

CLUBS

★ **Fodor'sChoice Rumours.** The after-work crowd loves this spot, which has dance videos, disco, and throbbing lights. On Saturday "Little Chill" nights, the club plays oldies from the '70s, '80s, and '90s and serves free pūpū. ⊠ *Ala Moana Hotel, 410 Atkinson St., Ala Moana* ☏ *808/955–4811.*

Venus Nightclub. This high-energy social bar, with leather couches ideal for a night of people-watching, features hip-hop, trance, and reggae with guest DJs five nights a week. Attention, ladies: there's a male dance revue Saturday evenings. ⊠ *1349 Kapi'olani Blvd., Ala Moana* ☏ *808/951–8671.*

ELSEWHERE IN O'AHU

BARS

Boardrider's Bar & Grill. Tucked away in Kailua Town, this spot has long been the venue for local bands to strut their stuff. Renovations have spruced up the space, which now includes pool tables, dartboards, foosball, and eight TVs for sports-viewing with the local and military crowd. Look for live entertainment—reggae to alternative rock to good old-fashioned rock-n-roll—Wednesday through Saturday from 10:30 PM to 1:30 AM. Cover ranges from $3 to $10. ⊠ *201-A Hamakua Dr., Kailua* ☏ *808/261–4600.*

Breaker's Restaurant. Just about every surf contest post-party is celebrated at this family-owned establishment, as the owner's son, Benji Weatherly, is a pro surfer himself. Surfing memorabilia, including surfboards hanging from the ceiling, fill the space. The restaurant/bar is open from 11 AM to 9:30 PM with a late-night menu until midnight. But things start to happen around 9 PM on Thursday for the 18-and-over crowd, who cruise while the DJ spins, and there's live music on Saturday. The party goes until 2 AM. ⊠ *Marketplace Shopping Center, 66-250 Kamehameha Hwy., Hale'iwa* ☏ *808/637–9898.*

The Shack. This sports bar and restaurant is about the only late-night spot you can find in Southeast O'ahu. After a day of snorkeling at Hanauma Bay, stop by to kick back, have a beer, eat a burger, watch some sports, or play a game of pool. It's open until 2 AM nightly. ⊠ *Hawai'i Kai Shopping Center, 377 Keahole St., Hawai'i Kai* ☏ *808/396–1919* ☾ *Nightly until 2 AM.*

Where to Eat

WORD OF MOUTH

"Make sure you have a shrimp plate lunch from one of the shrimp trucks. YUM YUM YUM! You will find them along the roadside in the North Shore area."
—annikany

By Trina
Kudlacek

O'AHU, WHERE THE MAJORITY of the Islands' 2,000-plus restaurants are located, offers the best of all worlds: it has the foreignness and excitement of Asia and Polynesia, but when the kids need McDonald's, or when you just have to have a Starbucks latte, they're here, too.

Budget for a pricey dining experience at the very top of the restaurant food chain, where chefs Alan Wong, Roy Yamaguchi, George Mavrothalassitis, and others you've read about in *Gourmet* put a sophisticated and unforgettable spin on local foods and flavors. Savor seared 'ahi tuna in sea urchin beurre blanc or steak marinated in Korean kimchi sauce.

Spend the rest of your food dollars where budget-conscious locals do: in plate-lunch places and small ethnic eateries, at roadside stands and lunch wagons, or at window-in-the-wall delis. Munch a musubi rice cake (a rectangular form of rice wrapped with seaweed and often topped with Spam), slurp shave ice with red-bean paste, order up Filipino pork adobo with two scoops of rice and macaroni salad.

In Waikīkī, where most visitors stay, you can find choices from gracious rooms with a view to surprisingly authentic Japanese noodle shops. But hop in the car, or on the trolley or bus, and travel just a few miles in any direction, and you can save your money and get in touch with the real food of Hawai'i.

Kaimukī's Wai'alae Avenue, for example, offers one of the city's best espresso bars, a hugely popular Chinese bakery, a highly recommended patisserie, an exceptional Italian bistro, a dim-sum restaurant, Mexican food (rare here), and a Hawai'i regional cuisine standout, 3660 on the Rise—all in three blocks, and 10 minutes from Waikīkī. Chinatown, 10 minutes in the other direction and easily reached by the Waikīkī Trolley, is another dining (and shopping) treasure, not only for Chinese but also Vietnamese, Filipino, Malaysian, and Indian food, and even a chic little tea shop.

RESERVATIONS

If you expect to dine at Alan Wong's, Chef Mavro, or Roy's, book your table from home weeks in advance. Also beware the brand-new restaurants: they get slammed by migratory hordes for the first few weeks. Otherwise, reserve when you get into town.

WHAT TO WEAR

You'll find people dress up for dinner on Oʻahu—especially in Waikīkī and Honolulu—more so than on any other Hawaiian Island. Even so, casual reigns supreme here; most top restaurants abide by the "dressy causal" standard, where dark jeans are acceptable as long as they're not worn with sneakers.

HOURS & PRICES

The most sought-after dinner reservations are between 6 and 6:30, but you can often have your pick of tables at 8. Exceptions: sushi bars and Japanese taverns, a few 24-hour diners, and some younger-spinning restaurants. Takeout places still open at dawn and close shortly after midday. Standard tipping for good service is 20%.

WHAT IT COSTS				
¢	$	$$	$$$	$$$$
RESTAURANTS				
under $10	$10–$17	$18–$26	$27–$35	over $35

Restaurant prices are for a main course at dinner.

WAIKĪKĪ

AMERICAN

$$-$$$ ✕**Duke's Canoe Club.** Named for the father of modern surfing, and outfitted with much Duke Kahanamoku memorabilia, Duke's is both an open-air bar and a very popular steak-and-seafood grill. It's known for its Big Island pork ribs, huli-huli (rotisserie) chicken, and grilled catch of the day, as well as for a simple and economical Sunday brunch. A drawback is that it's often loud and crowded, and the live contemporary Hawaiian music can stymie conversation. ⊠*Outrigger Waikīkī on the Beach, 2335 Kalākaua Ave., Waikīkī* ☎808/922–2268 ☖*Reservations essential* ▤*AE, DC, MC, V.*

¢-$ ✕**Eggs 'n Things.** A favorite of Waikīkī hotel workers for its late hours (11 PM–2 PM daily), this restaurant on the first floor of an obscure budget hotel has a hearty, country-style menu with a few island touches (tropical-fruit pancake syrups, fresh grilled fish), and a permanent line out front. ⊠*Ha-*

Where to Eat in Waikīkī

Caffelatte Italian Restaurant, **7**
dk Steakhouse, **13**
Duke's Canoe Club, **12**
Eggs 'n Things, **4**
Hau Tree Lānai, **16**
Hula Grill, **11**
Keo's in Waikīkī, **5**
La Mer, **9**
Nick's Fishmarket, **6**
Nobu, **8**
Orchids, **10**
Prince Court, **1**
Sansei Seafood Restaurant & Sushi Bar, **14**
Teddy's Bigger Burgers, **15**
Todai Restaurant Waikīkī, **3**
Wailana Coffee House, **2**

waiian Monarch Hotel, 1911–B Kalākaua Ave., Waikīkī
☎808/949–0820 ▭No credit cards ⊘No dinner.

$$–$$$ ✕**Hula Grill.** The placid younger sister of boisterous Duke's,
downstairs, this restaurant and bar resembles a plantation-
period summer home: open to the air, outfitted with kitschy
decor, stone-flagged floors, warm wood, and floral prints.
The food is carefully prepared and familiar—standard
breakfast items, steaks and grilled seafood at dinner—but
with local and Asian touches that add interest. There's a
fabulous Diamond Head view. ✉*Outrigger Waikīkī on
the Beach, 2335 Kalākaua Ave., Waikīkī* ☎808/923–4852
▭*AE, D, DC, MC, V* ⊘*No lunch.*

¢ ✕**Teddy's Bigger Burgers.** Though the focus at Teddy's is on
the burgers, fries, and shakes, their success has inspired
them to add a chicken, veggie, and fish sandwich to their
menu. But, for those who like a classic, the burgers are
beefy, the fries crisply perfect, the shakes rich and sweet.
The original location in Waikīkī combines burger shack
simplicity with surf-boy cool—there's even a place to store
your surfboard while you have your burger. This popular location has given birth to two others in Kailua and
Hawai'i Kai. ✉*134 Kapahulu Ave., Waikīkī* ☎808/926–
3444 ▭*MC, V.*

¢–$ ✕**Wailana Coffee House.** Despite the notoriously inattentive
waitstaff, budget-conscious snowbirds, night owls with a
yen for karaoke, all-day drinkers of both coffee and the
stronger stuff, hearty eaters, and lovers of local-style plate
lunches contentedly rub shoulders at this venerable diner
and cocktail lounge at the edge of Waikīkī. Most checks
are under $9; there's a $1.95 children's menu. It's open 24
hours a day, 7 days a week, 365 days a year but the place
fills up and a line forms around the corner at breakfast
time, so arrive early or late. ✉*Wailana Condominium,
ground floor, 1860 Ala Moana Blvd., corner of 'Ena Rd.
and Ala Moana, Waikīkī* ☎808/955–1674 ✍*Reservations
not accepted* ▭*AE, MC, V.*

ECLECTIC

$$$–$$$$ ✕**Hau Tree Lānai.** The vinelike hau tree is ideal for sitting
under, and it's said that the one that spreads itself over this
beachside courtyard is the very one that shaded Robert
Louis Stevenson as he mused and wrote about Hawai'i.
In any case, diners are still enjoying the shade, though the
view has changed—the gay-friendly beach over the low
wall is paved with hunky sunbathers. The food is unre-

markable island casual, but we like the place for late-afternoon or early-evening drinks, pūpū, and people-watching. ⊠*New Otani Kaimana Beach Hotel, 2863 Kalākaua Ave., Waikīkī* ☎*808/921–7066* ⚑*Reservations essential* ⊟*AE, D, DC, MC, V.*

$$$$ ✕**Prince Court.** This restaurant overlooking Ala Wai Yacht Harbor is a multifaceted success, with exceptional high-end lunches and dinners, daily breakfast buffets, weekly dinner seafood buffets, and sold-out weekend brunches. With a truly global mix of offerings, the overall style is Eurasian. Their ever-changing prix-fixe menu includes offerings such as Australian rack of lamb, Kahuku prawns, and medallions of New York Angus. ⊠*Hawai'i Prince Hotel, 100 Holomoana St., Waikīkī* ☎*808/944–4494* ⚑*Reservations essential* ⊟*AE, D, DC, MC, V.*

FRENCH

$$$$ ✕**La Mer.** Like the hotel in which it's housed (Halekūlani, or "House Befitting Heaven"), La Mer is pretty much heavenly: a softly lighted, low-ceiling room with windows open to the breeze, a perfectly framed vista of Diamond Head, and the faint sound of music wafting up from a courtyard below. The food captures the rich and sunny flavors of the south of France in one tiny, exquisite course after another. We recommend the degustation menu. Place yourself in the sommelier's hands for wine choices from the hotel's exceptional cellar. ⊠*Halekūlani, 2199 Kālia Rd., Waikīkī* ☎*808/923–2311* ⚑*Reservations essential. Jacket required* ⊟*AE, DC, MC, V* ⊗*No lunch.*

ITALIAN

$$$$ ✕**Caffelatte Italian Restaurant.** Every dish at this tiny trattoria run by a Milanese family is worth ordering, from the gnocchi in a thick, rich sauce of Gorgonzola to spinach ravioli served with butter and basil. The tiramisu is the best in town, and the sugared orange slices in Russian vodka are a perfect ending to a meal. Each person must order three courses (appetizer, soup or salad, and main course). ■TIP➔ **There's no parking, so walk here if you can.** There's no air-conditioning, so it can be warm and noisy due to open windows. ⊠*339 Saratoga Rd., 2nd level, Waikīkī* ☎*808/924–1414* ⊟*MC, V* ⊗*Closed Mon. and Tues.*

CLOSE UP

Best Breakfast

Big City Diner (Ala Moana & Kailua). Start the day like a local: rice instead of toast, fish or Portuguese sausage instead of bacon, or a bowl of noodles instead of cereal.

Cinnamon's Restaurant (Kailua). Voted best for breakfast in a local newspaper poll, Cinnamon's does all the breakfast standards.

Duke's Canoe Club and Hula Grill (Waikīkī). Duke's has an $11.95 buffet; Hula Grill has a pricier but carefully prepared à la carte breakfast.

Eggs 'n Things (Waikīkī). This is a longtime favorite for late hours and country-style food with Island touches.

Sam Choy's Breakfast, Lunch & Crab (Iwilei). This family-friendly restaurant showcases gigantic portions of the quintessential island breakfast dish, the loco moco (rice, egg, meat or fish, and gravy).

JAPANESE

$$$–$$$$ ✕**Nobu.** Famed chef Nobu Matsushida's is the master of innovative Japanese cuisine, and his Hawaiian outpost is definitely a *Waikīkī* hotspot. Fish is the obvious centerpiece, with entrées such as Tasmanian ocean trout with crispy spinach and yuzu soy, seafood harumaki with caviar and Maui onion salsa, and even Nobu's version of fish-and-chips. Cold dishes include tuna tataki with ponzu, yellowtail sashimi with jalapeno, and whitefish sashimi with dried miso. The warm decor and sexy lighting means there isn't a bad seat in the house. ✉ *Hawaii Parc Hotel, 2233 Helumoa Rd., Waikīkī* ☎*808/237–6999* ▭*AE, MC, V.*

$$$ ✕**Sansei Seafood Restaurant & Sushi Bar.** D. K. Kodama's Japanese-based Pacific Rim cuisine is an experience not to be missed, from early-bird dinners (from 5:30 PM) to late-night appetizers and sushi (until 1 AM Friday and Saturday, with karaoke). The specialty sushi here—mango-crab roll, foie gras nigiri with eel sauce, and more—leaves California rolls far behind. We fantasize about the signature calamari salad with spicy Korean sauce and crisp-tender squid. Cleverly named and beautifully prepared dishes come in big and small plates or in a multicourse tasting menu. Finish with tempura-fried ice cream or Mama Kodama's brownies. ✉ *Waikīkī Beach Marriott Resort and Spa, 2552 Kalākaua Ave., Waikīkī* ☎*808/931–6286* ▭*AE, DC, MC, V.*

6

SEAFOOD

$$$-$$$$ ✕ **Nick's Fishmarket.** Nick's is like a favorite soap opera—go away for a while, come back and very little has changed. And that's why we like it: the dim lighting, the expansive banquettes, the retro-ish Continental menu, tableside service for Caesar salad or flambéed desserts; it's like a window back to just the good part of the good old days. After the lobster bisque or sautéed abalone, leave room for signature Vanbana Pie, a decadent combination of bananas, vanilla-Swiss-almond ice cream, and hot caramel sauce. ☒ *Waikīkī Gateway Hotel, 2070 Kalākaua Ave., Waikīkī* ☎*808/955–6333* ▭*AE, D, DC, MC, V.*

$$$-$$$$ ✕ **Orchids.** Perched along the seawall at historic Gray's Beach, Orchids is beloved by power-breakfasters, ladies who lunch, and family groups celebrating at the elaborate Sunday brunch. La Mer, upstairs, is better known for the evening, but we have found dinner at Orchids equally enjoyable. The louvered walls are open to the breezes, the orchids add splashes of color, the seafood is perfectly prepared, and the wine list is intriguing. Plus, it is more casual and a bit less expensive than La Mer. Whatever your meal, finish with the hotel's signature coconut layer cake. ☒*Halekūlani, 2199 Kālia Rd., Waikīkī* ☎*808/923–2311* ⚑*Reservations essential* ▭*AE, D, MC, V.*

$$-$$$ ✕ **Todai Restaurant Waikīkī.** Bountiful buffets and menus that feature seafood are popular with Islanders, so this Japan-based restaurant is a local favorite. It's popular with budget-conscious travelers as well, for the wide range of hot dishes, sushi, and the 160-foot seafood spread. The emphasis here is more on quantity than quality. ☒*1910 Ala Moana Blvd., Waikīkī* ☎*808/947–1000* ⚑*Reservations essential* ▭*AE, D, DC, MC, V.*

STEAK HOUSE

$$$-$$$$ ✕ **dk Steakhouse.** Around the country, the steak house has returned to prominence as chefs rediscover the art of dry-aging beef and of preparing the perfect béarnaise sauce. D. K. Kodama's chic second-floor restaurant characterizes this trend with such presentations as a 22-ounce Paniolo ("cowboy") rib-eye steak, dry-aged 30 days on the bone with house-made rub, grilled local onions, and creamed corn. The restaurant shares space, but not a menu, with Kodama's Sansei Seafood Restaurant & Sushi Bar; sit at the bar perched between the two and you can order from either menu. ☒ *Waikīkī Beach Marriott Resort and Spa,*

ON THE MENU

Much of the Hawaiian language encountered during a stay in the Islands will appear on restaurant menus and lists of lū'au fare. Here's a quick primer.

'ahi: yellowfin tuna.

aku: skipjack, bonito tuna.

bento: a box lunch.

chicken lū'au: a stew made from chicken, taro leaves, and coconut milk.

haupia: a light, gelatinlike dessert made from coconut.

imu: the underground ovens in which pigs are roasted for lū'au.

kālua: to bake underground.

kaukau: food. The word comes from Chinese but is used in the Islands.

Kona coffee: coffee grown in the Kona district of the Big Island.

laulau: literally, a bundle. *Laulau* are morsels of pork, butterfish, or other ingredients wrapped with young taro shoots in ti leaves for steaming.

liliko'i: passion fruit, a tart, seedy yellow fruit that makes delicious desserts and jellies.

lomilomi: to rub or massage; also a massage. *Lomilomi* salmon is fish that has been rubbed with onions and herbs, commonly served with minced onions and tomatoes.

lū'au leaves: cooked taro tops with a taste similar to spinach.

mahimahi: mild-flavored dolphinfish, not the marine mammal.

mai tai: potent rum drink with orange and lime juice, from the Tahitian word for "good."

manō: shark.

niu: coconut.

'ōkolehao: a liqueur distilled from the ti root.

onaga: pink or red snapper.

ono: a long, slender mackerel-like fish; also called wahoo.

'opihi: a tiny shellfish, or mollusk, found on rocks; also called limpets.

pāpio: a young *ulua* or jack fish.

pohā: Cape gooseberry. Tasting a bit like honey, the pohā berry is often used in jams and desserts.

poi: a paste made from pounded taro root, a staple of the Hawaiian diet.

poke: chopped, pickled raw tuna, tossed with herbs and seasonings.

saimin: long thin noodles and vegetables in broth, often garnished with small pieces of fish cake, scrambled egg, luncheon meat, and green onion.

ti leaves: a member of the agave family, used to wrap food while cooking and removed before eating.

uku: deep-sea snapper.

6

2552 Kalākaua Ave., Waikīkī ☎*808/931–6280* ▤*AE, D, MC, V* ⊘*No lunch.*

THAI

$–$$ ✕**Keo's in Waikīkī.** Many Islanders—and many Hollywood stars—got their first taste of pad thai noodles, lemongrass, and coconut-milk curry at one of Keo Sananikone's restaurants. This one, perched right at the entrance to Waikīkī, characterizes his formula: a bright, clean space awash in flowers, with intriguing menu titles and reasonable prices. Evil Jungle Prince, a stir-fry redolent of Thai basil, flecked with chilies and rich with coconut milk, is a classic; also try the apple bananas (smaller, sweeter variety of banana) in coconut milk. The Eastern and Western breakfasts are popular. ✉*2028 Kūhiō Ave., Waikīkī* ☎*808/951–9355* ▤*AE, D, DC, MC, V.*

HONOLULU: ALA MOANA, DOWNTOWN & CHINATOWN

AMERICAN

$ ✕**Big City Diner.** Part of a chain of unfussy retro diners, Big City offer a short course in local-style breakfasts—rice instead of potatoes, fish or Portuguese sausage instead of bacon, steaming bowls of noodles—with generous portions, low prices, and pronounced flavors. Lunch and dinner focus on local-style comfort food—baby back ribs, kimchi fried rice—and burgers. ✉*Ward Entertainment Center, 1060 'Auahi St., Ala Moana* ☎*808/591–8891* ▤*AE, D, MC, V.*

¢–$ ✕**Contemporary Café.** This tasteful lunch spot in the Contemporary Museum offers light and healthful food from a short but well-selected menu of house-made soups, crostini of the day, innovative sandwiches garnished with fruit, and a hummus plate with fresh pita. In the exclusive Makīkī Heights neighborhood above the city, the restaurant spills out of the ground floor of the museum onto the lawn. ✉*The Contemporary Museum, 2411 Makīkī Heights Dr., Makīkī* ☎*808/523–3362* ▤*AE, DC, MC, V* ⊘*No dinner.*

$$ ✕**E & O Trading Co.** Named for the colonial-era Eastern & Orient Trading Co., this restaurant's decor recalls a bustling mercantile district in some Asian port. Like a merchant ship, the Southeast Asian grill menu hops from Singapore to Korea, Japan to India. The Indonesian corn fritters are a must, as are the Burmese ginger salad and the silky-textured, smoky-flavored marinated portobello satay.

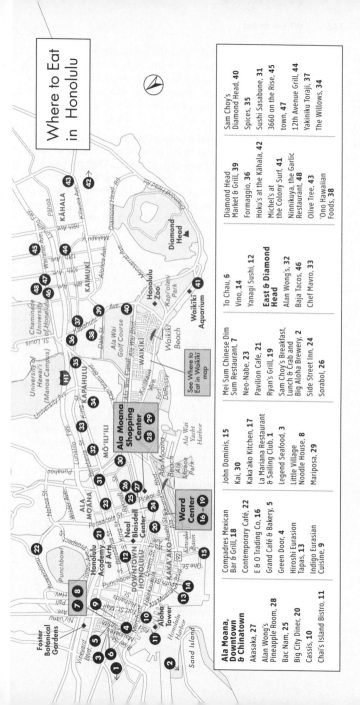

Where to Eat in Honolulu

Ala Moana, Downtown & Chinatown
Akasaka, **27**
Alan Wong's Pineapple Room, **28**
Bac Nam, **25**
Big City Diner, **20**
Cassis, **10**
Chai's Island Bistro, **11**

Compadres Mexican Bar & Grill, **18**
Contemporary Café, **22**
E & O Trading Co, **16**
Grand Café & Bakery, **5**
Green Door, **4**
Hiroshi Eurasion Tapas, **13**
Indigo Eurasian Cuisine, **9**

John Dominis, **15**
Kai, **30**
Kaka'ako Kitchen, **17**
La Mariana Restaurant & Sailing Club, **1**
Legend Seafood, **3**
Little Village Noodle House, **8**
Mariposa, **29**

Mei Sum Chinese Dim Sum Restaurant, **7**
Neo-Nabe, **23**
Pavilion Cafe, **21**
Ryan's Grill, **19**
Sam Choy's Breakfast, Lunch & Crab and Big Aloha Brewery, **2**
Side Street Inn, **24**
Sorabol, **26**

To Chau, **6**
Vino, **14**
Yanagi Sushi, **12**

East & Diamond Head
Alan Wong's, **32**
Baja Tacos, **46**
Chef Mavro, **33**

Diamond Head Market & Grill, **39**
Formaggio, **36**
Hoku's at the Kāhala, **42**
Michel's at the Colony Surf, **41**
Ninnikuya, the Garlic Restaurant, **48**
Olive Tree, **43**
'Ono Hawaiian Foods, **38**

Sam Choy's Diamond Head, **40**
Spices, **35**
Sushi Sasabune, **31**
3660 on the Rise, **45**
town, **47**
12th Avenue Grill, **44**
Yakiniku Toraji, **37**
The Willows, **34**

See Where to Eat in Waikiki map

To match the unusual menu, the bar creates some unusual mixtures with infusions and fresh juices. For a unique experience, ask the bartender to make a citrus or other fruit-flavored Elixir (a type of martini) for you. ⊠ *Ward Centre, 1200 Ala Moana Blvd., Kaka'ako* ☎ *808/591–9555* ⊟ *AE, D, DC, MC, V.*

$–$$ ✕ **La Mariana Restaurant & Sailing Club.** Just past downtown Honolulu, tucked away in the industrial area of Sand Island, is this friendly South Seas–style restaurant. Over the past 50 years, nonagenarian owner Annette Nahinu has bought up kitsch from other restaurants, so it's tikis to the max here. The food—grilled seafood, steaks—is just okay; but go for the sing-along fun and the feeling that Don the Beachcomber might walk in any minute. ⊠ *50 Sand Island Rd., Iwilei* ☎ *808/848–2800* ⊟ *AE, D, DC, MC, V.*

$ ✕ **Pavilion Cafe.** The cool courtyards and varied galleries of the Honolulu Academy of Arts are well worth a visit and, afterward, so is Mike Nevin's popular lunch restaurant. The café overflows onto a lānai from which you can ponder Asian statuary and a burbling-water feature while you wait for your salade niçoise or signature Piadina Sandwich (fresh-baked flatbread rounds stuffed with arugula, tomatoes, basil, and cheese). ⊠ *Honolulu Academy of Arts, 900 S. Beretania St., Downtown Honolulu* ☎ *808/532–8734* ⊟ *AE, D, DC, MC, V* ☉ *Closed Sun. and Mon. No dinner.*

$–$$ ✕ **Ryan's Grill.** An all-purpose food and drink emporium, lively and popular Ryan's has an exceptionally well-stocked bar, with 20 beers on tap, an outdoor deck, and TVs broadcasting sports. Lunch, dinner, and small plates are served from 11 AM to 2 AM. The eclectic menu ranges from an addictive hot crab-and-artichoke dip with focaccia to grilled fresh fish, pasta, salads, and sophisticated versions of local favorites, such as the Kobe beef hamburger steak. ⊠ *Ward Centre, 1200 Ala Moana Blvd., Kaka'ako* ☎ *808/591–9132* ⊟ *AE, D, DC, MC, V.*

¢–$ ✕ **Side Street Inn.** Famous as the place where celebrity chefs gather after hours, local boy Colin Nishida's pub is on an obscure side street near Ala Moana Shopping Center. It is worth searching for, despite the sometimes-surly staff, because Nishida makes what might be the best darned pork chops and fried rice in the world. Local-style bar food comes in huge, share-plate portions. This is a place to dress any way you like, nosh all night, watch sports on TV, and sing karaoke until they boot you out. Pūpū (in portions large enough for a dinner) are served from 4 PM to 12:30 AM daily. ⊠ *1225 Hopaka St., Ala Moana* ☎*808/591–0253* ▭*AE, D, MC, V* ⊗*No lunch.*

ASIAN

¢–$ ✕**Green Door.** Closet-size and fronted by a green door and a row of welcoming Chinese lanterns, this Chinatown café has introduced Honolulu to budget- and taste bud–friendly Malaysian and Singaporean foods, redolent of spices and crunchy with fresh vegetables. ⊠*4614 Kilauea Ave., Kahala* ☎*808/533–0606* ▭*No credit cards* ⚲*Reservations not accepted* ⊗*Closed Mon.*

$$–$$$ ✕**Hiroshi Eurasion Tapas.** Built around chef Hiroshi Fukui's signature style of "West & Japan" cuisine, this sleek dinner house focuses on small plates to share (enough for two servings each), with an exceptional choice of hard-to-find wines by the glass and in flights. Do not miss Hiroshi's braised veal cheeks (he was doing them before everyone else), the locally raised kampachi fish carpaccio, or the best-ever *misoyaki* butterfish (marinated in a rich miso-soy blend, then grilled). ⊠*1341 Kapi'olani Blvd., Ala Moana* ☎*808/955–0552* ▭*AE, D, MC, V* ⊗*No lunch.*

CHINESE

¢–$ ✕**Legend Seafood Restaurant.** Do as the locals do: start your visit to Chinatown with breakfast dim sum at Legend. If you want to be able to hear yourself think, get there before 9 AM, especially on weekends. And don't be shy: use your best cab-hailing technique and sign language to make the cart ladies stop at your table and show you their wares. The pork-filled steamed buns, hearty spare ribs, prawn dumplings, and still-warm custard tarts are excellent pre-shopping fortification. ⊠*Chinese Cultural Plaza, 100 N. Beretania St., Chinatown* ☎*808/532–1868* ▭*AE, D, DC, MC, V.*

★ **Fodor's**Choice ✕**Little Village Noodle House.** Unassuming and
¢–$ budget-friendly, Little Village sets a standard of congenial and attentive service. We have roamed the large, pan-China menu and found a new favorite in everything we've tried: shredded beef, spinach with garlic, Shanghai noodles, honey-walnut shrimp, orange chicken, dried green beans. Two words: go there. ■TIP→ **Two hours of free parking is available next door.** ⊠*1113 Smith St., Chinatown* ☎*808/545–3008* ▭*AE, DC, MC, V.*

SOME DIM SUM? Dim sum is the original small-plates meal, born of roadside tea stands in southern China and served from early morning to mid-afternoon. Dumplings and steamed dishes predominate, with some soup and sweets. You'll get tea, and a bill to mark your purchases in lieu of a menu. As food carts pass, be bold: wave to get the attention of the tea ladies; ask to see what's on the cart. Some things will look strange and taste even stranger, but popular with all are dumplings, buns, noodles, and custard tarts.

¢ ✕**Mei Sum Chinese Dim Sum Restaurant.** In contrast to the sprawling and noisy halls in which dim sum is generally served, Mei Sum is compact and shiny bright. It's open daily, serving nothing but small plates from 7:45 AM to 8:45 PM. Be ready to guess and point at the color photos of dim-sum favorites as not much English is spoken, but the delicate buns and tasty bits are exceptionally well-prepared and worth the charades. ⊠*65 N. Pauahi St., Chinatown* ☎*808/531–3268* ⊟*No credit cards.*

ECLECTIC

$$$ ✕**Chai's Island Bistro.** Chai Chaowasaree's stylish, light-bathed, and orchid-draped lunch and dinner restaurant expresses the sophisticated side of this Thai-born immigrant. He plays East against West on the plate in signature dishes such as *kataifi* (baked and shredded phyllo), macadamia-crusted prawns, 'ahi *katsu* (tuna steaks dredged with crisp Japanese breadcrumbs and quickly deep-fried), crispy duck confetti spring rolls, and seafood risotto. Some of Hawai'i's best-known contemporary Hawaiian musicians play brief dinner shows here Wednesday through Sunday. ⊠*Aloha Tower Marketplace, 1 Aloha Tower Dr., Downtown Honolulu* ☎*808/585–0012* ⊟*AE, D, DC, MC, V* ⊘*No lunch Sat.–Mon.*

$ ✕**Grand Café & Bakery.** This well-scrubbed, pleasantly furnished breakfast, brunch, and lunch spot is ideal for taking a break before or after a trek around Chinatown. Its period feel comes from the fact that chef Anthony Vierra's great-grandfather had a restaurant of this name in Chinatown nearly 100 years ago. The delicious and well-presented food ranges from retro diner dishes (chicken pot pie) to contemporary creations such as beet-and-goat-cheese salad. ⊠*31 N. Pauahi, Chinatown* ☎*808/531–0001* ⊟*MC, V.*

$$$ ✕**Indigo Eurasian Cuisine.** Indigo sets the right mood for an evening out on the town: the walls are red brick, the ceilings are high, and from the restaurant's lounge next door comes the sultry sound of late-night jazz. Take a bite of goat-cheese wontons with four-fruit sauce followed by rich Mongolian lamb chops. After dinner, duck into the hip Green Room lounge or Opium Den & Champagne Bar for a nightcap. If you're touring downtown at lunchtime, the Eurasian buffet with trio of dim sum is a good deal at around $16 per person. ⊠ *1121 Nu'uanu Ave., Downtown Honolulu* ☎*808/521–2900* ⊟*AE, D, DC, MC, V.*

FRENCH

$$$ ✕**Cassis.** When Chef Mavro decided to develop a new restaurant for Honolulu, he went back to memories of his boyhood home in Cassis for inspiration and brought French comfort food to Hawai'i. Though the atmosphere is contemporary and chic, Mavro's French Bistro offers old-world favorites such as cassoulet and steak frites (steak and fries). His exceptionally tender huli-huli chicken with fresh Kahuku creamed corn and Hamakua mushroom risotto demonstrate Mavro's commitment to fresh local products. Lunches are a real treat, with views of the harbor, and a *pau hana* (after-work) drink at the wine bar is a memorable experience. ⊠ *66 Queen St., Downtown Honolulu* ☎*808/545–8100* ⊟*AE, MC, V* ⊙*Closed Sun.*

MALASADAS. Doughnuts without a hole, malasadas are a contribution of the Portuguese, who came to the Islands to work on the plantations. Roughly translated, the name means "half-cooked," which refers to the origin of these deep-fried, heavily sugared treats: they are said to have been created as a way to use up scraps of rich, buttery egg dough. A handful of bakeries specialize in malasadas (Leonard's on Kapahulu, Agnes in Kailua, Champion on Beretania); restaurants sometimes serve an upscale version stuffed with fruit puree; they're inevitable at fairs and carnivals. Eat them hot or not at all.

ITALIAN

$$–$$$ ✕**Vino.** Small plates of Italian-inspired appetizers, a wine list selected by the state's first Master Sommelier, a relaxed atmosphere, and periodic special tastings are the formula for success at this wine bar. ■TIP→ **Vino is well-situated for stopping off between downtown sightseeing and a return to your Waikīkī hotel.** ⊠*Restaurant Row, 500 Ala Moana Blvd.,*

6

Downtown Honolulu ☎*808/524–8466* ▤*AE, D, DC, MC, V* ☉*Closed Sun.–Tues.*

JAPANESE

$–$$ ✕**Akasaka.** Step inside this tiny sushi bar tucked behind the Ala Moana Hotel, and you'll swear you're in an out-of-the-way Edo neighborhood in some indeterminate time. Greeted with a cheerful "Iraishaimasu!" (Welcome!), sink down at a diminutive table or perch at the handful of seats at the sushi bar. It's safe to let the sushi chefs here decide (omakase-style) or you can go for the delicious grilled specialties, such as scallop *battayaki* (grilled in butter). Reservations are accepted for groups only. ▨*1646 B Kona St., Ala Moana* ☎*808/942–4466* ▤*AE, D, DC, MC, V* ☉*No lunch Sun.*

¢–$ ✕**Kai.** This chic little spot introduced Honolulu to *okonomi-yaki*, the famous savory pancakes that are a specialty of Osaka, with mix-and-match ingredients scrambled together on a griddle then drizzled with various piquant sauces. The combinations may at times strike you as bizarre, but you can always order simpler grilled dishes. ▨*1427 Makaloa St., Ala Moana* ☎*808/944–1555* ▤*AE, D, DC, MC, V* ☉*Closed Mon. No lunch.*

$–$$ ✕**Neo-Nabe.** Pronounced "nee-oh nah-bay," this hip restaurant and bar minutes from Waikīkī specializes in a contemporary version of the cook-at-the-table Japanese hot pot called nabe. You choose the broth and ingredients; they light up the tabletop brazier and bring you hot rice and a range of dipping sauces to go with the meal you cook. Geared to clubbers and night workers, Neo-Nabe is open 5 PM to 2 AM Sunday through Thursday and 5 PM to 5 AM Friday and Saturday. Don't miss the ojia, a folksy Asian risotto made with your leftovers and some secret ingredients. It's filling, fun food. ▨*2065 S. King St., Suite 110, Ala Moana* ☎*808/944–6622* ▤*MC, V* ☉*Closed Mon. No lunch.*

$–$$ ✕**Yanagi Sushi.** One of relatively few restaurants to serve the complete menu until 2 AM (Sunday only until 10 PM), Yanagi is a full-service Japanese restaurant offering not only sushi and sashimi around a small bar, but also *taishoku* (combination menus), tempura, stews, and grill-it-yourself shabu-shabu. The fish here can be depended on for freshness and variety. ▨*762 Kapi'olani Blvd., Downtown Honolulu* ☎*808/597–1525* ▤*AE, D, DC, MC, V.*

KOREAN

$–$$ ✕Sorabol. The largest Korean restaurant in the city, this 24-hour eatery, with its impossibly tiny parking lot and maze of booths and private rooms, offers a vast menu encompassing the entirety of day-to-day Korean cuisine, plus sushi. English menu translations are cryptic at best. Still, it's great for wee-hour "grinds" (local slang for food): *bi bim bap* (veggies, meats, and eggs on steamed rice), *kal bi* and *bulgogi* (barbecued meats), and meat or fish *jun* (thin fillets fried in batter). ✉*805 Keʻeaumoku St., Ala Moana* ☎*808/947–3113* ⊟*AE, DC, MC, V.*

MEXICAN

$–$$ ✕Compadres Mexican Bar and Grill. The after-work crowd gathers here for potent margaritas and yummy pūpū. The outdoor terrace is best for cocktails only. Inside, the wooden floors, colorful photographs, and lively paintings create a festive setting. Compadres defines itself as "Western cooking with a Mexican accent": fajitas, baby back ribs, pork *carnitas* (slow-roasted shredded pork), and fish tacos are specialties. At the bar, choose from over 80 brands of tequila. A late-night appetizer menu is available until midnight. ✉*Ward Centre, 1200 Ala Moana Blvd., Ala Moana* ☎*808/591–8307* ⊟*AE, D, DC, MC, V.*

MODERN HAWAIIAN

¢–$ ✕Kakaʻako Kitchen. Russell Siu was the first of the local-boy fine dining chefs to open a place of the sort he enjoys when he's off-duty, serving high-quality plate lunches (house-made sauce instead of from-a-mix brown gravy, for example). Here you can get your two scoops of either brown or white rice, green salad instead of the usual macaroni salad, grilled fresh fish specials, and vegetarian fare. Breakfast is especially good, with combos like corned-beef hash and eggs, and exceptional baked goods. ✉*Ward Centre, 1200 Ala Moana Blvd., Kakaʻako* ☎*808/596–7488* ⊟*Reservations not accepted* ⊟*AE, MC, V.*

PACIFIC RIM

$$–$$$ ✕Alan Wong's Pineapple Room. This is not your grandmother's department-store restaurant. It's über-chef Alan Wong's more casual second spot, where the chef de cuisine plays intriguing riffs on local food themes. Warning: the spicy chili-fried soybeans are addictive. Their house burger, made with locally raised grass-fed beef, bacon, cheddar cheese, hoisin-mayonnaise spread, and avocado, won a local tasting hands-down. Surroundings are pleasant and service

Non-native dishes—such as salt salmon and chicken long-rice—have joined seafood, taro, fruits, and sweet potatoes to create the Hawaiian cuisine we know today.

is very professional. ⊠*Macy's, Ala Moana Center, 1450 Ala Moana Blvd., Ala Moana* ☎*808/945–6573* ⊟*AE, D, DC, MC, V.*

$–$$ ✕**Mariposa.** Yes, the popovers and the wee little cups of bouillon are here at lunch, but in every other regard, this Neiman-Marcus restaurant menu departs from the classic model, incorporating a clear sense of Pacific place. The veranda, open to the breezes and view of Ala Moana Park, twirling ceiling fans, and life-size hula-girl murals say Hawai'i. The popovers come with a butter-pineapple-papaya spread; the oxtail osso buco is inspired; and local fish are featured nightly in luxuriant specials. ⊠*Nieman-Marcus, Ala Moana Center, 1450 Ala Moana, Ala Moana* ☎*808/951–3420* ♨*Reservations essential* ⊟*AE, D, DC, MC, V.*

SEAFOOD

$$$–$$$$ ✕**John Dominis.** "Legendary" is the word for the Sunday brunch buffet at this long-established restaurant, named for a Hawaiian kingdom chamberlain who became the consort of the last queen, Lili'uokalani. With a network of koi ponds running through the multilevel restaurant, a view of Diamond Head and a favorite surfing area, and over-the-top seafood specials, it's the choice of Oahuans with something to celebrate. An appetizer-and-small-plates menu is available in the bar. ⊠*580 Nimitz Hwy.,Iwilei* ☎*808/523–0955* ⊟*AE, D, DC, MC, V.*

$$–$$$ ✕ **Sam Choy's Breakfast, Lunch & Crab and Big Aloha Brewery.** In this casual, family-friendly setting, diners can down crab and lobster—but since these come from elsewhere, we recommend the catch of the day, the *char siu* (Chinese barbecue), baby back ribs, or Sam's special fried *poke* (flash-fried tuna). This eatery's warehouse size sets the tone for its *bambucha* (huge) portions. An on-site microbrewery brews seven varieties of Big Aloha beer. Sam Choy's is in Iwilei past Downtown Honolulu on the highway heading to Honolulu International Airport. ⊠ *580 N. Nimitz Hwy., Iwilei* ☎ *808/545–7979* ⊟ *AE, D, DC, MC, V.*

VIETNAMESE

¢–$ ✕ **Bac Nam.** Tam and Kimmy Huynh's menu is much more extensive than that of most Vietnamese restaurants, ranging far beyond the usual *pho* (beef noodle soup) and *bun* (cold noodle dishes). Coconut-milk curries, an extraordinary crab noodle soup, and other dishes hail from both North and South Vietnam. The atmosphere is welcoming and relaxed, and they'll work with you to make choices. Reservations are not accepted for groups of fewer than six. ⊠ *1117 S. King St., Downtown Honolulu* ☎ *808/597–8201* ⊟ *MC, V.*

¢ ✕ **To Chau.** If you need proof that To Chau is highly regarded for its authentic *phô* (Vietnamese beef noodle soup), just check the lines that form in front every morning of the week. It's said that the broth is the key, and it won't break the bank for you to find out, as the average check is less than $10. Open only until 12:30 PM. ⊠ *1007 River St., Chinatown* ☎ *808/533–4549* ⊟ *No credit cards* ⊘ *No dinner.*

HONOLULU: EAST & DIAMOND HEAD

AMERICAN

¢–$ ✕ **Diamond Head Market & Grill.** Kelvin Ro's one-stop spot is a plate-lunch place, a gourmet market, a deli and bakery and espresso bar, too—and it's a five-minute hop from Waikīkī hotels. A take-out window offers grilled sandwiches or plates ranging from teriyaki beef to portobello mushrooms. The market's deli case is stocked with a range of heat-and-eat entrées from risotto cakes to lamb stew; specials change daily. There are packaged Japanese bento lunchboxes, giant scones, enticing desserts, and even a small wine selection. ⊠ *3158 Monsarrat Ave., Diamond Head* ☎ *808/732–0077* ⚑ *Reservations not accepted* ⊟ *AE, D, MC, V.*

Musubi

Musubi needs translation. Here are cakes of steamed rice like thick decks of cards, topped with something that resembles spoiled luncheon meat, and bound with a strip of black, like a paper band around a stack of new bills. Swathed in plastic, they sit on the counter of every mom-and-pop store and plate-lunch place in Hawai'i, selling for $1.50 to $1.95. And everyone from T-shirted surfers with sandy feet, girls in pareus, and *tutus* (grandmas) in mu'umu'u are munching these oddities with apparent delight.

"Huh?" says the visitor.

So, a quick dictionary moment: *musubi* (*moo*-sue-bee), a cake of steamed Japanese-style rice topped with some sweet-salty morsel and held together with *nori* (*no*-ree; seaweed). Most common form: Spam musubi, popularized in the early 1980s by vendor Mitsuko Kaneshiro.

Kaneshiro turned her children's favorite snack into a classic—Spam slices simmered in a sugar-soy mixture atop rectangular rice cakes, with nori for crisp contrast. The flavor is surprisingly pleasant and satisfying, like a portable rice bowl.

Musubi has its roots in Japan, where rice cakes are standard festival, funeral, and family fare. But Islanders carried the tradition far afield, topping rice with slices of teriyaki chicken, sandwiching tuna salad between two cakes, dressing the rice in piquant slivers of scarlet pickled plum, toasted sesame, and strips of seaweed.

These ubiquitous tidbits are Hawai'i's go-food, like hot dogs or pretzels on a New York street. Quality varies, but if you visit a craft fair or stumble on a school sale and see homemade musubi—grab one and snack like a local.

FRENCH

$$$$ ✕**Michel's at the Colony Surf.** With its wide-open windows so close to the water that you feel the soft mist at high tide, this is arguably the most romantic spot in Waikīkī for a sunset dinner for two. Venerable Michel's is synonymous with fine dining in the minds of Oahuans who have been coming here for more than 40 years. The menu is très, très French with both classic choices (escargot, foie gras) and contemporary items (Hardy's Hawaiian Bouillabaisse—named after the chef who created a Hawaiian twist on a French classic). There's a Sunday brunch. ⊠*Colony Surf, 2895 Kalākaua Ave., Waikīkī* ☎*808/923–6552* ⌂*Reservations essential* ⊟*AE, D, DC, MC, V* ⊗*No lunch.*

HAWAIIAN

¢-$ ✕**'Ono Hawaiian Foods.** The adventurous in search of a real local food experience should head to this no-frills hangout. You know it has to be good if residents are waiting in line to get in. Here you can sample *poi (*a paste made from pounded taro root), *lomi lomi* salmon (salmon massaged until tender and served with minced onions and tomatoes), laulau, *kālua* pork (roasted in an underground oven), and *haupia* (a light, gelatinlike dessert made from coconut milk). Appropriately enough, the Hawaiian word *'ono* means "delicious." ✉*726 Kapahulu Ave., Kapahulu* ☎*808/737–2275* ⌨*Reservations not accepted* ⊟*No credit cards* ☉*Closed Sun.*

$$-$$$ ✕**The Willows.** An island dream, this buffet restaurant is made up of pavilions overlooking a network of ponds (once natural streams flowing from mountain to sea). The Island-style comfort food includes the trademark Willows curry along with Hawaiian dishes such as *laulau* (a steamed bundle of ti leaves containing pork, butterfish, and taro tops) and local favorites such as Korean barbecue ribs. ✉*901 Hausten St., Mō'ili'ili* ☎*808/952–9200* ⌨*Reservations essential* ⊟*AE, D, MC, V.*

ITALIAN

¢-$ ✕**Formaggio.** All but invisible on the back side of a strip mall, this wine bar seeks to communicate the feel of a catacomb in Italy and largely succeeds, with dim lighting and soft, warm tones. Choose a small sip or an entire bottle from the many wines they offer, enjoy the music, then ponder the small-dish menu of pizzas, panini, and hot and cold specialties such as eggplant Napoléon and melting short ribs in red wine. ✉*Market City Shopping Center, rear, lower level, 2919 Kapi'olani Blvd., Kaimukī* ☎*808/739–7719* ⌨*Reservations not accepted* ⊟*AE, MC, V* ☉*Closed Sun. No lunch.*

JAPANESE

$$$ ✕**Ninnikuya, the Garlic Restaurant.** Chef-owner Endo Eiyuki picked a powerful focus for his charming restaurant in a converted Kaimukī bungalow: garlic. He calls the menu Euro-Asian but the spicing and approach—except for the prevalence of garlic—are distinctly Japanese. Don't miss the Black Angus steak served on a sizzling stone. ✉*3196 Waīalae Ave., Kaimukī* ☎*808/735–0784* ⌨*Reservations essential* ⊟*AE, D, DC, MC, V* ☉ *Closed Sun. No lunch.*

6

$$ ✕**Sushi Sasabune.** Meals here are unforgettable, though you may find the restaurant's approach exasperating and a little condescending. It's possible to order from the menu, but you're strongly encouraged to order omakase-style (oh-*mah*-ka-*say*, roughly, "trust me"), letting the chef send out his choices for the night. The waiters keep up a steady mantra to instruct patrons in the proper way to eat their delicacies: "Please, no shoyu on this one." "One piece, one bite." But any trace of annoyance vanishes with the first bite of California baby squid stuffed with Louisiana crab, or unctuous *toro* ('ahi belly) smeared with a light soy reduction, washed down with a glass of the smoothest sake you've ever tasted. A caution: the courses come very rapidly—ask the server to slow down the pace a bit. An even bigger caution: the courses, generally two pieces of sushi or six to eight slices of sashimi, add up fast. ✉*1419 S. King St., Mōʻiliʻili* ☎*808/947–3800* ⌖*Reservations essential* ▱*AE, D, DC, MC, V* ☉*Closed Sun. No lunch Sat. and Mon.*

$-$$ ✕**Yakiniku Toraji.** Trendy Yakiniku Toraji resembles a Japanese country inn and features, in addition to the usual meats and vegetables grilled at the table, *ishikyaki*, which are meats and vegetables baked on a bed of rice in a stone bowl heated to broiling, forming a delicious crust. This is a particularly visitor-friendly spot, as the menus offer a cartoon to explain yakiniku how-tos. ✉*949 Kapahulu Ave., Kapahulu* ☎*808/732–9996* ▱*AE, D, MC, V* ☉*No lunch.*

MEDITERRANEAN

¢–$ ✕**Olive Tree.** Mediterranean food is scarce in the Islands, so Olive Tree keeps insanely busy; expect a wait for your hummus, fish souvlaki, Greek egg-and-lemon soup, and other specialties at this small spot behind Kāhala Mall. ✉*4614 Kīlauea Ave., Kāhala* ☎*808/737–0303* ⌖*Reservations not accepted* ▱*No credit cards* ☉*No lunch.*

MEXICAN

¢ ✕**Baja Tacos.** One of the first California-style taquerias in the Islands, Baja Tacos offers authentic flavors, house-made salsas, Mexican-style small plates, enchiladas, pork carnitas (slow-roasted and shredded), and *adobada* (marinated pork) and, of course, tacos—to take out or eat in. It's a perfect postbeach stop. ✉*3040 Waiʻalae Ave., Kaimukī* ☎*808/737–5893* ⌖*Reservations not accepted* ▱*No credit cards.*

CLOSE UP

Shave Ice

Island-style shave ice (never shaved ice—it's a pidgin thing) is said to have been born when neighborhood kids hung around the ice house, waiting to pounce on the shavings from large blocks of ice, carved with ultrasharp Japanese planes that created an exceptionally fine-textured granita.

In the 1920s, according to the historian for syrup manufacturer Malolo Beverages Co., Chinese vendors developed sweet fruit concentrates to pour over the ice.

The evolution continued with mom-and-pop shops adding their own touches, such as hiding a nugget of sweet bean paste, Japanese-style, in the center; placing a small scoop of ice cream at the bottom; adding *li hing* powder (a sweet spice); or using multitoned cones.

There's nothing better on a sticky hot day. Try **Waiola** (⊠*525 Kapahulu Ave., Mō'ili'ili*) or **Aoki's** (⊠*66-117 Kamehameha Hwy., Hale'iwa*).

6

MODERN HAWAIIAN

$$ ╳ **12th Avenue Grill.** At this clean, well-lighted place on a back street, chef Kevin Hanney dishes up diner chic, including macaroni-and-cheese glazed with house-smoked Parmesan and topped with savory breadcrumbs. The kimchi steak, a sort of teriyaki with kick, is a winner. Go early (5 PM) or late (8:30 PM) to avoid the crowds. Enjoy wonderful, homey desserts. There's a small, reasonably priced wine list. ⊠*1145C 12th Ave., Kaimukī* ☎*808/732–9469* ⌂*BYOB* ═*MC, V* ⊙*Closed Sun. No lunch.*

$$$ ╳ **3660 on the Rise.** This casually stylish eatery is a 10-minute drive from Waikīkī in the up-and-coming culinary mecca of Kaimukī. Sample Chef Russell Siu's New York Steak Alae (steak grilled with Hawaiian clay salt), the crab cakes, or the signature 'ahi katsu wrapped in nori and deep-fried with a wasabi-ginger butter sauce. Siu combines a deep understanding of local flavors with a sophisticated palate, making this place especially popular with homegrown gourmands. The dining room can feel a bit snug when it's full (as it usually is); go early or late. ⊠*3660 Wai'alae Ave., Kaimukī* ☎*808/737–1177* ═*AE, DC, MC, V.*

★ **Fodor's**Choice ╳ **Alan Wong's.** This not-to-be-missed restaurant
$$$–$$$$ is like that very rare shell you stumble upon on a perfect day at the beach—well polished and without a flaw. We've

never had a bad experience here, and we've never heard of anyone else having one either. The "Wong Way," as it's not-so-jokingly called by his staff, includes an ingrained understanding of the aloha spirit, evident in the skilled but unstarched service, and creative and playful interpretations of Island cuisine. Try Da Bag (seafood steamed in an aluminum pouch), Chinatown Roast Duck Nachos, and Poki Pines (rice-studded seafood wonton appetizers). With a view of the Koʻolau Mountains, warm tones of koa wood, and lauhala woven mats, you forget you're on the third floor of an office building. ⊠*McCully Court, 1857 S. King St., 3rd fl., Mōʻiliʻili* ☎*808/949–2526* ═*AE, MC, V* ⊗*No lunch.*

★ **Fodor'sChoice** ✕**Chef Mavro.** George Mavrothalassitis, who
$$$$ took two hotel restaurants to the top of the ranks before founding this James Beard Award–winning restaurant, admits he's crazy. Crazy because of the care he takes to draw out the truest and most concentrated flavors, to track down the freshest fish, to create one-of-a-kind wine pairings that might strike others as mad. But for this passionate Provençal transplant, there's no other way. The menu changes quarterly, every dish (including dessert) matched with a select wine. We recommend the multicourse tasting menus (beginning at $65 for three courses without wine; up to $225 for 11 courses with wine). Etched-glass windows screen the busy street-corner scene and all within is mellow and serene with starched white tablecloths, fresh flowers, wood floors, and contemporary Island art. ⊠*1969 S. King St., Mōʻiliʻili* ☎*808/944–4714* ⚲*Reservations essential* ═*AE, DC, MC, V* ⊗*No lunch.*

$$$$ ✕**Hoku's at the Kāhala.** Everything about this room speaks of quality and sophistication: the wall of windows with their beach views, the avant-garde cutlery and dinnerware, the solicitous staff, and Pacific Rim cuisine. Though the prices are eye-popping, you get good value in such dishes as the melting salt-crusted rack of lamb for two ($94) and the warm Tristan de Cunha Salad ($27). An excellent choice for special occasions. The dress code is collared shirts, no beachwear. ⊠*The Kāhala, 5000 Kāhala Ave., Kāhala* ☎*808/739–8780* ═*AE, D, MC, V* ⊗*No lunch Sat.*

Izakaya

Japanese pub-restaurants, called *izakaya* (ee-ZAH-ka-ya), are sprouting up all over the Islands like *matsutake* mushrooms in a pine forest. They began as oases for homesick Japanese nationals but were soon discovered by adventurous locals, who appreciated the welcoming atmosphere, sprawling menus, and later dining hours.

You can find *yakitori* (grilled dishes), tempura (deep-fried dishes), *donburi* (rice bowls), sushi and sashimi, *nabemono* and *shabu-shabu* (hot pots), noodles (both soup and fried), okonomiyaki (chop suey-type omelets), and a bizarre assortment of *yoshoku* dishes (Western foods prepared in Japanese style).

Full bars are usual; a wide choice of lager-type beers and good-to-great sakes are universal. Many specialize in single-malt scotch, but wine lists are generally short.

Izakaya menus are often confusing, many staff speak marginal English, and outings can get expensive fast. Prices range from $5 for a basket of edamame (steamed and salted soybeans) to $20 or more for wafu (seasoned, grilled steak, sliced for sharing). Start by ordering drinks and *edamame* or silky-textured braised *kabocha* pumpkin. This will keep the waiter happy. Then give yourself a quarter of an hour to examine the menu, ogle other people's plates, and seek recommendations.

Imanas Tei. Go early to this cozy, out-of-the-way restaurant for its tasteful, simple decor and equally tasteful and simply perfect sushi, sashimi, *nabe* (hot pots prepared at the table), and grilled dishes; reservations are taken from 5 to 7; after that, there's always a line. ✉ *2626 S. King St., Mōʻiliʻili* 🕾 *808/941–2626 or 808/934–2727* 🖃 *AE, DC, MC, V* 🍴 *$8–$25.*

Izakaya Nonbei. Teruaki Mori designed this pub to put you in mind of a northern inn in winter in his native Japan; dishes not to miss—*karei kara-age* (delicate deep-fried flounder) and *dobinmushi* (mushroom consommé presented in a teapot). ✉ *3108 Olu St., Kapahulu* 🕾 *808/734–5573* 🖃 *AE, D, DC, MC, V* 🍴 *$7–$20.*

Tokkuri-Tei. This is a favorite of locals for the playful atmosphere that belies the excellence of the food created by chef Hideaki "Santa" Miyosh. Just say "Moriwase, kudasai" ("chef's choice, please"), and he'll order for you. ✉ *611 Kapahulu Ave., Kapahulu* 🕾 *808/739–2800* 🖃 *AE, D, DC, MC, V* 🍴 *$13–$25.*

—Wanda Adams

6

PACIFIC RIM

$$$ ✕ **Sam Choy's Diamond Head.** Sam Choy has been called the Paul Prudhomme of Hawai'i and aptly so: both are big, welcoming men with magic in their hands and a folksy background in small, rural towns. Choy grew up cooking for his parents' lū'au business and now has an empire—restaurants, TV show, cookbooks, commercial products— and his two best chef-friends are Prudhomme and Emeril Lagasse. Here, Choy and executive chef Aaron Fukuda interpret local favorites in sophisticated ways, and the fresh fish is the best. The portions, like Sam's smile, are huge. ✉ *449 Kapahulu Ave., Kapahulu* ☎ *808/732–8645* 🖃 *AE, D, MC, DC, V.*

$$ ✕ **town.** The motto at town (with a lowercase "t") is "local first, organic whenever possible, with aloha always." Pretty much everyone agrees that chef-owner Ed Kenney's Mediterranean-eclectic menu ranges from just fine (pastas and salads) to just fabulous (polenta with egg and asparagus or buttermilk panna cotta). But the over-forty crowd tends to be put off by the minimalist decor, the shrieking-level acoustics, and the heedlessly careless waitstaff, who have a tendency to get lost. The predominantly twenty- and thirtysomething clientele don't seem bothered by these circumstances. The restaurant serves an inexpensive continental breakfast, as well as lunch and dinner. ✉ *3435 Wai'alae Ave., Kaimukī* ☎ *808/735–5900* 🖃 *MC, V* ⊘ *Closed Sun.*

THAI

$ ✕ **Spices.** Created by a trio of well-traveled friends who enjoy the foods of Southeast Asia, Spices is alluringly decorated in spicelike oranges and reds and offers a lunch and dinner menu far from the beaten path, even in a city rich in the cuisine of this region. They claim inspiration but not authenticity and use Island ingredients to everyone's advantage. The menu is vegetarian friendly. ✉ *2671 S. King St., Mō'ili'ili* ☎ *808/949–2679* 🖉 *Reservations not accepted* 🖃 *MC, V* ⊘ *Closed Mon.*

SOUTHEAST O'AHU: HAWAI'I KAI

PACIFIC RIM

$$–$$$ ✕ **BluWater Grill.** Time your drive along Honolulu's South Shore to allow for a stop at this relaxed restaurant on Kuapa Pond. The savvy chef-manager team left a popular chain restaurant to found this "American eclectic" eatery, serving wok-seared moi fish, mango and guava ribs, and lots

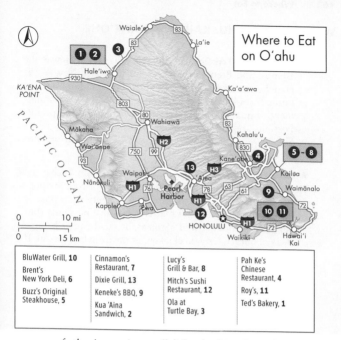

BluWater Grill, **10**	Cinnamon's Restaurant, **7**	Lucy's Grill & Bar, **8**	Pah Ke's Chinese Restaurant, **4**
Brent's New York Deli, **6**	Dixie Grill, **13**	Mitch's Sushi Restaurant, **12**	Roy's, **11**
Buzz's Original Steakhouse, **5**	Keneke's BBQ, **9**	Ola at Turtle Bay, **3**	Ted's Bakery, **1**
	Kua ʻAina Sandwich, **2**		

of other interesting small dishes for $5 to $10. They're open until 11 PM Monday through Thursday and on Sunday, and until midnight Friday and Saturday. ⊠*Hawaiʻi Kai Shopping Center, 377 Keahole St., Hawaiʻi Kai* ☎*808/395–6224* ▭*AE, DC, MC, V.*

$$–$$$ ✕**Roy's.** Roy Yamaguchi's flagship restaurant across the highway from Maunalua Bay attracts food-savvy visitors like the North Shore attracts surfers. But it also has a strong following among well-heeled Oahuans from surrounding neighborhoods, who consider the place an extension of their homes and Roy's team their personal chefs. For this reason, Roy's is always busy and sometimes overly noisy. It's best to visit later in the evening if you're sensitive to pressure to turn the table. The wide-ranging and ever-interesting Hawaiian fusion menu changes daily except for signature dishes like Roy's Original blackened ʻahi with soy-mustard-butter sauce, and a legendary meat loaf. There's an exceptional wine list. ⊠*Hawaiʻi Kai Corporate Plaza, 6600 Kalanianaʻole Hwy., Hawaiʻi Kai* ☎*808/396–7697* ☝*Reservations essential* ▭*AE, D, DC, MC, V.*

WINDWARD O'AHU: KAILUA & KĀNE'OHE

AMERICAN

¢–$ ✕ **Brent's New York Deli.** Jewish-style delis are very few in the Islands, and Brent's is a mecca for homesick New Yorkers who need a knish or a Reuben. But you don't have to know from blintzes to appreciate Brent Brody's commitment to quality. Breakfasts are particularly scrumptious. Portions are ample and prices right. ⊠ *629-A Kailua Rd., Suite 108, Kailua* ☎ *808/262–8588* ⚐ *Reservations not accepted* ☰ *MC, V.*

★ **Fodor's Choice** ✕ **Buzz's Original Steakhouse.** Virtually unchanged
$–$$ since it opened in 1967, this cozy maze of rooms opposite Kailua Beach Park is filled with the enticing aroma of grilling steaks. It doesn't matter if you're a bit sandy (but bare feet are not allowed). Stop at the salad bar, order up a steak, a burger, teriyaki chicken, or the fresh fish special. If you sit at the bar, expect to make friends. ⊠ *413 Kawailoa Rd., Kailua* ☎ *808/261–4661* ☰ *No credit cards.*

¢ ✕ **Cinnamon's Restaurant.** Known for uncommon variations on common breakfast themes (pancakes, eggs Benedict, French toast, home fries, and eggs), this neighborhood favorite is tucked into a hard-to-find Kailua office park; call for directions. Lunch and dinner feature local-style plate lunch and a diner-style menu (meat loaf, baked beans). ⊠ *315 Uluniu, Kailua* ☎ *808/261–8724* ☰ *D, DC, MC, V* ☽ *No dinner Sun.–Wed.*

$$ ✕ **Lucy's Grill and Bar.** This Windward eatery offers outdoor lānai seating and an open-air bar that shakes up a mean martini to go with its eclectic and innovative menu. The indoor seating, though attractive, gets very noisy. Begin with the deep-fried kālua pig (pork roasted in an underground oven) pastry triangles with a mandarin orange–plum dipping sauce. Seafood offerings include daily fish specials with your choice of preparations. For meat lovers, there are Indonesian lamb chops or rib-eye steak. Brunch is served on Sunday. ⊠ *33 Aulike St., Kailua* ☎ *808/230–8188* ☰ *MC, V* ☽ *No lunch.*

CHINESE

$ ✕ **Pah Ke's Chinese Restaurant.** Chinese restaurants tend to be interchangeable, and while the ambience here may be standard, this one—named for the local pidgin term for Chinese (literally translated this is Chinese's Chinese Restaurant)—is worth the drive from Honolulu for its focus on healthier cooking techniques and use of local ingredients, its seasonal specials such as cold soups and salads made from locally raised produce, and its exceptional East–West desserts. The menu offers all the usual suspects, some with a distinct Hawaiian flourish, but ask the owner and chef Raymond Siu, a former hotel pastry cook, if he's got anything different and interesting in the kitchen, or call ahead to ask for a special menu. ✉46-018 Kamehameha Hwy., Kāne'ohe ☎808/235–4505 ▤AE, DC, MC, V.

FAST FOOD

¢ ✕**Keneke's BBQ.** When you're sightseeing between Hanauma Bay and Makapu'u, the food pickings are slim. But every day, 365 days a year, there's Keneke's in Waimanālo town. It's the home of plate lunches, shave ice, and Scriptural graffiti on the walls (Keith "Keneke" Ward, the burly, weight-lifting, second-generation owner of the place, is a born-again Christian). The food is diet-busting, piled high, and mostly pretty good, particularly the Asian-style barbecue (including teriyaki chicken or beef and Korean kalbi (barbecue), Puerto Rican guisantes (pork and peas in tomato gravy), and Filipino adobo (piquant pork stew). If you want a treat, try the shave ice with ice cream. ✉41-855 Kalaniana'ole Hwy., Waimānalo ☎808/259–9800 ▤No credit cards.

THE NORTH SHORE: HALE'IWA

AMERICAN

¢ ✕**Kua 'Aina Sandwich.** A must-stop spot during a drive around the island, this North Shore eatery specializes in large, hand-formed burgers heaped with bacon, cheese, avocado, and pineapple; or try the grilled mahimahi sandwich. The crispy shoestring fries alone are worth the trip. Kua 'Aina also has a south-shore location across from the Ward Centre in Honolulu. ✉66-160 Kamehameha Hwy., Hale'iwa ☎808/637–6067 ✉1200 Ala Moana Blvd., Ala Moana ☎808/591–9133 ⚏Reservations not accepted ▤No credit cards.

★ Fodor'sChoice ✕**Ola at Turtle Bay Resort.** In a pavilion literally
$$ on the sand, this casual but refined restaurant wowed critics from the moment it opened, both with its idyllic location on Kuilima Cove and with chef Fred DeAngelo's reliably wonderful food. Ola means "life, living, healthy," an apt name for a place that combines a commitment to freshness and wholesomeness with a discriminating and innovative

palate in such dishes as a vegan risotto made with local mushrooms and orzo pasta, slow-poached salmon with caramelized cane sugar and Okinawan sweet potatoes. It is absolutely worth the drive. ⊠*57-091 Kamehameha Hwy., Kahuku* ☎*808/293–0801* ⚞*Reservations essential* ═*AE, DC, MC.*

¢ ✕**Ted's Bakery.** Across from Sunset Beach and famous for its chocolate *haupia* pie (layered coconut and chocolate puddings topped with whipped cream), Ted's Bakery is also favored by surfers and area residents for quick breakfasts, sandwiches, or plate lunches, to-go or eaten at the handful of umbrella-shaded tables outside. ⊠*59-024 Kamehameha Hwy., Hale'iwa* ☎*808/638–8207* ⚞*Reservations not accepted.* ═*DC, MC, V.*

CENTRAL & LEEWARD O'AHU

AMERICAN

$ ✕**Dixie Grill.** Casual and family-friendly, the Dixie Grill, just off the freeway in Pearl City, brings a taste of the South to the Islands with barbecue (including a variety of spicy sauces to choose from), seafood specialties (creole mahimahi, fried catfish), coleslaw, and hush puppies. ■TIP→ **This place is convenient if you're visiting Pearl Harbor or the swap meet.** ⊠*99-016 Kamehameha Hwy., 'Aiea* ☎*808/485–2722* ⚞*Reservations not accepted* ═*AE, D, DC, MC, V.*

JAPANESE

$$–$$$ ✕**Mitch's Sushi Restaurant.** This microscopic sushi bar (15 seats) is an adjunct of a wholesale seafood market operated by gregarious South African expatriate Douglas Mitchell, who oversees the sushi chefs and keeps customers chatting. The fish, air-freighted from around the world, is ultrafresh, well-cut, and nicely presented. You can spend as much or as little as you like—$40 for a half-dozen pieces of prime bluefin tuna belly, or just a few dollars for pickled plum sushi. ⊠*524 Ohohia St., near Honolulu International Airport, Airport area* ☎*808/837–7774* ⚞*Reservations essential* ═*MC, V.*

Where to Stay

WORD OF MOUTH

"The simplest thing would be to stay in Waikīkī. The beach there is beautiful and everything in Waikīkī is within walking distance of the beach. There are hotels in all price ranges."

—aloha

By Trina
Kudlacek

THE 2½-MI STRETCH OF SAND KNOWN AS WAIKĪKĪ BEACH is a 24-hour playground and the heartbeat of Hawai'i's tourist industry. Waikīkī has a lot to offer—namely, the beach, shopping, restaurants, and nightlife, all within walking distance of your hotel.

Business travelers stay on the western edge, near the Hawai'i Convention Center, Ala Moana, and downtown Honolulu. As you head east, Ala Moana Boulevard turns into Kalākaua Avenue, Waikīkī's main drag. This is hotel row (mid-Waikīkī), with historic boutique hotels, newer high-rises, and megaresorts. Bigger chains like Sheraton, Outrigger, ResortQuest, and Ohana have multiple properties along the strip, which can be confusing. Surrounding the hotels and filling their lower levels is a flurry of shopping centers, restaurants, bars, and clubs. As you get closer to Diamond Head Crater, the strip opens up again, with the Honolulu Zoo and Kapi'olani Park providing green spaces. This end has a handful of smaller hotels and condos for those who like their Waikīkī with a "side of quiet."

Waikīkī is still the resort capital of this island and the lodging landscape is constantly changing. The Waikīkī Beach Walk opened in 2007 on 8 acres within the confines of Beach Walk, Lewers and Saratoga streets, and Kālia Road. It comprises a multitiered entertainment complex, cultural center, hotels, and vacation ownership properties, all accented by lush tropical landscaping. Ko Olina Resort and Marina, about 15 minutes from the airport in West O'ahu, looms large on the horizon—this ongoing development already contains the J. W. Marriott 'Ihilani Resort, Marriott's Ko Olina Beach Club, and some outstanding golf courses, but it is slated, over the coming decade, to see the construction of an extensive planned resort community and marina, an aquarium, dozens of restaurants and shops, more hotels, and yet more vacation-ownership rentals.

Casual Windward and North Shore digs are shorter on amenities but have laid-back charms all their own. O'ahu offers a more limited list of B&Bs than other islands because the state stopped licensing them here in the 1980s; many of those operating here now do so under the radar. If you can't find your match below, contact a reservation service to make reservations at one of O'ahu's reputable B&Bs. Legislators on O'ahu are taking another look at this industry, and it's possible that B&Bs will flourish here again in the next decade.

For a list of hotel and condominium accommodations on the island, go to the Hawai'i Visitors & Convention Bureau's Web site (⊕ *www.gohawaii.com*).

RESERVATIONS

After your online research but before you book a room, try calling the hotels directly. Sometimes on-property reservationists can hook you up with the best deals, and they usually have the most accurate information about rooms and hotel amenities. If you use a toll-free number, ask for the location of the calling center you've reached. If it's not in O'ahu, double-check information and rates by calling the hotel's local number.

PRICES

The lodgings we list are the cream of the crop in each price category. Assume that hotels have private bath, phone, and TV and that they do not serve meals unless we state otherwise. We always list facilities but not whether you'll be charged an extra fee to use them, so when pricing accommodations, find out what's included.

WHAT IT COSTS				
¢	$	$$	$$$	$$$$
HOTELS				
under $100	$100–$180	$181–$260	$261–$340	over $340

Hotel prices are for two people in a standard double room in high season. Condo price categories reflect studio and one-bedroom rates.

WAIKĪKĪ

HOTELS & RESORTS

$$ ⚁ **Doubletree Alana Waikīkī.** The location (a 10-minute walk from the Hawai'i Convention Center), three phones in each room, and the 24-hour business center and gym meet the requirements of the Doubletree's global business clientele, but the smallness of the property, the staff's attention to detail, and the signature Doubletree chocolate-chip cookies upon arrival, resonate with vacationers. All rooms in the 19-story high-rise have lānai, but they overlook the city and busy Ala Moana Boulevard across from Fort DeRussy. To get to the beach, you either cross Fort DeRussy or head

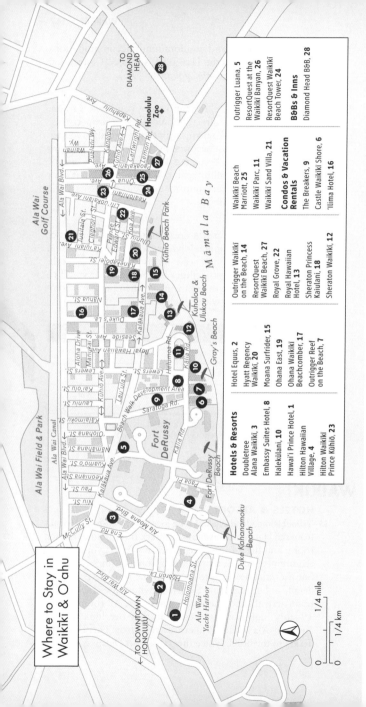

Where to Stay in Waikīkī & O'ahu

Hotels & Resorts
Doubletree
Alana Waikīkī, **3**
Embassy Suites Hotel, **8**
Halekūlani, **10**
Hawai'i Prince Hotel, **1**
Hilton Hawaiian
Village, **4**
Hilton Waikīkī
Prince Kūhiō, **23**

Hotel Equus, **2**
Hyatt Regency
Waikīkī, **20**
Moana Surfrider, **15**
Ohana East, **19**
Ohana Waikīkī
Beachcomber, **17**
Outrigger Reef
on the Beach, **7**

Outrigger Waikīkī
on the Beach, **14**
ResortQuest
Waikīkī Beach, **27**
Royal Grove, **22**
Royal Hawaiian
Hotel, **13**
Sheraton Princess
Kaiulani, **18**
Sheraton Waikīkī, **12**

Waikīkī Beach
Marriott, **25**
Waikīkī Parc, **11**
Waikīkī Sand Villa, **21**

**Condos & Vacation
Rentals**
The Breakers, **9**
Castle Waikīkī Shore, **6**
'Ilima Hotel, **16**

Outrigger Luana, **5**
ResortQuest at the
Waikīkī Banyan, **26**
ResortQuest Waikīkī
Beach Tower, **24**

B&Bs & Inns
Diamond Head B&B, **28**

through the Hilton Hawaiian Village. **Pros:** Professional staff, pleasant public spaces. **Cons:** Beach is a bit of a walk. ☒*1956 Ala Moana Blvd., Waikīkī*☎*808/941–7275 or 800/222–8733* ⊕*www.alana-doubletree.com* ⤏*272 rooms, 45 suites* ♿*In-room: safe, dial-up. In-hotel: restaurant, room service, bar, pool, gym, parking (fee), no-smoking rooms*☐*AE, D, MC, V.*

$$$$ 🖫**Embassy Suites Hotel–Waikīkī Beach Walk.** In a place where space is at a premium, the only all-suites resort in Hawai'i offers families and groups traveling together a bit more room to move about, with two 21-story towers housing one- and two-bedroom suites. All rooms have at least two balconies, some with ocean views; most overlook the 1,965-square-foot Grand Lānai with its pool, bar, restaurant, and meeting areas. The experience begins with a sit-down check-in and a manager's reception with free appetizers and drinks, and ends with an aloha lei ceremony. Rooms are done in Tommy Bahama–meets–Island beach home style (carved-wood tables, pineapple-print upholstery, hula-dancer artwork), and have relaxing earth tones, with amenities like pull-out beds and wet bars with microwaves and mini-refrigerators inviting longer stays. Developed by locally based Outrigger Enterprises, the hotel is steeped in Hawaiiana, with tapa-pattern murals adorning the exterior and cultural programs available for adults and youth. **Pros:** Great location next to Waikīkī Beach Walk, great vibe, nice pool deck. **Cons:** No direct beach access. ☒*201 Beachwalk St., Waikīkī*☎*800/362–2779* ⊕*www.embassy suiteswaikikibeachwalk.com* ⤏*353 1-bedroom suites, 68 2-bedroom suites* ♿*In-room: safe, refrigerator, dial-up. In-hotel: 4 restaurants, room service, bar, pool, concierge, parking (fee)*☐*AE, D, MC, V.*

★ **Fodor's**Choice 🖫**Halekūlani.** Honeymooners, and others seek-
$$$$ ing seclusion amid the frenetic activity of the Waikīkī scene, find it here. Halekūlani exemplifies the translation of its name—the "house befitting heaven." From the moment you step inside the lobby, the attention to detail and service wraps you in luxury. It begins with private registration in your guest room and extends to the tiniest of details, such as complimentary tickets to the Honolulu Symphony, Contemporary Art Museum, and Honolulu Academy of Arts. Spacious guest rooms, artfully appointed in marble and wood, have ocean views and extra-large lānai. If you want to honeymoon in the ultimate style, consider the 4,300-square-foot Vera Wang Suite, created by the

7

noted wedding-dress designer herself. It's entirely Vera, right down to the signature soft-lavender color scheme. For a day of divine pampering, check into the Halekūlani Spa. Outside, the resort's freshwater pool has an orchid design created from more than 1½ million glass mosaic tiles. Gray's Beach, which fronts the hotel just beyond the pool, is small and has been known to disappear at high tide. **Pros:** Heavenly interior spaces and wonderful dining opportunities in house. **Cons:** Might feel a bit formal for Waikīkī. ✉2199 Kālia Rd., Waikīkī☎808/923–2311 or 800/367–2343 ⊕www.halekulani.com ⇨412 rooms, 43 suites ⊘In-room: dial-up, DVD, safe. In-hotel: 3 restaurants, room service, bars, pool, spa, beachfront, laundry service, concierge, public Internet, public Wi-Fi, parking (fee), no-smoking rooms☰AE, DC, MC, V.

$$$$ ⊡**Hawai'i Prince Hotel & Golf Club Waikīkī.** This slim high-rise fronts Ala Wai Yacht Harbor at the 'ewa (west) edge of Waikīkī, close to Honolulu's downtown business districts, the convention center, and Ala Moana's outdoor mall. There's no beach here, but Ala Moana Beach Park is a 10-minute stroll away along the harbor, and the hotel also offers complimentary shuttle service around Waikīkī and its surrounding beaches. It's the only resort in Waikīkī with a golf course—the 27-hole Arnold Palmer–designed course is in 'Ewa Beach, about a 45-minute ride via complimentary shuttle from the hotel. The sleek, modern Prince looks to Asia both in its high-style decor and such pampering touches as the traditional *oshiburi* (chilled hand towel) for refreshment upon check-in. Floor-to-ceiling windows overlooking the harbor—ideal for sunsets—make up for the lack of lānai. **Pros:** Fantastic views, all very elegant, easy exit from complicated-to-maneuver Waikīkī. **Cons:** Can feel a bit stuffy as it caters more to business travelers. ✉100 Holomoana St., Waikīkī☎808/956–1111 or 866/774–6236 ⊕www.hawaiiprincehotel.com ⇨521 rooms, 57 suites ⊘In-room: safe, refrigerator, dial-up. In-hotel: 3 restaurants, room service, bar, golf course, pool, gym, spa, concierge, parking (fee), no-smoking rooms☰AE, DC, MC, V.

$$ ⊡**Hilton Hawaiian Village Beach Resort and Spa.** Location, location, location: this megaresort and convention destination sprawls over 22 acres on Waikīkī's widest stretch of beach, with the green lawns of neighboring Fort DeRussy creating a buffer zone from the high-rise lineup of central Waikīkī. The Hilton makes the most of its prime real estate—surrounding the six hotel towers with lavish gardens, an aquatic playground of pools, a 5-acre lagoon, cascading waterfalls, koi ponds, penguins, and pink flamingos. Rainbow Tower, with its landmark 31-story mural, has knockout views of Diamond Head. Rooms in all towers have lānai with ocean, city, or Waikīkī Beach views. More of a city than a village, the HHV has an ABC sundries store, a bookstore, a Louis Vuitton store, and a post office. Culture comes in the form of an outpost of the Bishop Museum and the contemporary Hawaiian art gracing the public spaces. It even has its own pier, docking point for the Atlantis submarine. The sheer volume of options, including free activities (lei-making, 'ukulele lessons, and fireworks), makes the HHV a good choice for families. **Pros:** Activities and amenities can keep you busy for weeks; big-resort perks like check-in kiosks (complete with room keys) in the baggage-claim area at the airport. **Cons:** Temptation to stay on-site, missing out on the "real" Hawai'i; frequent renovations and construction; size of property can be overwhelming. ⊠ *2005 Kālia Rd., Waikīkī* ☎ *808/949–4321 or 800/221–2424* ⊕ *www. hiltonhawaiianvillage.com* ⤵ *3,432 rooms, 365 suites, 264 condominiums* ⚙ *In-room: safe, refrigerator. In-hotel: 20 restaurants, room service, bars, pools, gym, spa, beach- front, children's programs (ages 5–12), laundry service, public Wi-Fi, parking (fee), no-smoking rooms* ⊟ *AE, D, DC, MC, V.*

$$ 🏨 **Hilton Waikīkī Prince Kūhiō.** You enter through a lobby of rich wood detailing, contemporary fabrics, and magnificent tropical floral displays whose colors match the hibiscus reds of the carpeting. Two blocks from Kūhiō Beach, this 37-story high-rise is on the Diamond Head end of Waikīkī. The Lobby Bar mixes up tropical cocktails and an island-style pūpū menu and has wireless access and a wide-screen plasma TV for sports fans and news junkies while their restaurant MAC 24-7 offers their version of modern comfort food 24 hours a day, 7 days a week. If marriage is on your mind, note the wedding gazebo anchoring the hotel gardens. Book on an upper floor for an ocean view from your lānai. **Pros:** Good value, central location, and pleasant, comfortable public spaces. **Cons:** A bit of a distance to the beach, very few rooms with views. ⊠ *2500 Kūhiō Ave., Waikīkī* ☎ *808/922–0811 or 800/445–8667* ⊕ *www. princekuhiohotel.com* ⤵ *620 rooms* ⚙ *In-room: safe, Eth- ernet. In-hotel: restaurant, room service, bar, pool, gym, laundry facilities, parking (fee), no-smoking rooms* ⊟ *AE, D, DC, MC, V.*

7

Halekūlani

$–$$ ⊡**Hotel Equus.** Formerly the Hawaii Polo Inn, this small hotel has been completely renovated with a Hawaiian country theme that pays tribute to Hawai'i's polo-playing history. It fronts busy Ala Moana Boulevard, on the 'ewa end of Waikīkī and is one block from both Ala Moana shopping center and Ala Moana Beach Park. All rooms are equipped with refrigerators, microwaves, and TVs that can access any channel in the world; some have balconies and partial ocean views; daily continental breakfast is included. The front desk staff is happy to assist with driving directions to the polo-playing fields at Mokuleia and Waimānalo, where guests receive free tickets in season—pack a picnic if you go. **Pros:** Casual, fun atmosphere, attentive staff, nicely furnished rooms. **Cons:** On a very busy road you must cross to get to the beach. ⊠*1696 Ala Moana Blvd., Waikīkī*☏*808/949–0061 or 800/535–0085* ⊕*www.hawaiipolo.com* ⌑*69 rooms* ⊡*In-room: safe. In-hotel: pool, public Wi-Fi, laundry facilities, parking (fee)*▭*AE, DC, MC, V.*

$$$$ ⊡**Hyatt Regency Waikīkī Resort and Spa.** Though it's across the street from the Kūhiō Beach section of Waikīkī, the Hyatt is actually on the oceanfront, as there's no resort between it and the Pacific Ocean. A pool-deck staircase leads directly to street level, for easy beach access. An open-air atrium with three levels of shopping, a two-story waterfall, and free nightly live entertainment make this one of the liveliest lobbies anywhere. An activity center offers kids' programs, including lei-making lessons, 'ukulele lessons, and field trips to the aquarium and zoo. **Pros:** Public spaces are airy and waterfall is spectacular. **Cons:** In a very busy and crowded part of Waikīkī. ⊠*2424 Kalākaua Ave., Waikīkī*☏*808/923–1234 or 800/633–7313* ⊕*www.waikiki.hyatt.com* ⌑*1,230 rooms, 18 suites* ⊡*In-room: safe, refrigerator, Wi-Fi. In-hotel: 5 restaurants, room service, bars, pool, gym, spa, children's programs (ages 5–12), concierge, parking (fee), no-smoking rooms*▭*AE, D, DC, MC, V.*

7

OPEN AIR. Islanders love their porches, balconies, and verandas—all wrapped up in the single Hawaiian word: lānai. When booking, ask about the lānai and be sure to specify the view (understanding that top views command top dollars). Also, check that the lānai is not merely a step-out or Juliet balcony, with just enough room to lean against a railing—you want a lānai that is big enough for patio seating.

$$$$ 🏨**Moana Surfrider.** Outrageous rates of $1.50 per night were the talk of the town when the "First Lady of Waikīkī" opened her doors in 1901. The Hawai'i Calls radio program was broadcast from the veranda during the 1940s and '50s. Today this historic beauty is still a wedding and honeymoon favorite with a sweeping main staircase and period furnishings in its main wing, the Moana. In the late 1950s, the hotel's Diamond Head Tower was built. In the '70s, the Surfrider hotel went up next door; all three merged into one hotel in the 1980s. The newly refurbished Surfrider has oceanfront suites with two separate lānai, one for sunrise and one for sunset viewing. Relax on the private beach or in a cabana by the pool. Enjoy live music and hula at the Banyan Court each evening or dine at the Beach House restaurant. **Pros:** Elegant, historic property, best place on Waikīkī Beach to watch hula and have a drink. **Cons:** You might feel you have to tiptoe around formal public spaces. ⊠*2365 Kalākaua Ave., Waikīkī*☎*808/922–3111, 888/488–3535, or 866/500–8313* ⊕*www.moana-surfrider.com* ⊃*793 rooms, 46 suites* ⌂*In-room: safe, dial-up. In-hotel: 2 restaurants, spa, room service, bars, pool, beachfront, laundry service, children's programs (ages 5–12), concierge, parking (fee), no-smoking rooms*☐*AE, DC, MC, V.*

$$$ 🏨**Ohana East.** If you want to be in central Waikīkī and don't want to pay beachfront lodging prices, consider the flagship property for Ohana Hotels in Waikīkī. Next to the Sheraton Princess Kaiulani on the corner of Kaiulani and Kūhiō avenues, it's a mere two blocks from the beach and within walking distance of shopping, restaurants, and nightlife. Its location and reasonable rates tend to attract plenty of group travelers. Don't expect any fancy lobbies or outdoor gardens here. Certain rooms on lower floors have no lānai, and some rooms have showers only. Suites have kitchenettes. **Pros:** Close to the beach and reasonable rates. **Cons:** No lānai and very basic public spaces. ⊠*150 Kaiulani Ave., Waikīkī*☎*808/922–5353 or 800/462–6262* ⊕*www.ohanahotels.com* ⊃*420 rooms, 20 suites* ⌂*In-room: safe, kitchen (some), refrigerator. In-hotel: 3 restaurants, bar, pool, gym, laundry facilities, parking (fee)*☐*AE, D, DC, MC, V.*

$$$–$$$$ 🏨**Ohana Waikīkī Beachcomber Hotel.** Ohana took over the beloved old Beachcomber in 2005 and has given her a comprehensive facelift while retaining the Polynesian theme. At this and other Ohana hotels, the Ohana Waikīkī Connection

offers several free services: unlimited rides on the Waikīkī Trolley Pink Line, long-distance phone service to the United States and Canada, and a daily newspaper. Early check-in guests can leave their bags, pick up a pager, and hit the beach; they'll be alerted when their rooms are ready. This Ohana hotel hosts the popular Blue Hawai'i show and is almost directly across from the Royal Hawaiian Shopping Center and next door to the International Marketplace. The third-floor pool deck is front-row seating for any of Waikīkī's year-round parades or Ho'olaulea street-party festivals. It's a family-friendly place, with cultural activities that include 'ukulele and hula lessons as well as arts and crafts. On the hotel's ground level is an entrance to Macy's, and across the street is a public access-way that opens up to the beach fronting the Royal Hawaiian hotel. **Pros:** Lots of freebees, in the thick of Waikīkī action. **Cons:** Very busy area, no direct beach access. ✉*2300 Kalākaua Ave., Waikīkī* ☎*808/922–4646 or 800/462–6262* ⊕*www. ohanahotels.com* ⌀*493 rooms, 7 suites* ⌂*In-room: refrigerator. In-hotel: restaurant, snack bar, pool, laundry facilities, public Wi-Fi, parking (fee), no-smoking rooms* ▤*AE, DC, MC, V.*

$$$–$$$$ ⊡**Outrigger Reef on the Beach.** At this writing, the Outrigger Reef is undergoing a thorough renovation, to be completed in mid-2008. The project incorporates a Hawaiian voyaging-design theme, expanded room size, larger and more contemporary bathrooms—including full-size bathtubs in what was previously an all-shower hotel—and a new signature restaurant, though the Shore Bird and Ocean House remain. What had been a plain but pleasant oceanfront bargain now offers polished elegance in keeping with its prime location. Though the inland Pacific Tower, which reopens mid-year, will have been renovated more recently, it's worthwhile to go for an ocean view or oceanfront accommodation in the already-completed Ocean Tower; other rooms have less enchanting views, and noisy construction on the Trump Towers across the street will continue into 2009. New features include smoke-free rooms, flat-screen TVs, and free long distance to the U.S. mainland and Canada. **Pros:** On beach, direct access to Waikīkī Beach Walk. **Cons:** Proximity to Trump Tower construction. ✉*2169 Kālia Rd., Waikīkī* ☎*808/923–3111 or 800/688–7444* ⊕*www. outrigger.com* ⌀*631 rooms, 44 suites* ⌂*In-room: refrigerator, bar, dial-up. In-hotel: 2 restaurants, pool, gym, beachfront, children's programs (ages 5–12), laundry facilities,*

7

public Internet, public Wi-Fi, parking (fee), no-smoking rooms ⊟*AE, D, DC, MC, V.*

$$$$　🖵**Outrigger Waikīkī on the Beach.** This star jewel of Outrigger Hotels & Resorts sits on one of the finest strands of Waikīkī Beach. The guest rooms in the16-story no-smoking resort have rich dark-wood furnishings, Hawaiian art, and lānai that offer either ocean or Waikīkī-skyline views. The popular Duke's Canoe Club has beachfront concerts under the stars. Waikīkī Plantation Spa offers Hawaiian seaweed wraps, hot-stone massages, and wedding packages. **Pros:** The best bar on the beach is downstairs, free Wi-Fi in lobby. **Cons:** The lobby feels a bit like an airport with so many people using it as a throughway to the beach. ✉*2335 Kalākaua Ave., Waikīkī*☎*808/923–0711 or 800/688–7444* ⊕*www.outrigger.com* ☞*524 rooms, 30 suites* ⌂*In-room: safe, kitchen (some), refrigerator, dial-up. In-hotel: 3 restaurants, room service, bars, pool, gym, beachfront, children's programs (ages 5–13), laundry service, laundry facilities, concierge, public Wi-Fi, parking (fee), no-smoking rooms* ⊟*AE, D, DC, MC, V.*

$$$–$$$$　🖵**ResortQuest Waikīkī Beach Hotel.** A three-story volcano, backlighted in a faux eruption, crawls up the side of this hotel opposite Kūhiō Beach and near Kapi'olani Park. Rooms are furnished in dark tropical woods with lava-red floral-print fabrics. The Tiki Bar and Grill completes the tropical-island experience. Breakfast, evening music, and gatherings take place on the third-floor pool deck. In the early mornings, there's an international food court where guests can choose complimentary breakfast munchies to pack in a take-out cooler bag and head to the beach across the street to catch some early-morning wave action. A good choice for families, it is directly across the street from a protected stretch of Kūhiō Beach and there are in-room movies and games and free hula lessons twice weekly. In the evenings, the poolside bar breaks out with Hawaiian music that ranges from traditional to Jawaiian (Hawaiian sound with a reggae beat). **Pros:** Fun for families, great beach access. **Cons:** Active lobby area and crowded elevators. ✉*2570 Kalākaua Ave., Waikīkī*☎*808/922–2511 or 877/997–6667* ⊕*www.rqWaikikibeachhotel.com*☞*644 rooms, 40 suites* ⌂*In-room: safe, refrigerator, dial-up. In-hotel: 3 restaurants, pool, gym, public Wi-Fi, laundry facilities, parking (fee), no-smoking rooms* ⊟*AE, D, DC, MC, V.*

¢ ⚁**Royal Grove Hotel.** Two generations of the Fong family have put their heart and soul into the operation of this tiny (by Waikīkī standards), six-story hotel that feels like a throwback to the days of boarding houses, where rooms were outfitted for function, not style, and served up with a wealth of home-style hospitality at a price that didn't break the bank. During the hot summer months, seriously consider splurging on the highest-end accommodations, which have air-conditioning, lānai, and small kitchens. The hotel's pool is its social center in the evenings, when you can usually find one or more members of the Fong family strumming a 'ukulele, dancing hula, and singing songs in the old Hawaiian style. On special occasions, the Fongs host a potluck dinner by the pool. Little touches that mean a lot include free use of boogie boards, surfboards, beach mats, and beach towels. The hotel is two blocks from Waikīkī's Kūhiō Beach. On property are a tiny sushi bar, a natural foods deli, and an authentic Korean barbecue plate-lunch place. For extra value, inquire about the Grove's weekly rates. Parking is available in a public lot down the street. **Pros:** Very economical Waikīkī option, lots of character. **Cons:** No air-conditioning in some rooms. ✉*151 Uluniu Ave., Waikīkī* 🕾*808/923–7691* ⊕*www.royalgrovehotel. com* ➳*78 rooms, 7 suites* ♿*In-room: kitchen. In-hotel: pool*═*AE, D, DC, MC, V.*

$$$$ ⚁**The Royal Hawaiian Hotel.** At this writing, the Royal Hawaiian is scheduled to close for renovations between June and December 2008. Beginning in 2009, you'll be able to enjoy the outdoor Mai Tai Bar again—and its famous high-octane cocktail. The Matson Navigation Company built the Pink Palace of the Pacific, so nicknamed for its cotton-candy color, in 1927 for its luxury-cruise passengers. A modern tower has since been added, but we're partial to the romance and architectural detailing of the historic wing, with its canopy beds, Queen Anne–style desks, and color motifs that range from soft mauve to soothing sea foam. If you want a lānai for sunset viewing, rooms in the oceanfront tower are your best bet. The Royal's weekly lū'au—the only oceanfront lū'au in Waikīkī—is held Monday evenings underneath the stars on the Ocean Lawn. **Pros:** Can't be beat for history, mai tais and sunsets are amazing. **Cons:** Closed for half of 2008. ✉*2259 Kalākaua Ave., Waikīkī* 🕾*888/488–3535, 808/923–7311, or 866/500–8313* ⊕*www.royal-hawaiian.com* ➳ *528 rooms, 53 suites* ♿*In-room: refrigerator, Ethernet. In-hotel: restaurant, room*

7

service, pool, spa, beachfront, bar, children's programs (ages 5–12), concierge, public Internet, parking (fee), no-smoking rooms⊟AE, DC, MC, V.

$$ ⬚**Sheraton Princess Kaiulani.** This hotel sits across the street from its sister property, the Sheraton Moana Surfider. You can sleep at the Princess Kaiulani, taking advantage of the lower rates of a non-beachfront hotel, oversee the bustle of Waikīkī from your private lānai, and dine at any of the more-pricey oceanfront Sheratons, charging everything back to your room at the Princess Kaiulani. Rooms are in two towers—some peer at the ocean over the Moana's low-rise historic wing. It's a two-minute stroll to the beach. The hotel's pool is street-side, facing Kalākaua Avenue. **Pros:** In the heart of everything in Waikīkī. **Cons:** No direct beach access, kid's activities offsite. ⊠*120 Kaiulani Ave., Waikīkī*☎*808/922–5811, 888/488–3535, or 866/500–8313*⊕*www.princesskaiulani.com* ⬚*1,150 rooms, 14 suites* ⬚*In-room: dial-up. In-hotel: 2 restaurants, room service, bars, pool, gym, children's programs (ages 5–12), no-smoking rooms*⊟*AE, D, DC, MC, V.*

$$$$ ⬚**Sheraton Waikīkī.** Towering over its neighbors on the prow of Waikīkī's famous sands, the Sheraton is center stage on Waikīkī Beach. Designed for the convention crowd, it's big and busy; the ballroom, one of O'ahu's largest, hosts convention expos, concerts, and boxing matches. A glass-wall elevator, with magnificent views of Waikīkī, ascends 30 stories to the Hano Hano Room's skyline Cobalt lounge and restaurant in the sky. The resort's best beach is on its Diamond Head side, fronting the Royal Hawaiian Hotel. Lānai afford views of the ocean, Waikīkī, or mountains. If you don't shy away from crowds, this could be the place for you. It's so large that even the walk to your room could hike off a few of those calories consumed in mai tais. The advantage here is that you have at your vacation fingertips a variety of amenities, venues, and programs, as well as a location smack-dab in the middle of Waikīkī. **Pros:** Location in the heart of everything. **Cons:** Busy atmosphere clashes with laid-back Hawaiian style. ⊠*2255 Kalākaua Ave., Waikīkī*☎*888/488–3535, 808/922–4422, or 866/500–8313*⊕*www.sheratonwaikiki.com* ⬚*1,695 rooms, 128 suites* ⬚*In-room: refrigerator. In-hotel: 2 restaurants, room service, bars, pools, beachfront, laundry service, children's programs (ages 5–12), concierge, parking (fee), no-smoking rooms*⊟*AE, DC, MC, V.*

$$$–$$$$ ▥**Waikīkī Beach Marriott Resort & Spa.** On the eastern edge of Waikīkī, this flagship Marriott sits across from Kūhiō Beach and close to Kapiʻolani Park, the zoo, and the aquarium. Deep Hawaiian woods and bold tropical colors fill the hotel's two towers, which have ample courtyards and public areas open to ocean breezes and sunlight. Rooms in the Kealohilani Tower are some of the largest in Waikīkī, and the Paoakalani Tower's Diamond Head–side rooms offer breathtaking views of the crater and Kapiʻolani Park. All rooms have private lānai. The hotel's Spa Olakino, owned by Honolulu celebrity stylist Paul Brown, is one of the largest in Waikīkī and specializes in use of Hawaiʻi-based materials and treatments. Daily activities are offered for children and adults alike and surf lessons are available from surfer Tony Moniz at the Faith Surf School. **Pros:** Stunning views of Waikīkī, professional service, airy tropical public spaces. **Cons:** Noise from Kalākaua Avenue can drown out surf below. ⊠*2552 Kalākaua Ave., Waikīkī*☎*808/922–6611 or 800/367–5370* 2⊕*www.marriottwaikiki.com* ⇗*1,310 rooms, 13 suites* ⏃*In-room: dial-up, Wi-Fi. In-hotel: 6 restaurants, room service, bars, 2 pools, gym, spa, concierge, parking (fee), no-smoking rooms*⊟*AE, D, MC, V.*

$$$–$$$$ ▥**Waikīkī Parc.** Contrasting the stately vintage-Hawaiian elegance of her sister hotel, the Halekūlani, the Waikīkī Parc makes a chic and contemporary statement to its Gen-X clientele, offering the same attention to detail in service and architectural design but lacking the beachfront location and higher prices. The guest rooms in this high-rise complex have modern minimalist furnishings but give a nod to the tropics by keeping plantation-style shutters that open out to the lānai. A complimentary evening manager's reception features wine specially made for the hotel. Its heated pool and sundeck are eight floors up, affording a bit more privacy and peace for sunbathers, and guests can take advantage of the spa at the Halekūlani across the street. Nobu Waikīkī, of the world-renowned Nobu restaurant family, opened here in 2007, serving Japanese food with a South American accent. **Pros:** Stunningly modern, high-design rooms, great access to Waikīkī Beach Walk. **Cons:** No direct beach access. ⊠*2233 Helumoa Rd., Waikīkī*☎*808/921–7272 or 800/422–0450* ⊕*www. Waikikiparc.com* ⇗*297 rooms* ⏃*In-room: safe, dial-up. In-hotel: restaurant, room service, pool, gym, concierge, parking (fee)*⊟*AE, D, DC, MC, V.*

7

$ 🖭 **Waikīkī Sand Villa.** Families and others looking for a good rate without sacrificing proximity to Waikīkī's beaches, dining, and shopping return to the Waikīkī Sand Villa year after year. It's on the corner of Kaiulani Avenue and Ala Wai Boulevard, a three-block walk to restaurants and the beach. There's a high-rise tower and a three-story building (no elevator) of studio accommodations with kitchenettes. Rooms are small but well planned. Corner deluxe units with lānai overlook Ala Wai Canal and the golf course. The fitness center has 24-hour access. Complimentary continental breakfast is served poolside beneath shady coconut trees, and the hotel's Sand Bar comes alive at happy hour with a great mix of hotel guests and locals who like to hang out and "talk story." The Sand Bar also has computers and Web cams, so that you not only can keep in touch with family by e-mail, you can also taunt them with your developing tan. **Pros:** Fun bar, economical choice. **Cons:** The noise from the bar might annoy some, 10-minute walk to the beach. ⊠*2375 Ala Wai Blvd., Waikīkī* ☎*808/922–4744 or 800/247–1903* ⊕*www.sandvillahotel.com* ⤏*214 rooms* ⌂*In-room: safe, refrigerator. In-hotel: restaurant, bar, gym, parking (fee)* ⊟*AE, D, DC, MC, V.*

CONDOS & VACATION RENTALS

$–$$ 🖭 **The Breakers.** Despite an explosion of high-rise construction all around it, the low-rise Breakers continues to offer a taste of '60s Hawai'i in this small complex a mere half block from Waikīkī Beach. The Breakers' six two-story buildings surround its pool and overlook gardens filled with tropical flowers. Guest rooms have Japanese-style shoji doors that open to the lānai, plus kitchenettes, and bathrooms with showers only. Some have views of the Urasenke Teahouse. The Breakers enjoys enviable proximity to the Waikīkī Beach Walk entertainment, dining, and retail complex. The resort is very popular thanks to its reasonable prices and great location. **Pros:** Intimate atmosphere, great location. **Cons:** Parking space is limited. ⊠*250 Beach Walk, Waikīkī* ☎*808/923–3181 or 800/426–0494* ⊕*www.breakers-hawaii.com* ⤏*63 units* ⌂*In-room: kitchen. In-hotel: restaurant, pool, parking (no fee)* ⊟*AE, DC, MC, V.*

$$$–$$$$ 🖭 **Castle Waikīkī Shore.** Nestled between Fort DeRussy Beach Park and the Outrigger Reef on the Beach, this is the only condo right on Waikīkī Beach. Units include studios and one- and two-bedroom suites, each with private lānai and panoramic views of the Pacific Ocean. All units have washers and dryers, and many have full kitchens, but some only

CONDO COMFORTS

The local **Foodland** grocery-store chain has two locations near Waikīkī. ✉ Market City, 2939 Harding Ave., near intersection with Kapahulu Ave. and highway overpass, Kaimukī ☎808/734–6303 ✉ Ala Moana Center, 1450 Ala Moana Blvd., ground level, Ala Moana ☎808/949–5044.

A smaller version of larger Foodland, **Food Pantry** also has apparel, beach stuff, and tourist-oriented items. ✉2370 Kūhiō Ave., across from Miramar hotel, Waikīkī ☎808/923–9831. ✉2370 Kūhiō Ave., across from Miramar hotel, Waikīkī ☎808/923–9831.

Blockbuster Video ✉Ala Moana Shopping Center, 451 PiikoiSt., Ala Moana ☎808/593–2595.

Pizza Hut ☎808/643–1111 for delivery statewide.

If you want to expand your culinary horizons without leaving your condo, call **Room Service in Paradise** (☎808/941–3463). They will drop off a list with the menus from all the restaurants where you can place your order and for a slight handling and delivery free, RSP will deliver it right to your condo door or hotel room.

have kitchenettes, so be sure to inquire when booking. Families love this place for its spaciousness, while others love it for its quiet location on the 'ewa end of Waikīkī. However, through 2008 and into 2009, there will be construction on the new Trump Towers directly across Kālia Road. **Pros:** Great security, great views, great management. **Cons:** Ongoing construction on Diamond Head side of property. ✉2161 Kālia Rd., Waikīkī☎808/952–4500 or 800/367–2353 ⊕www.castleresorts.com ⊅168 units ⌂In-room: safe, kitchen (some), dial-up. In-hotel: beachfront, parking (fee), no-smoking rooms⊟AE, D, DC, MC, V.

$$–$$$ ⊡ **'Ilima Hotel.** Tucked away on a residential side street near Waikīkī's Ala Wai Canal, this locally owned 17-story condominium-style hotel is a gem. The glass-wall lobby with koa-wood furnishings, original Hawaiian artwork, and friendly staff create a Hawaiian home-away-from-home. Rates are decent for the spacious studios with kitchenettes and the one- and two-bedroom suites with full kitchens, Jacuzzi baths, cable TV with free HBO and Disney channels, multiple phones, and spacious lānai. It's a two-block walk to Waikīkī Beach, shopping, and Kalākaua Avenue restaurants. The parking is free but limited. When the spots are full, you park on the street. **Pros:** Big rooms are great for families. **Cons:** Limited hotel parking and street parking can be difficult to find. ✉ *445 Nohonani St., Waikīkī* ☎ *808/923–1877 or 800/801–9366* ⊕ *www. ilima.com* ⬥ *98 units* ⌂ *In-room: safe, kitchen. In-hotel: pool, gym, laundry facilities, free parking, no-smoking rooms* ⊟ *AE, DC, MC, V.*

$$$–$$$$ ⊠ **Outrigger Luana.** At the entrance to Waikīkī near Fort DeRussy is this welcoming hotel offering both rooms and condominium units. Luana's two-story lobby is appointed in rich, Hawaiian-wood furnishings with Island-inspired fabrics, and the mezzanine lounge is as comfortable as any living room back home. Units are furnished with a mix of rich woods with etched accents of pineapples and palm trees. At bedside, hula-dancer and beach-boy lamps add another Hawaiian residential touch. The recreational deck has a fitness center, pool, and barbecue area with tables that can be enclosed cabana-style for privacy when dining outdoors. One-bedroom suites each have two lānai. If you like Hawaiiana and appreciate a bit of kitsch this is a great option. **Pros:** Two lānai in suites, barbecue area (rare for Waikīkī). **Cons:** No direct beach access. ✉ *2045 Kalākaua Ave., Waikīkī* ☎ *808/955–6000 or 800/688–7444* ⊕ *www. outrigger.com* ⬥ *218 units* ⌂ *In-room: safe, kitchen (some), dial-up. In-hotel: pool, gym, laundry facilities, public Wi-Fi, parking (fee)* ⊟ *AE, D, DC, MC, V.*

$$–$$$ ⊠ **ResortQuest at the Waikīkī Banyan.** The recreation deck at this family-oriented property has outdoor grills, a heated swimming pool, two hot tubs, a playground, a miniputting green, and volleyball, basketball, and tennis courts. The welcoming lobby is decorated in warm tropical woods with plenty of seating to enjoy the trade winds. There is also a koi pond and mini-waterfall. One-bedroom suites contain island-inspired decor and have complete kitchens and lānai that offer Diamond Head or ocean views. **Pros:** Many rooms have great views. **Cons:** Trekking to the beach with all your gear. ✉ *201 Ohua Ave., Waikīkī* ☎ *808/922–0555 or 866/774–2924* ⊕ *www.rqwaikikibanyan.com* ⬥ *876 units* ⌂ *In-room: kitchen, dial-up. In-hotel: tennis court, pool, parking (fee), laundry facilities, no-smoking rooms* ⊟ *AE, D, DC, MC, V.*

$$$$ ⊠ **ResortQuest Waikīkī Beach Tower.** You'll find the elegance of a luxury all-suite condominium combined with the intimacy and service of a boutique hotel at this Kalākaua

Avenue address. Facing Kūhiō Beach, this 40-story resort offers spacious (1,100- to 1,400-square-foot) one- and two-bedroom suites with gourmet kitchens and windows that open to sweeping views of Waikīkī and the Pacific Ocean. Amenities include twice-daily maid service, washer-dryers, and spacious private lānai. **Pros:** Very large rooms—big enough to move into. **Cons:** No on-site restaurants, you must cross a busy street to the beach. ⊠*2470 Kalākaua Ave., Waikīkī* ☎*808/926–6400 or 866/774–2924* ⊕*www. rqwaikikibeachtower.com* ⊃ *140 units* ᗄ*In-room: safe, kitchen, DVD, dial-up. In-hotel: room service, pool, tennis court, laundry facilities, concierge, parking (no fee), no-smoking rooms*⊟*AE, D, DC, MC, V.*

B&BS & INNS

$ ⓣ**Diamond Head Bed and Breakfast.** Many a traveler and resident would love to own a home like this art-filled B&B at the base of Waikīkī's famous Diamond Head crater, one of the city's most exclusive neighborhoods. Each of the three guest rooms feature koa-wood furnishings and private bath, and they open to a lānai and a big backyard filled with the sounds of birds and rustling trees. The more private ground-floor suite has a separate living room and a bedroom with a queen bed. To experience a bit of Hawaiian history, request the room that includes the extra-large hand-carved koa bed that once belonged to a Hawaiian princess. The closest beach is the intimate Sans Souci near the Natatorium; it's hard to believe that the hustle and bustle of Waikīkī is a short stroll from the house. Reserve three to four months in advance. **Pros:** Secluded and peaceful. **Cons:** Small and therefore difficult to book. ⊠*3240 Noela Dr., Waikīkī* ⌇*Reservations: Hawai'i's Best Bed and Breakfasts, Box 485, Laupahoehoe 96767* ☎*808/962–0100, 800/262–9912 reservations* ⊕*www.bestbnb.com* ⊃*2 rooms, 1 suite* ᗄ*In-room: no a/c, no phone. In-hotel: no-smoking rooms*⊟*No credit cards.*

HONOLULU BEYOND WAIKĪKĪ

$$ ⓣ**Ala Moana Hotel.** Shoppers might wear out their Manolos here; this renovated condo-hotel is connected to O'ahu's biggest mall, the Ala Moana Shopping Center, by a pedestrian ramp, and it's a four-block stroll away from the Victoria Ward Centers. Business travelers can walk one block in the opposite direction to the Hawai'i Convention Center. Swimmers, surfers, and beachgoers make the two-minute

walk to Ala Moana Beach Park across the street. Rooms are like small, comfortable apartments, with cherrywood furnishings, a soothing blue color scheme, kitchenettes, flat-screen TVs, and balconies with outdoor seating. The recreation deck features a pool with cabanas and a bar, outdoor yoga and Pilates studios, and a fitness center. **Pros:** Adjacent to Ala Moana shopping center, rooms nicely appointed. **Cons:** Lobby feels a bit like an airport, beach across busy Ala Moana Boulevard. ✉*410 Atkinson Dr., Ala Moana* ☎*808/955–4811 or 888/367–4811* ✪*www. alamoanahotel.com* ⤳*1,150 studios, 67 suites* ⚷*In-room: safe, refrigerator. In-hotel: 4 restaurants, room service, bars, pool, gym, laundry facilities, parking (fee), no-smoking rooms* ⊟*AE, DC, MC, V.*

★ **Fodor's**Choice ⚏ **The Kāhala.** Hidden away in the wealthy resi-
$$$$ dential neighborhood of Kāhala (on the other side of Diamond Head from Waikīkī), this elegant oceanfront hotel has played host to both presidents and princesses as one of Hawai'i's very first luxury resorts. The Kāhala is flanked by the exclusive Waialae Golf Links and the Pacific Ocean—surrounding it in a natural tranquility. Pathways meander out along a walkway with benches tucked into oceanfront nooks for lazy viewing offering an "outer island" experience 10 minutes from Waikīkī and Honolulu. The expansive oceanfront Chi Fitness Center offers outdoor yoga and Pilates. Fine dining is available at Hokus, or the poolside bar and grill will serve at your lounge chair on the beach. The reef not far from shore makes the waters here calm enough for young kids. You can also sign up for dolphin interactions in the 26,000-square-foot-lagoon. The rooms, decorated in an understated Island style with mahogany furniture, are spacious (550 square feet), with bathrooms with two vanities, and lānai big enough for a lounge chair. If you're a golf-lover visiting the second week of January, ask for a room overlooking the course for a bird's-eye view of the PGA Sony Open from your lānai. **Pros:** Away from hectic Waikīkī, beautiful rooms and public spaces, heavenly spa. **Cons:** Waikīkī is a drive away. ✉*5000 Kāhala Ave., Kāhala* ☎*808/739–8888 or 800/367–2525* ✪*www. kahalaresort.com* ⤳*312 rooms, 31 suites* ⚷*In-room: safe, refrigerator, dial-up. In-hotel: 5 restaurants, room service, bars, pool, gym, spa, beachfront, bicycles, children's programs (ages 5–12), concierge, parking (fee), no-smoking rooms* ⊟*AE, D, DC, MC, V.*

7

The Kāhala

$$$ ⊞ **ResortQuest at the Executive Centre Hotel.** Downtown Hono-
lulu's only hotel is an all-suites high-rise in the center of
the business district, within walking distance of the historic
Capitol District, Honolulu's Chinatown, and a 10-minute
drive from Honolulu International Airport. It's also three
blocks from Aloha Tower Marketplace and the cruise-ship
terminal at Pier 10. Accommodations occupy the top 10
floors of a 40-story glass tower, and have magnificent views
of downtown Honolulu and Honolulu Harbor. Many hotels
offer their guests free continental breakfast each morning,
but here it's served in the top-floor Executive Club with
views so mesmerizing, you might linger over your morning
coffee past sunset. The slew of amenities is a boon to those
staying for several days or longer. Each spacious suite has a
separate living area, three phones, deep whirlpool tubs, and
kitchenette stocked with cold beverages. Some units have
washer-dryers. The major disadvantage is that, after work
hours, there are few nearby dining options, so if you like to
dine out, you should consider renting a car. **Pros:** Central
to downtown businesses, transportation, and sights. **Cons:**
Few restaurants within walking distance at night, no beach
within walking distance. ⊠*1088 Bishop St., Downtown
Honolulu* ☎*808/539–3000 or 866/774–2924* ⊕*www.rq
executivecentre.com* ⌁*116 suites* ⚲*In-room: safe, kitchen.
In-hotel: restaurant, pool, gym, laundry facilities, parking
(fee), no-smoking rooms* ⊟*AE, DC, MC, V.*

WINDWARD O'AHU

$ ⊞ **Ingrid's.** This B&B in the Windward bedroom commu-
nity of Kailua features a one-bedroom upstairs studio with
decor that mimics that of a traditional Japanese inn, with
shoji screen doors and black-tile counters. Ingrid is one
of the island's most popular hosts, and she has created a
space of Zen-like tranquility in this unit, which also has a
kitchenette and deep soaking tub, and a private entrance.
Guests have access to the pool, and Kailua Beach is less
than 1 mi away. Three- to four-month advance reserva-
tions are advised. **Pros:** In Kailua, one of the most desir-
able locations on O'ahu. **Cons:** You'll need a car or bike
to get to the beach, must reserve months ahead. ⊠*Pauku
St., Kailua* ⊕*Reservations: Hawai'i's Best Bed and Break-
fasts, Box 485, Laupahoehoe 96767* ☎*808/962–0100,
800/262–9912 reservations* ⊕*www.bestbnb.com* ⌁*1 2-
room unit* ⚲*In-room: no phone, kitchen, DVD. In-hotel:
pool* ⊟*No credit cards.*

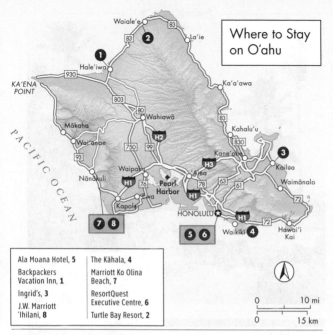

Ala Moana Hotel, **5**	The Kāhala, **4**
Backpackers Vacation Inn, **1**	Marriott Ko Olina Beach, **7**
Ingrid's, **3**	ResortQuest Executive Centre, **6**
J.W. Marriott 'Ihilani, **8**	Turtle Bay Resort, **2**

NORTH SHORE

⟨ ⌆ **Backpackers Vacation Inn and Plantation Village.** Laid-back Hale'iwa surfer chic at its best, Backpackers is Spartan in furnishings, rustic in amenities, and definitely very casual in spirit. At Pūpūkea Beach Marine Sanctuary, otherwise known as Three Tables Beach, it's a short stroll to Waimea Bay. This is the place to catch z's between wave sets. Accommodations in this property's 10 buildings include hostel-type dorm rooms, double rooms (some with a double bed, others with two single beds), studios, and cabins. Some have kitchenettes while others have full kitchens. TVs are available in every building and pay phones and barbecues are on the property. It's a three-minute walk to the supermarket. **Pros:** Friendly, laid-back staff; prices you won't find anywhere else. **Cons:** Many rooms are plainly furnished. ⊠*59-788 Kamehameha Hwy., Hale'iwa* ☎*808/638–7838* ⊕*www.backpackers-hawaii.com 25 rooms*⌂*In-room: no a/c, no phones, kitchen (some), no TV (some). In-hotel: laundry facilities* ⊟*DC, MC, V.*

★ **Fodor's**Choice ⌆**The Turtle Bay Resort.** Some 880 acres of raw
$$$$ natural Hawai'i landscape are your playground at this

Turtle Bay Resort

glamorous resort on O'ahu's scenic North Shore. On the edge of Kuilima Point, the Turtle Bay has spacious guest rooms averaging nearly 500 square feet, with lānai that showcase stunning peninsula views. In winter, when the big waves roll ashore, you get a front-row seat for the powerful surf. The sumptuous oceanfront beach cottages have Brazilian-walnut floors, teak rockers on the lānai, and beds you can sink right into while listening to the sounds of the ocean. Turtle Bay has a Hans Heidemann Surf School, horse stables, a spa, and the only 36-hole golf facility on O'ahu to keep you busy. There are two swimming pools, one with an 80-foot waterslide. While out exploring Turtle Bay's 12 mi of nature trails, don't be surprised if you suddenly find yourself *Lost*. The hit television series has been known to frequent the resort's beaches, coves, and natural forests for location filming. **Pros:** Great open, public spaces in a secluded area of O'ahu. **Cons:** Very far from anything else—even Hale'iwa is a 20-minute drive. ⊠*57-091 Kamehameha Hwy., Box 187, Kahuku* ☎*808/293–8811 or 800/203–3650* ⊕*www.turtlebayresort.com* ⌨*373 rooms, 40 suites, 42 beach cottages, 56 ocean villas* ⌂*In-room: refrigerator. In-hotel: 4 restaurants, room service, bars, golf courses, tennis courts, pools, gym, spa, beachfront, children's programs (ages 5–12), no-smoking rooms* ▤*AE, D, DC, MC, V.*

WEST O'AHU

$$$$ ☒**J. W. Marriott 'Ihilani Resort & Spa.** Forty-five minutes and a world away from the bustle of Waikīkī, this sleek, 17-story resort anchors the still-developing Kō' Ōlina Resort and Marina on O'ahu's Leeward coastline. Honeymooners, NFL Pro-Bowlers, and even local residents looking for a Neighbor Island experience without the hassle of catching a flight come to 'Ihilani for first-class R&R. The resort sits on one of Kō'Ōlina's seven lagoons and has a lū'au cove, tennis garden, wedding chapel, yacht marina, spa, and a Ted Robinson–designed 18-hole championship golf facility. The 650-square-foot rooms are luxurious, with lulling color schemes, marble bathrooms with deep soaking tubs, spacious private lānai with teak furnishings; and high-tech control systems for lighting and temperature. Introduced in 2007, Hawai'i's only allergy-friendly rooms are equipped with tea-tree-oil-infused air purifiers that remove allergens from the room within 15 minutes and with hypoallergenic fabrics, specially treated to reduce contaminants and irri-

7

tants. Most rooms have views. **Pros:** Beautiful property, impeccable service, pool is stunning at night. **Cons:** A bit of a drive from Honolulu, rental car a necessity. ⊠*92-1001 'Ōlani St., Kapolei* ☎*808/679–0079 or 800/626–4446* ⊕*www.ihilani.com* ⌕*387 rooms, 36 suites* ⌂*In-room: safe. In-hotel: 3 restaurants, room service, golf course, tennis courts, pools, spa, beachfront, children's programs (ages 5–12), concierge, no-smoking rooms*⊟*AE, DC, MC, V.*

$$$$ ⌨**Marriott's Ko Olina Beach Club.** If you have your heart set on getting away to O'ahu's western shores, check out this hotel and (primarily) vacation-ownership property. Rooms range from hotel-style standard guest rooms to expansive and elegantly appointed one- or two-bedroom apartments. Interior decor soothes in rich reds, greens, and creamy soft yellows, with furnishings made of rare Hawaiian koa wood. The larger villas (1,240 square feet) have three TVs, full kitchens, and separate living and dining areas. On 30 acres of Ko Olina, fronting a lagoon, this resort has two pools (one with sandy-beach bottom), a fitness center, barbecue areas, and four outdoor hot tubs, including one overlooking the ocean that's ideal for sunset soaks. Guests can choose from two restaurants on the property or purchase groceries at the Market, on-site. **Pros:** Suites are beautifully decorated and ample for families, nice views. **Cons:** 40-minute drive to Honolulu, ongoing construction at other properties nearby. ⊠*92-161 Waipahe Pl., Kapolei* ☎*808/679–4900 or 877/229–4484* ⊕*www.marriott vacationclub.com* ⌕*300 units* ⌂*In-room: safe, kitchen, DVD, Wi-Fi. In-hotel: 2 restaurants, bar, golf course, tennis courts, pools, gym, beachfront, children's programs (ages 5–12), parking (fee)*⊟*AE, DC, MC, V.*

O'ahu Essentials

There are planners and there are those who, excuse the pun, fly by the seat of their pants. We happily place ourselves among the planners. Our writers and editors try to anticipate all the issues you may face before and during any journey, and then they do their research. This section is the product of their efforts. Use it to get excited about your trip to O'ahu, to inform your travel planning, or to guide you on the road should the seat of your pants start to feel threadbare.

GETTING STARTED

We're really proud of our Web site: Fodors.com is a great place to begin any journey. Scan "Travel Wire" for suggested itineraries, travel deals, restaurant and hotel openings, and other up-to-the-minute info. Check out "Booking" to research prices and book plane tickets, hotel rooms, rental cars, and vacation packages. Head to "Talk" for on-the-ground pointers from travelers who frequent our message boards. You can also link to loads of other travel-related resources.

▌ RESOURCES

ONLINE TRAVEL TOOLS

ALL ABOUT O'AHU

Resources Hawai'i Beach Safety (⊕ www.hawaiibeachsafety.org) has the latest updates on O'ahu's beaches, including surf forecasts and safety tips.

Hawai'i Department of Land and Natural Resources (⊕ www.state.hi.us/dlnr) has information on hiking, fishing, and camping permits and licenses; online brochures on hiking safety and mountain and ocean preservation; and details on volunteer programs.

Hawai'i Tourism Authority (⊕ www.travelsmarthawaii.com) sponsors a Web site that offers tips on everything from packing to flying.

O'ahu Visitors Bureau (⊕ www.visit-oahu.com) is a good place to start to discover all that there is to see and do on this very special

island. And, you can access the online travel planner and sports adventure brochures or take a look at 12 sample itineraries that will help you plan the perfect vacation. The Web site also has an online yellow-pages listing of accommodations, activities and sports, attractions, dining venues, services, transportation, travel professionals, and wedding information.

VISITOR INFORMATION

Before you go, contact the O'ahu Visitors Bureau (OVB) for a free vacation planner and map. You can also request brochures on the island's romance, golf, and family activities. For general information on all of the Islands, contact the Hawai'i Visitors & Convention Bureau. The HVCB Web site has a calendar section that allows you to see what local events will be taking place during your stay.

Contacts Hawai'i Visitors & Convention Bureau (⊠ 2270 Kalakaua Ave., Suite 801, Honolulu ☎ 808/923–1811, 800/464–2924 for brochures ⊕ www.gohawaii.com). **O'ahu Visitors Bureau** (⊠ 733 Bishop St., Suite 1520, Honolulu ☎ 808/524–0722 ⊕ www.visit-oahu.com).

■ THINGS TO CONSIDER

GEAR

O'ahu is casual: sandals, bathing suits, and comfortable, informal clothing are the norm. In summer synthetic slacks and shirts, although easy to care for, can be uncomfortably warm.

There's a saying that when a man wears a suit during the day, he's either going for a loan or he's a lawyer trying a case. Only a few upscale restaurants require a jacket for dinner. The aloha shirt is accepted dress on O'ahu for business and most social occasions. Shorts are acceptable daytime attire, along with a T-shirt or polo shirt. There's no need to buy expensive sandals on the mainland—here you can get flip-flops for a couple of dollars and off-brand sandals for $20. Golfers should remember that many courses have dress codes requiring a collared shirt; call courses you're interested in for details. If you're not prepared, you can pick up appropriate clothing at resort pro shops. If you're visiting in winter or planning to visit a high-altitude area, bring a sweater or light- to medium-weight jacket. A polar fleece pullover is ideal, and makes a great impromptu pillow. If you're planning on doing any hiking, a good pair of boots is essential.

TRIP INSURANCE

What kind of coverage do you honestly need? Do you even need trip insurance at all? Take a deep breath and read on.

We believe that comprehensive trip insurance is especially valuable if you're booking a very expensive or complicated trip (particularly to an isolated region) or if you're booking far in advance. Who knows what could happen six months down the road? But whether or not you get insurance has more to do with how comfortable you are assuming all that risk yourself.

Comprehensive travel policies typically cover trip-cancellation and interruption, which let you cancel or cut your trip short because of a personal emergency, illness, or, in some cases, acts of terrorism in your destination. Such policies also cover evacuation and medical care. Some also cover you for trip delays because of bad weather or mechanical problems as well as for lost or delayed baggage. Another type of coverage to look for is financial default—that is, when your trip is disrupted because a tour operator, airline, or cruise line goes out of business. Generally you must buy this when you book your trip or shortly thereafter, and it's only available to you if your operator isn't on a list of excluded companies.

Expect comprehensive travel-insurance policies to cost about 4% to 7% or 8% of the total price of your trip (it's more like 8% to 12% if you're over age 70). A medical-only policy may or may not be cheaper than a comprehensive policy. Always read the fine print of your policy to make sure that you are covered for the risks that are of most concern to you. Compare several policies to make sure you're getting the best price and range of coverage available.

Trip-Insurance Resources

INSURANCE COMPARISON SITES		
Insure My Trip.com	800/487–4722	www.insuremytrip.com
Square Mouth.com	800/240–0369 or 727/490–5803	www.squaremouth.com
COMPREHENSIVE TRAVEL INSURERS		
Access America	800/284-8300	www.accessamerica.com
CSA Travel Protection	800/873–9855	www.csatravelprotection.com
HTH Worldwide	610/254–8700 or 888/243–2358	www.hthworldwide.com
Travelex Insurance	800/228–9792	www.travelex-insurance.com
Travel Guard International	715/345–0505 or 800/826–4919	www.travelguard.com
Travel Insured International	800/243–3174	www.travelinsured.com
MEDICAL-ONLY INSURERS		
International Medical Group	800/628–4664 or 317/655–4500	www.imglobal.com
International SOS		www.internationalsos.com
Wallach & Company	800/237–6615 or 540/687–3166	www.wallach.com

BOOKING YOUR TRIP

Is it truly better to book directly on an airline or hotel Web site? And when does a real live travel agent come in handy? Read on.

▌ ONLINE

You really have to shop around. A travel wholesaler such as Hotels.com or HotelClub.net can be a source of good rates, as can discounters such as Hotwire or Priceline, particularly if you can bid for your hotel room or airfare. Indeed, such sites sometimes have deals that are unavailable elsewhere. They do, however, tend to work only with hotel chains (which makes them just plain useless for getting hotel reservations outside of major cities) or big airlines (so that often leaves out upstarts like jetBlue and some foreign carriers like Air India).

Also, with discounters and wholesalers you must generally prepay, and everything is nonrefundable. And before you fork over the dough, be sure to check the terms and conditions, so you know what a given company will do for you if there's a problem and what you'll have to deal with on your own.

▌ WITH A TRAVEL AGENT

If this is your first visit to O'ahu, a travel agent or vacation packager specializing in Hawai'i can be extremely helpful in planning a memorable vacation. Not only do they have the knowledge of the destination, but they can save you money by packaging the costs of airfare, hotel, activities, and car rental. In addition, many Hawai'i-specialist travel agents may offer added value or special deals (i.e., resort food and beverage credit, free night's stay) when you book a vacation with them. The OVB provides a list of member travel agencies and tour operators.

Agent Resources American Society of Travel Agents (☎703/739–2782 ⊕www.travelsense.org).

O'ahu Travel Agents AA Vacations (☎800/321-2121 ⊕www.aavacations.com). **AAA Travel** (☎800/436–4222 ⊕www.aaa.com). **All About Hawai'i** (☎800/274–8687 ⊕www.allabouthawaii.com). **Continental Airlines Vacations** (☎800/301–3800 ⊕www.covacations.com).**Delta Vacations** (☎800/654–6559 ⊕www.deltavacations.com).**Funjet Vacations**(☎888/558–6654 ⊕www.funjet.com).**Hawaiian Vacations**(☎888/834–2924 ⊕www.gohawaiianvacations.com).

▌ RENTAL CARS

Depending on where you're staying and what you're planning on seeing and doing while on O'ahu, there are lots of ways to keep your ground transportation costs affordable. If you are staying in Waikīkī, you can easily walk or use public or shuttle transportation to get to many of the attractions in and

Online Booking Resources

AGGREGATORS		
Kayak	www.kayak.com	looks at cruises and vacation packages.
Mobissimo	www.mobissimo.com	examines airfare, hotels, cars, and tons of activities.
Qixo	www.qixo.com	compares cruises, vacation packages, and even travel insurance.
Sidestep	www.sidestep.com	compares vacation packages and lists travel deals and some activities.
BOOKING ENGINES		
Expedia	www.expedia.com	large online agency that charges a booking fee for airline tickets.
Hotwire	www.hotwire.com	discounter.
Orbitz	www.orbitz.com	charges a booking fee for airline tickets, but gives a clear breakdown of fees and taxes before you book.
Travelocity	www.travelocity.com	charges a booking fee for airline tickets, but promises good problem resolution.
ONLINE ACCOMMODATIONS		
Hotelbook.com	www.hotelbook.com	focuses on independent hotels worldwide.
Hotels.com	www.hotels.com	big Expedia-owned wholesaler that offers rooms in hotels all over the world.
Quikbook	www.quikbook.com	offers "pay when you stay" reservations that allow you to settle your bill when you check out, not when you book; best for trips to U.S. and Canadian cities.

around the resort area. Since hotel parking garages charge upward of $20 per day, you may want to rent a car only on the days you plan to sightsee around the island.

If you are staying outside of Waikīkī, your best bet is to rent a car. Even though the city bus is a wonderfully affordable way to

get around the island, you'll want the flexibility of having your own transportation, especially if you're planning lots of dining and sightseeing adventures.

■TIP→ Make sure that a confirmed reservation guarantees you a car. Agencies sometimes overbook, particularly for busy weekends and holiday periods.

You can rent anything from an econobox and motorcycle to a Ferrari while on Oʻahu. Rates are usually better if you reserve through a rental agency's Web site. It's wise to make reservations far in advance, especially if visiting during peak seasons or for major conventions or sporting events.

Rates in Honolulu begin at about $25 a day for an economy car with air-conditioning, automatic transmission, and unlimited mileage. This does not include the airport concession fee, general excise tax, rental-vehicle surcharge or vehicle-license fee. When you reserve a car, ask about cancellation penalties and drop-off charges should you plan to pick up the car in one location and return it to another. Many rental companies offer coupons for discounts at various attractions that could save you money later on in your trip.

In Hawaiʻi you must be 21 years of age to rent a car and you must have a valid driver's license and a major credit card. Those under 25 will pay a daily surcharge of $15 to $25. Request car seats and extras such as GPS when you make your reservation. Hawaiʻi's Child Restraint Law requires that all children three years and younger be in an approved child safety seat in the backseat of a vehicle. Children ages four to seven must be seated in a rear booster seat or child restraint such as a lap and shoulder belt. Car seats and boosters range from $8 to $12/day.

In Hawaiʻi your unexpired mainland driver's license is valid for rental for up to 90 days.

Be sure to allow plenty of time to return your vehicle so that you can make your flight. Traffic in Honolulu is terrible during morning and afternoon rush hours, especially between Waikīkī and Honolulu International Airport. Give yourself about 3½ to 4 hours before departure time to return your vehicle if you're traveling during these peak times; otherwise plan on about 2½ to 3 hours.

CAR-RENTAL INSURANCE

If you own a car and carry comprehensive car insurance for both collision and liability, your personal auto insurance will probably cover a rental, but read your policy's fine print to be sure. Some credit cards offer CDW coverage, but it's usually supplemental to your own insurance and rarely covers SUVs, minivans, luxury models, and the like. If your coverage is secondary, you may still be liable for loss-of-use costs from the car-rental company (again, read the fine print). But no credit-card insurance is valid unless you use that card for *all* transactions, from reserving to paying the final bill.

■TIP→**Diners Club offers primary CDW coverage on all rentals reserved and paid for with the card. This means that Diners Club's company—not your own car insurance—pays in case of an accident. It doesn't mean that your car-insurance company won't raise your rates once it discovers you had an accident.**

You may also be offered supplemental liability coverage; the car-rental company is required to carry a minimal level of liability coverage insuring all renters, but it's rarely enough to cover claims in a really serious accident if you're at fault. Your own auto-insurance policy will protect you if you own a car; if you don't, you have to decide whether you are willing to take the risk.

U.S. rental companies sell CDWs and LDWs for about $15 to $25 a day; supplemental liability is usually more than $10 a day. The car-rental company may offer you all sorts of other policies, but they're rarely worth the cost. Personal accident insurance, which is basic hospitalization coverage, is an especially egregious rip-off if you already have health insurance.

■TIP→You can decline the insurance from the rental company and purchase it through a third-party provider such as Travel Guard (www.travelguard.com)—$9 per day for $35,000 of coverage. That's sometimes just under half the price of the CDW offered by some car-rental companies.

▌ VACATION PACKAGES

About half of O'ahu's visitors book package tours. All of the wholesalers specializing in Hawai'i offer a range of packages from the low to the high end. Because of the volume of business they do, wholesalers typically have great deals. Combine that with their knowledge of the destination and wholesale packages make a lot of sense.

However, shop around and compare before you book to make sure you are getting a good deal.

Hawai'i Tour Operators American Express Vacations (☎800/528–4800 ⊕www.americanexpress vacations.com). **Apple Vacations** (☎800/517–2000 ⊕www.apple vacations.com). **Classic Vacations** (☎800/635–1333 ⊕www.classic vacations.com). **Creative Leisure** (☎800/413–1000 ⊕www.creative leisure.com). **Pleasant Holidays** (☎800/742–9244 ⊕www.pleasant holidays.com).

■TIP→Local tourism boards can provide information about lesser-known and small-niche operators that sell packages to only a few destinations.

Car-Rental Resources

AUTOMOBILE ASSOCIATIONS

American Automobile Association	800/763–9900 or 315/797–5000	www.aaa.com; most contact with the organization is through state and regional members.
National Automobile Club	650/294–7000	www.thenac.com; membership open to CA residents only.

LOCAL AGENCIES

AA Aloha Cars-R-Us	800/655–7989	www.hawaiicarrental.com
Discount Hawai'i Car Rental	888/292–3307	www.discounthawaiicarrental.com
Hawai'i Harley Rental	808/831–2600	www.hawaiiharleyrental.com
Hawaiian Discount Car Rentals	800/882–9007	www.hawaiidrive-o.com
JN Car and Truck Rentals	800/475–7522, 808/831–2724 on O'ahu	www.jnautomotive.com
VIP Car Rentals	808/922–4605 in Waikīkī	www.vipcarrentalhawaii.com

MAJOR AGENCIES

Advantage	800/777–5500	www.tradewindsudrive.com
Alamo	800/462–5266	www.alamo.com
Avis	800/331–1212	www.avis.com
Budget	800/527–0700	www.budget.com
Dollar	800/800–4000	www.dollar.com
Enterprise	800/261–7331	www.enterprise.com
Hertz	800/654–3131	www.hertz.com
National Car Rental	800/227–7368	www.nationalcar.com
Thrifty	800/847–4389	www.thrifty.com

TRANSPORTATION

Yes, O'ahu is a wonderful tourist destination and on any given day there are more than 100,000 visitors on the island. It's also home to about 75% of the 1.3 million people who live in Hawai'i. And, as the capital of the state and the financial crossroads to Asia and the Pacific, Honolulu is among the nation's largest cities. So, needless to say, you'll find lots of cars and traffic, especially during the morning and afternoon drive times. Visitors may be able to navigate more easily by orienting themselves to a few major landmarks. O'ahu is made up of two extinct volcanoes, which form what is today the island's two mountain ranges: Wai'anae and Ko'olau. The Wai'anae range curves from Ka'ena State Park, on the island's westernmost point, past Makaha, Wai'anae, and Nānākuli to Kō'Ōlina, a growing resort on the sunny Leeward shore. The extinct craters of Diamond Head and Koko Head are usually visible from anywhere along the island's Leeward coast. The Ko'olau Range forms a jagged spine that runs from the island's eastern tip along the Windward coast to the famous surfing center on the North Shore.

The island's volcanic origins have limited O'ahu's developments to tide flats and ridge lines, and as a result the city and county have many one-way streets and limited public parking. Honolulu's public transportation system, TheBus, is a stress-free, affordable, and convenient way to get around. There are routes that will take you to all of the major attractions, neighborhoods, and sightseeing locations around the island.

▐ BY AIR

Flying time is about 10 hours from New York, 8 hours from Chicago, and 5 hours from Los Angeles.

All of the major airline carriers serving Hawai'i fly direct to Honolulu; some also offer nonstops to Maui, Kaua'i, and the Big Island. Honolulu International Airport, although open-air and seemingly more casual than airports in most major U.S. hubs, can be very busy. Allow extra travel time during morning and afternoon traffic periods.

Plants and plant products are subject to regulation by the Department of Agriculture, both on entering and leaving O'ahu. Upon leaving, you'll have to have your bags X-rayed and tagged at the airport's agricultural inspection station before you proceed to check-in. Pineapples and coconuts with the packer's agricultural inspection stamp pass freely; papayas must be treated, inspected, and stamped. All other fruits are banned for export to the U.S. mainland. Flowers pass except for gardenia, rose leaves, jade vine, and mauna loa. Also banned are insects, snails, soil, cotton, cacti, sugarcane, and all berry plants.

You'll have to leave dogs and other pets at home. A 120-day quarantine is imposed to keep out rabies, which is nonexistent in Hawai'i. If specific pre- and postarrival requirements are met, animals may qualify for 30-day or 5-day-or-less quarantine.

■TIP→ If you travel frequently, look into the TSA's Registered Traveler program. The program, which is still being tested in several U.S. airports, is designed to cut down on gridlock at security checkpoints by allowing prescreened travelers to pass quickly through kiosks that scan an iris and/or a fingerprint. How sci-fi is that?

Airlines & Airports Airline and Airport Links.com (⊕www.airlineandairportlinks.com) has links to many of the world's airlines and airports.

Airline Security Issues Transportation Security Administration (⊕www.tsa.gov) has answers for almost every question that might come up.

Air-Travel Resources in O'ahu State of Hawai'i Airports Division Offices (☎808/836-6413 ⊕www.hawaii.gov/dot/airports).

AIRPORTS
Honolulu International Airport (HNL) is 20 minutes (9 mi) west of Waikīkī, and is served by most of the major domestic and international carriers. To travel interisland from Honolulu, you can depart from either the interisland terminal or the commuter-airline terminal, located in two separate structures adjacent to the main

overseas terminal building. A free Wiki Wiki shuttle bus operates between terminals.

If you have time after you've checked in for your flight home, visit the Pacific Aerospace Museum, open daily, in the main terminal. It includes a full-scale space-shuttle flight deck and hands-on exhibits such as a mission-control computer program tracing flights in the Pacific.

■TIP→ Long layovers don't have to be only about sitting around or shopping. These days they can be about burning off vacation calories. Check out www.airportgyms.com for lists of health clubs that are in or near many U.S. and Canadian airports.

Airport Information Honolulu International Airport (HNL) (☎808/836-6413 ⊕www.hawaii.gov/dot/airports).

GROUND TRANSPORTATION
Some hotels have their own pickup service. Check when you book accommodations.

Taxi service is available on the center median just outside baggage claim areas. Look for the taxi dispatchers wearing green shirts who will radio for a taxi. The fare to Waikīkī runs approximately $35 to $40, plus $0.50 per bag, and tip. If your baggage is oversized, there is an additional charge of $4.60.

Roberts Hawai'i runs a 24-hour airport shuttle from the airport to most of the major hotels in Waikīkī. The fare is $9 one-way, $15 round-trip; paid in cash to your driver. Look for a representative at the baggage claim. Call for return reservations only.

TheBus, the municipal bus, will take you into Waikīkī for only $2, but you are allowed only one bag, which must fit on your lap.

Contacts Roberts Hawaiʻi (☎808/539–9400 ⊕ www.robertshawaii.com). **TheBus** (☎808/848–5555 ⊕www.thebus.org).

FLIGHTS

From the U.S. mainland, ATA, Alaska Airlines, America West, American, Continental, Delta, Northwest, and United serve Honolulu.

Airline Contacts ATA (☎800/435–9282 ⊕www.ata.com). **Alaska Airlines** (☎800/252–7522 ⊕www.alaskaair.com). **Aloha Airlines** (☎800/367–5250 ⊕www.alohaairlines.com). **America West/US Airways** (☎800/428–4322 ⊕www.usairways.com). **American Airlines** (☎800/433–7300 ⊕www.aa.com). **Continental Airlines** (☎800/523–3273 for U.S. and Mexico reservations, 800/231–0856 for international reservations ⊕www.continental.com). **Delta Airlines** (☎800/221–1212 for U.S. reservations, 800/241–4141 for international reservations ⊕www.delta.com). **Hawaiian Airlines** (☎800/367–5320 ⊕www.hawaiianair.com). **Northwest Airlines** (☎800/225–2525 ⊕www.nwa.com). **Southwest Airlines** (☎800/435–9792 ⊕www.southwest.com). **United Airlines** (☎800/864–8331 for U.S. reservations, 800/538–2929 for international reservations ⊕www.united.com).

INTERISLAND FLIGHTS

If you've allotted more than a week for your vacation, you may want to consider visiting a neighbor island. From Honolulu, there are departing flights to the Neighbor Islands leaving almost every half hour from early morning until evening.

Aloha Airlines, go! Airlines/go! Express, Hawaiian Airlines, Island Air, Mokulele Airlines, and Pacific Wings/PWExpress offer regular service between the Islands. In addition to offering very competitive rates and online specials, all have frequent-flyer programs that entitle you to rewards and upgrades the more you fly. Be sure to compare prices offered by all of the interisland carriers. If you are somewhat flexible with your dates and times for island-hopping, you should have no problem getting a very affordable round-trip ticket. There are also a number of wholesalers that offer neighbor island packages including air, hotel, rental car, and even visitor attractions or activities.

Interisland Flights Aloha Airlines (☎800/367–5250 ⊕www.alohaairlines.com). **go! Airlines/go! Express** (☎888/435–9462 ⊕www.iflygo.com). **Hawaiian Airlines** (☎800/367–5320 ⊕www.hawaiianair.com). **IslandAir** (☎800/323–3345 ⊕www.islandair.com).

❚ BY BOAT

The City and County of Honolulu runs TheBoat, one-hour passenger ferry service from Kalaeloa on Oʻahu's west coast to Aloha Tower in downtown Honolulu. Designed primarily to ease the commute for West O'ahu residents, there are three departures each way in the morning and again in the afternoon/evening. The one-way fare is $2/person. A four-day pass for unlimited rides is $20 and can be purchased at ABC stores in Waikīkī and in the Ala Moana Shopping Center, at selected 7-Eleven stores, and at TheBus Pass Office. This is a great alternative to driving for visitors staying at Kō'Ōlina who want to spend one or more days in Honolulu, or for those staying in Honolulu who want to spend time at Kō'Ōlina or Hawaiian Waters Adventure Park. There is connecting bus service for most of the trips; check the Web site or call to confirm.

Information Hawai'i Superferry (☎877/443–3779 ⊕www.hawaiisuperferry.com). **TheBoat** (☎808/848–5555 ⊕www.trytheboat.com).

▌ BY BUS

Getting around by bus is a convenient and affordable option on O'ahu. In Waikīkī, in addition to TheBus and the Waikīkī Trolley, there are a number of brightly painted private buses, many of which are free, that will take you to such commercial attractions as dinner cruises, garment factories, and the like.

You can go all around the island or just down Kalākaua Avenue for $2 on Honolulu's municipal transportation system, affectionately known as TheBus. It's one of the island's best bargains. Taking TheBus in the Waikīkī and downtown

Honolulu areas is especially easy, with buses making stops in Waikīkī every 15 minutes to take passengers to nearby shopping areas, such as Ala Moana Center.

You're entitled to one free transfer per fare if you ask for it when boarding. Exact change is required, and dollar bills are accepted. A four-day pass for visitors costs $20 and is available at ABC convenience stores in Waikīkī and in the Ala Moana Shopping Center. Monthly passes cost $40.

There are no official bus-route maps, but you can find privately published booklets at most drugstores and other convenience outlets. The important route numbers for Waikīkī are 2, 4, 8, 19, 20, 58, and City Express Route B. If you venture farther afield, you can always get back on one of these.

Bus Information TheBus (☎808/848–5555 ⊕www.thebus.org).

▌ BY CAR

O'ahu can be circled except for the roadless west-shore area around Ka'ena Point. Elsewhere, major highways follow the shoreline and traverse the island at two points. Rush-hour traffic (6:30 to 9:30 AM and 3:30 to 6 PM) can be frustrating around Honolulu and the outlying areas, as many thoroughfares allow no left turns due to contraflow lanes. Parking along many streets is curtailed during these times, and towing is strictly practiced. Read curbside parking signs before leaving your vehicle, even at a meter.

When asking for directions, remember that Hawai'i residents refer to places as being either *mauka* (toward the mountains) or *makai* (toward the ocean) from one another. Other directions depend on your location: in Honolulu, for example, people say to "go Diamond Head," which means toward that famous landmark, or to "go *'ewa*," meaning in the opposite direction. A shop on the mauka–Diamond Head corner of a street is on the mountainside of the street on the corner closest to Diamond Head. It all makes perfect sense once you get the lay of the land.

DRIVING TIMES FROM WAIKĪKĪ	
To	
Diamond Head	10–15 minutes
Downtown Honolulu	15 minutes
Hale'iwa	50 minutes
Hanauma Bay	30 minutes
Honolulu International Airport	30 minutes
Kailua	35 minutes
Kō'Ōlina	40 minutes
North Shore	1 hour
USS Arizona Memorial	30 minutes

GASOLINE
You can pretty much count on having to pay more at the pump for gasoline on O'ahu than on the U.S. mainland.

ROAD CONDITIONS
O'ahu is a relatively easy island to navigate. Roads and streets, although they may challenge the visitor's tongue, are well marked; just watch out for the many one-way streets in Waikīkī and downtown Honolulu. Keep an eye open for the Hawai'i Visitors and Convention Bureau's red-caped King Kamehameha signs, which mark major attractions and scenic spots. Ask for a map at the car-rental counter. Free publications containing good-quality road maps can be found at most hotels and resorts and throughout Waikīkī.

ROADSIDE EMERGENCIES
If you find yourself in an emergency or accident, pull over if you can. If you have a cell phone with you, call the roadside assistance number on your rental-car contract or AAA Help. If you find that your car has been broken into or stolen, report it immediately to your rental-car company and they can assist you. If it's an emergency and someone is hurt, call 911 immediately.

Emergency Services AAA Help (☎800/222–4357).

RULES OF THE ROAD
Be sure to buckle up. Hawai'i has a strictly enforced seat-belt law for front-seat passengers. Children under four must be in a car seat (available from car-rental agencies). Children 18 and under, riding in the backseat, are also required by state law to use seat belts. The highway speed limit is usually 55 mph. In-town traffic moves from 25 to 40 mph. Jaywalking is very common, so be particularly watch-

ful for pedestrians, especially in congested areas such as Waikīkī and downtown Honolulu. Unauthorized use of a parking space reserved for persons with disabilities can net you a $150 fine.

▌ BY TAXI

Taxis can be found at the airport, through your hotel doorman, in the more popular resort areas, or by contacting local taxi companies by telephone. Rates are $2.75 at the drop of the flag and each additional mile is $3. Drivers are generally courteous and the cars are in good condition, many of them air-conditioned. In addition, taxi and limousine companies on the island can provide a car and driver for half-day or daylong island tours if you absolutely don't want to rent a car, and a number of companies also offer personal guides. Remember, however, that rates are quite steep for these services, ranging from $100 to $200 or more per day.

Taxi Companies Carey Hawai'i Chauffeured Services (☎888/563–2888 or 808/572–3400 ⊕www.careyhawaii.com). **Charley's Taxi & Limousine** (☎808/531–1333 ⊕www.charleystaxi.com). **Elite Limousine Service** (☎800/776–2098 or 808/735–2431 ⊕www.elitelimohawaii.com). **The Cab Hawai'i** (☎808/422–2222 ⊕www.thecabhawaii.com).

▌ BY TROLLEY

The Waikīkī Trolley has four lines and dozens of stops that allow you to design your own itinerary while riding on brass-trimmed, open-air trolleys. The Honolulu City Line (Red Line) travels between Waikīkī and the Bishop Museum and includes stops at Aloha Tower, Ala Moana, and downtown Honolulu, among others. The Ocean Coast Line (Blue Line) provides a tour of O'ahu's southeastern coastline, including Diamond Head Crater, Hanauma Bay, and Sea Life Park. The Blue Line also has an express trolley to Diamond Head, which runs twice daily. The Ala Moana Shuttle Line (Pink Line) stops at Ward Warehouse, Ward Centers, and Ala Moana Shopping Center. These trolley lines depart from the DFS Galleria Waikīkī or Hilton Hawaiian Village. The Local Shopping & Dining Line (Yellow Line) starts at Ala Moana Center and stops at Ward Farmers' Market, Ward Warehouse, Ward Centers, and other shops and restaurants. A one-day, four-line ticket costs $25. Four-day tickets, also good for any of the four lines, are $45. You can order online and there are often online specials including a "buy one adult 4-day pass and get a second for free."

Information Waikīkī Trolley (☎808/591–2561 or 800/824–8804 ⊕www.waikikitrolley.com).

ON THE GROUND

▌ COMMUNICATIONS

INTERNET

If you've brought your laptop with you to O'ahu, you should have no problem checking e-mail or connecting to the Internet. Most of the major hotels and resorts offer high-speed access in rooms and/or lobbies. You should check with your hotel in advance to confirm that access is wireless; if not, ask whether in-room cables are provided. In some cases there will be an hourly or daily charge posted to your room. If you're staying at a small inn or B&B without Internet access, ask the proprietor for the nearest café or coffee shop with wireless access.

Contacts Cybercafes (⊕www. cybercafes.com) lists more than 4,000 Internet cafés worldwide. **JiWire** (⊕www.jiwire.com) features a directory of Wi-Fi hotspots around the world.

▌ HEALTH

Hawai'i is known as the Health State. The life expectancy here is 79 years, the longest in the nation. Balmy weather makes it easy to remain active year-round, and the low-stress aloha attitude certainly contributes to general well-being. When visiting the Islands, however, there are a few health issues to keep in mind.

The Hawai'i State Department of Health recommends that you drink 16 ounces of water per hour to avoid dehydration when hiking or spending time in the sun. Use sunblock, wear UV–reflective sunglasses, and protect your head with a visor or hat for shade. If you're not acclimated to warm, humid weather you should allow plenty of time for rest stops and refreshments. When visiting freshwater streams, be aware of the tropical disease leptospirosis, which is spread by animal urine and carried into streams and mud. Symptoms include fever, headache, nausea, and red eyes. If left untreated it can cause liver and kidney damage, respiratory failure, internal bleeding, and even death. To avoid this, don't swim or wade in freshwater streams or ponds if you have open sores and don't drink from any freshwater streams or ponds.

On the Islands, fog is a rare occurrence, but there can often be "vog," an airborne haze of gases released from volcanic vents on the Big Island. During certain weather conditions such as "Kona Winds," the vog can settle over the Islands and wreak havoc with respiratory and other health conditions, especially asthma or emphysema. If susceptible, stay indoors and get emergency assistance if needed.

The Islands have their share of bugs and insects that enjoy the tropical climate as much as visitors do. Most are harmless but annoying. When planning to spend time outdoors in hiking areas, wear long-sleeved clothing and pants and use mosquito repellent containing deet. In very damp places you may encounter the dreaded local centipede. On the Islands they usually come in two colors, brown and blue, and they range from the size of a worm to an 8-inch cigar. Their sting is very painful, and the reaction is similar to bee- and wasp-sting reactions. When camping, shake out your sleeping bag before climbing in, and check your shoes in the morning, as the centipedes like cozy places. If planning on hiking or traveling in remote areas, always carry a first-aid kit and appropriate medications for sting reactions.

▌ HOURS OF OPERATION

Even people in paradise have to work. Generally local business hours are weekdays 8 to 5. Banks are usually open Monday to Thursday 8:30 to 3 and until 6 on Friday. Some banks have Saturday-morning hours.

Many self-serve gas stations stay open around-the-clock, with full-service stations usually open from around 7 AM until 9 PM. U.S. post offices are open weekdays 8:30 AM to 4:30 PM and Saturday 8:30 to noon. On O'ahu, the Ala Moana post office branch is the only branch, other than the main Honolulu International Airport facility, that stays open until 4 PM on Saturday.

Most museums generally open their doors between 9 AM and 10 AM and stay open until 5 PM Tuesday to Saturday. Many museums operate with afternoon hours only on Sunday and close on Monday. Visitor-attraction hours vary, but most sights are open daily with the exception of major holidays such as Christmas. Check local newspapers upon arrival for attraction hours and schedules if visiting over holiday periods. The local dailies carry a listing of "What's Open/What's Not" for those time periods.

Stores in resort areas sometimes open as early as 8, with shopping-center opening hours varying from 9 to 10 on weekdays and Saturday, a bit later on Sunday. Bigger malls stay open until 9 weekdays and Saturday and close at 5 on Sunday. Boutiques in resort areas may stay open as late as 11.

▌ MONEY

Prices throughout this guide are given for adults. Substantially reduced fees are almost always available for children, students, and senior citizens.

ATMS & BANKS

Automatic-teller machines, for easy access to cash, can be found at many locations throughout O'ahu including shopping centers, small convenience and grocery stores, inside hotels and resorts, as well as outside most bank branches. For a directory of locations, call 800/424–7787 for the MasterCard/Cirrus/Maestro network or 800/843–7587 for the Visa/Plus network.

CREDIT CARDS

Throughout this guide, the following abbreviations are used: **AE**, American Express; **D**, Discover; **DC**, Diners Club; **MC**, MasterCard; and **V**, Visa.

Reporting Lost Cards American Express (☎800/528–4800 in the U.S. or 336/393–1111 collect from abroad ⊕www.americanexpress.com). **Diners Club** (☎800/234–6377 in the U.S. or 303/799–1504 collect from abroad ⊕www.dinersclub.com). **Discover** (☎800/347–2683 in the U.S. or 801/902–3100 collect from abroad ⊕www.discovercard.com). **MasterCard** (☎800/627–8372 in the U.S. or 636/722–7111 collect from abroad ⊕www.mastercard.com). **Visa** (☎800/847–2911 in the U.S. or 410/581–9994 collect from abroad ⊕www.visa.com).

▌ SAFETY

O'ahu is generally a safe tourist destination, but it's still wise to follow the same common-sense safety precautions you would normally follow in your own hometown. Hotel and visitor-center staff can provide information should you decide to head out on your own to more remote areas. Rental cars are magnets for break-ins, so don't leave any valuables in the car, not even in a locked trunk. Avoid poorly lighted areas, beach parks, and isolated areas after dark as a precaution. When hiking, stay on marked trails, no matter how alluring the temptation might be to stray. Weather conditions can cause landscapes to become muddy, slippery, and tenuous, so staying on marked trails will lessen the possibility of a fall or getting lost.

Be wary of those hawking "too good to be true" prices on everything from car rentals to attractions. Many of these offers are just a lure to get you in the door for time-share presentations. When handed a flyer, read the fine print before you make your decision to participate.

Women traveling alone are generally safe on the Islands, but always follow the safety precautions you would use in any major destination. When booking hotels, request rooms closest to the elevator, and always keep your hotel-room door and balcony doors locked. Stay away from isolated areas after dark; camping and hiking solo are not advised. If you stay out late visiting nightclubs and bars, use caution when exiting nightspots and returning to your lodging.

■TIP→ Distribute your cash, credit cards, IDs, and other valuables between a deep front pocket, an inside jacket or vest pocket, and a hidden money pouch. Don't reach for the money pouch once you're in public.

▌ TAXES

There's a 4.16% state sales tax on all purchases, including food. A hotel-room tax of 7.25%, combined with the sales tax of 4%, equals an 11.41% rate added onto your hotel bill. A $3-per-day road tax is also assessed on each rental vehicle.

▌TIME

Hawai'i is on Hawaiian Standard Time, 5 hours behind New York, and 2 hours behind Los Angeles.

When the U.S. mainland is on daylight saving time, Hawai'i is not, so add an extra hour of time difference between the Islands and U.S. mainland destinations. You may also find that things generally move more slowly here. That has nothing to do with your watch—it's just the laid-back way called Hawaiian time.

▌TIPPING

As this is a major vacation destination and many of the people who work at the hotels and resorts rely on tips to supplement their wages, tipping is not only common but expected. Bartenders expect a $1 or more per round of drinks; bellhops expect $1 to $5 per bag, depending on the hotel and kinds of items you have; hotel concierges expect to be tipped if they render you a service (usually $5 or more); hotel maids expect $1 to $3 per day (it's best to tip your maid daily in cash because the cleaner may be different on different days of your stay); taxi drivers expect 15% to 20%, but round up the fare to the next dollar amount; waiters expect to be tipped at about the same rate they would receive in a major city (15% to 20%, with 20% being the norm at upscale restaurants).

INDEX

Photo Credits: 1, Douglas Peebles/eStock Photo. 2, Peebles/Mauritius/age fotostock. 6, Joe Viesti/viestiphoto.com. **Chapter 1: Experience Oahu:** 8-9, Grant Studios/eStock Photo. 10, Ken Ross/viestiphoto.com. 11 (left), Michael S. Nolan/age fotostock. 11 (right), dancing_star. 14, Tor Johnson/Photo Resource Hawaii/Alamy. 15 (left), Ann Cecil/Photo Resource Hawaii/Alamy. 15 (right), Oahu Visitors Bureau. 16, Bill Gleasner/viestiphoto.com. 18, Angelita Trujillo. 19, Oahu Visitors Bureau. 20, Starwood Hotels & Resorts. 21, Oahu Visitors Bureau. 22, Robert Gerard. **Chapter 2: Exploring Oahu:** 23, David Schrichte/Aurora Photos. 25, Tor Johnson/Photo Resource Hawaii/Alamy. 29, Oahu Visitors Bureau. 33, David L. Moore/Alamy. 41, Corbis. 49, Giovanni Simeone/SIME/eStock Photo. 52, Douglas Peebles/eStock Photo. 58, Kenny Williams/Alamy. 58, Luca Tettoni/viestiphoto.com. **Chapter 3: Beaches & Outdoor Activities:** 63, J.D.Heaton/Picture Finders/age fotostock. 67, David Schrichte/Photo Resource Hawaii/Alamy. 72, SuperStock/age fotostock. 79, Photo Resource Hawaii/Alamy. 84, Douglas Peebles/eStock Photo. 88, Photo Resource Hawaii/Alamy. 93, Karen Wilson/ASP. 98, Douglas Peebles/eStock Photo. 103, Tor Johnson/Aurora Photos. **Chapter 4: Shops & Spas:** 109, Beauty Photo Studio/age fotostock. 120, Linda Ching/HVCB. **Chapter 5: Entertainment & Nightlife:** 123, Polynesian Cultural Center. 127, Ann Cecil/Photo Resource Hawaii/Alamy. 132, Giovanni Simeone/SIME/eStock Photo. **Chapter 6: Where to Eat:** 135, David L. Moore/Alamy. 152, Douglas Peebles/Aurora Photos. **Chapter 7: Where to Stay:** 165, Waikiki Parc Hotel. 172 (top), Halekulani. 172 (bottom), Halekulani. 185 (top), Kahala. 185 (bottom), Kahala. 188 (top and bottom), Turtle Bay Resort.

ABOUT OUR WRITERS

Don Chapman is the editor of the award-winning *MidWeek,* Hawai'i's largest-circulated newspaper. The golf writer for this guide, Don has played 88 golf courses in Hawai'i and writes about golf for a variety of national publications. He is also the author of four books.

Trina Kudlacek splits her time between her home in Hawai'i, where she is a faculty member at the University of Hawai'i, and Italy where she is a tour guide. Before moving back to Hawai'i, she spent a year guiding and guidebook writing in Northern Italy and vagabonding throughout Europe.

Chad Pata is a freelance writer who has spent the past 15 years falling in love with Hawai'i. Originally hailing from Georgia he has gladly traded in Southern hospitality for the Aloha spirit. He married a local girl and has two hapa kids, Honu and Calogero, through whom his life moves and gains its beauty.

Cathy Sharpe was born and reared on O'ahu. For 13 years, she worked at a Honolulu public-relations agency representing major travel-industry clients. Now living in Maryland, she is a marketing consultant. Cathy returns home once a year to visit family and friends, relax at her favorite beaches, and enjoy island cuisine.